More praise for *Getting to Calm: The Early Years*

"How can parents know what's best for their kids? Kastner offers keen insight into the inner world of children, providing practical tools that help parents navigate some of the most persistent problems of the early years. Fabulous!"

— Marsha Linehan, Ph.D.
Professor of psychology and adjunct professor of psychiatry
and behavioral sciences at the University of Washington

"Dr. Kastner does what she set out to do from the beginning: help parents get to calm. With clarity and an engaging style, she masterfully guides parents through the complex maze of parenting, encouraging them to embrace the paradox embedded in all healthy development: practicing unconditional acceptance of their children, even while encouraging them to grow, evolve, and change.

Kastner teaches parents how to respond mindfully, trust their own intuition, and become reflective and self-aware — invaluable skills for laying a foundation of secure attachment and creating a calm home."

— Yaffa Maritz
Psychologist and director, Community of Mindful Parenting

Praise for *Getting to Calm*

"Required reading for parents who struggle with their teen. Here is true insight into the mental and emotional world of adolescents."

— T. Berry Brazelton, M.D., and Joshua Sparrow, M.D.
Harvard Medical School

"An ideal guide book for parenting teens ... indispensable!"

— John Gottman, Ph.D.

"This is a smart book ... a wonderful contribution to every parent's library of support. Bravo!"

— Daniel J. Siegel, M.D.
Author, *Parenting from the Inside Out*

Praise for *Wise-Minded Parenting*

"One of the most articulately expressed, useful sets of research-validated parenting strategies you'll ever find ... a magnificent tool kit to help you become the parent you will be proud to be."

—Daniel J. Siegel, M.D.
Author, *Brainstorm* and *The Developing Mind*

"How rewarding to see scientifically proven practices given to parents, where it can do so much good!"

Carol S. Dweck, Ph.D.
Author, *Mindset: How You Can Fulfill Your Potential*

"This wonderfully thoughtful, wise, and comprehensive guide maps out the latest research and knowledge about what our tweens and teens need to thrive."

—Myla and Jon Kabat-Zinn
Authors, *Everyday Blessings: The Inner Work of Mindful Parenting*

"This is a great book — a must-read for all parents."

—John Gottman, Ph.D.
Author, *Raising an Emotionally Intelligent Child*

" ... one of those rarities in the world of parenting guides: a thoughtful and practical resource that is grounded in the scientific study of child development and parent-child relationships. I recommend it enthusiastically."

—Laurence Steinberg, Ph.D.
Author, *The 10 Basic Principles of Good Parenting*
and *You and Your Adolescent*

Getting to CALM

THE EARLY YEARS

Cool-Headed Strategies for Raising Happy, Caring,
and Independent Three- to Seven-Year-Olds

Laura S. Kastner, Ph.D.

ParentMap is a Seattle-based resource for
award-winning parenting information.

parentmap.com

Printed in the United States of America
Published by ParentMap
Distributed by Ingram Publisher Services

Cover photograph: Will Austin
Cover design: Amy Chinn

ISBN-13: 978-0-9904306-1-2

ParentMap dba Gracie Enterprises
4742 42nd Ave SW, #399
Seattle, WA 98116-4553
206-709-9026

ParentMap books are available at special discounts when purchased in bulk for premiums and sales promotions as well as for fundraisers or educational use. Place book orders at *parentmap.com* or 206-709-9026.

"Love isn't a state of perfect caring.
It is an active noun like struggle.
To love someone is to strive to accept that person exactly
the way he or she is, right here and now."

—*Fred Rogers*

Table of Contents

Acknowledgments

I am indebted to all of the families who have *trained me* over the three decades of my career. Throughout this book, I have created composites of similar cases to illustrate parenting strategies and tools, while protecting the confidentiality of my actual patients.

The contents of this book pay homage to the valuable, evidence-based research that is conducted for the benefit of parents but which often does not reach them directly. I consider my books on parenting to serve as a conduit from the ivory tower to the home plate. My academic origins influenced me deeply: I will be forever grateful to Mary Ainsworth, who inspired me during my graduate school years at the University of Virginia and enlightened me to the importance of secure attachment; Dickon Reppucci, who pushed me (kindly) toward community psychology; and David Waters, who taught me the physics of family systems.

A huge boatload of thanks goes to the team at ParentMap, whose members work together to promote child health. *ParentMap*'s publisher, Alayne Sulkin, is a community superhero; she initiates more civically minded projects in a month than most people do in a lifetime. Thanks also to my trustworthy copy editor Sunny Parsons and to graphic designer Amy Chinn.

I am beyond fortunate to have Kristen Russell as my editor. With her background as magazine editor, author, and resident genius in her job settings, she generously offered her fairy dust by adding clarity, zest, and brainpower.

Lastly, I would like to express my gratitude to my family of origin — my parents, Joan and Rex, and my siblings, Hank, Janet, and Linda — who have always supported me and put up with my irritating predilection for starting sentences with "Research indicates ...." I would be lost without my North Star and beloved husband, Philip Mease, who joins me in the pursuit of wise mind. We are fortunate beyond words to have parented our children, Cameron and Lindley, whom we love deeply; they taught us humility and inspire us daily with their grace, strong character, and dedication to making the world a better place. Parenting is, indeed, a trip.

Introduction

As much as I celebrate the breadth of rich information about child development that's available to today's parent, I worry about an increasingly troubling downside: Anxiety has become a national stress disorder for parents. Amid the cacophony of advice and input coming at parents from all quarters, how can they make sense of what is best for their child?

Is baby talk bad for your infant? Does praise raise confident kids — or self-important brats? Does your baby need gym class, swim lessons, French classes — or more time rolling in the grass? Is your child gritty enough? Vaccinated enough? Too addicted to screens? Are you wrecking your bond with time-outs? Compromising your marriage with the family bed? Are you glad that you avoid spanking, but worried that you yell too much? Do your attempts to impose discipline result in epic power struggles?

Parents have solid intuition about what's good for children, but many forces generate self-doubt, and we are all influenced by "the next big thing," especially when it relates to our beloved babes. Fads and gizmos — such as "IQ-boosting" educational tools and tricycle GPS systems — will come and go. What keeps them coming? The relentless parental drive to give our children every possible advantage, a drive that is often fueled by fear.

We all naturally fear that we'll fail somehow at this massive, outrageously daunting undertaking of parenting. We're afraid that our children will pay for our mistakes in lost potential, poor health, sluggish achievement, less success. We are painfully aware that it's a competitive world out there. And we are 100 percent dedicated to helping our wee ones achieve in all the ways that really matter: health, happiness, character, and an enduring, loving bond with us.

Being informed is good, but becoming anxious and doubting your own instincts is not. Parental anxiety is only helpful if it motivates you to improve your effectiveness and skillfulness as a parent so you can get back to the joy of parenting. But all too often, pressures, fears, and anxiety drive well-meaning people into unproductive and even harmful habits of parenting. Take a look at some common anxiety-driven parenting traits — and their unintended consequences for children:

Overprotectiveness	→ Less exploring and competency building
Academic pressure	→ Focus on grades instead of learning and curiosity
Competitiveness	→ Focus on performance instead of effort
Preoccupation with accomplishment	→ Less play, and less parent-child closeness
Drive to rescue child from any distress	→ Less resilience, coping, and self-reliance
Goal-oriented emphasis	→ Risks to security, self-worth, and emotional health
Extremely busy lifestyle	→ Less family bonding time and mindful parenting

You may be thinking about the positive aspects of the things in the left column; after all, it's good to be protective, value achievement, engage in competition, strive for academic excellence, set goals, and spring into action if your child is in danger. These assets are good qualities — in the right doses. But when they show up as anxiety-driven forces that propel parents into overdrive, parenting becomes corrosive, and the child experiences the outcomes in the right column, and worse.

My goal with this book is to quell anxiety and quiet the noise that saps energy, so that you can focus on the important stuff in parenting. It will become eminently clear that by "getting to calm," you can be your best self and nurture your children optimally. My hope is to be part neighborhood elder, part friendly shrink, and part synthesizer of the vast ocean of evidence-based research available today, the kind of research that is tested over decades and supported by scientific investigation.

From that ocean of research, I've extracted a string of pearls about child development and effective parenting. Beyond the fads and trends that come and go are tried-and-true methods that really will help you achieve those ultimate goals of raising happy, successful kids with healthy, loving bonds. In the coming pages, I'll describe many of these methods and help you evaluate which of them to try in your family — and which to (confidently) leave behind. With these tools, you'll learn to access your wise mind and listen to your natural intuition.

More than fifty years ago, the famous baby doctor Dr. Benjamin Spock assured parents, "You know more than you think you do." Now, we have research from brain science and dialectical behavior therapy to back up that declaration and illustrate the importance of intuition. When parents are rested, supported by others, and have a chance to reflect on their own childhoods and past experiences, they can develop their parenting skills, empathy, and intuition. However, these conditions don't always exist for parents in the twenty-first century.

A mother of a three-year-old recently consulted with me about a quandary: How could she support her daughter's independence while still maintaining a secure attachment? She had been getting all kinds of advice from friends and family, and media sources, everything from "You shouldn't let her cry like that — she needs to depend on you!" to "You are spoiling her!"

As it turns out, this very self-aware mother was hitting the sweet spot with her parenting. She was attuned to her daughter's needs, sensitive, and nurturing, but she often resisted intervening. She sometimes let her daughter experience frustration by letting her wait a few moments before being picked up. She also said "no" to all the usual things: cookies for dinner, staying up past bedtime, and refusing the car seat. This mom discovered that at many of these junctures, her daughter figured out ways to entertain herself while she waited. She also discovered her child could tolerate feeling anger or sadness when confronted with limits — *and that she could manage her own distress* in the face of her child's strongest emotions.

When her daughter was frustrated, angry, or sad, this mom tried her best to stay calm and validate her daughter's feelings, giving her choices and seeking her ideas for solving problems. This approach allowed mother and daughter to collaborate on solutions to conflicts over cookies, bedtime, and car seats. Importantly, this mom knew intuitively that a big part of her job was setting limits and talking to her child about feelings. By accepting her daughter's negative feelings and helping her put them into words (even when they were directed at her!), this mom was building a bridge to understanding, helping her child understand herself and other people, and developing her emotional competence.

Before our consultation, this mom was fretting over the misguided idea that maintaining a secure attachment with her child required her to try to eliminate distress and rescue her daughter from negative feelings. But this went against her own instincts as a mom. All on her own, she had naturally uncovered one of the most important paradoxes of parenting: *We love our children exactly as they are — and we want them to evolve.* We support our children emotionally so that they feel secure, *and* we challenge them to develop new competencies. Acceptance and change are part of every healthy, loving relationship. As parents, we change to adapt to their growth, development, and temperament. But all of our parenting needs to be embedded in a rock-solid foundation of acceptance.

The story about this mother's confusion is not unusual. Too much of what is in the media today is tipped to one side of the paradox or the other. In this book, you'll see how parents can maintain a secure attachment with their child *and* help them build competencies at the same time. Instead of emphasizing academic achievement as the be-all and end-all, you'll see why nurturing social and emotional skills is critical to your child's success in school (and in life). And you'll learn to trust that your relationship with your child can withstand the natural jolts of anger and upset caused by your setting necessary boundaries.

Based on my thirty years of clinical practice and teaching in psychology and psychiatry, I have compiled a toolbox of techniques and skills that help parents address the typical problems of raising three- to seven-year-olds, with special attention to the hot-button challenges of defiance, noncompliance, and meltdowns. Each of the following seven chapters is focused on one of the big predictors of success among children: secure attachment, self-control, academic success, social thriving, emotional flourishing, character, and physical health.

As you read, you'll see a common theme running through all seven chapters: Coping effectively with your own emotions creates a significant, enduring advantage in all of your parenting endeavors. Your own emotional regulation not only serves as a model for your ever-observant child, it's also guaranteed to reduce yelling and regret over parenting mistakes, and increase the frequency of positive and loving interactions. It's a cornerstone for building and maintaining a secure attachment with your child, a foundation so imperative to effective parenting that it inspired the title of this book (and that of its sequel).

I freely admit that managing your own emotions effectively at all times is impossible, especially given the significant and ever-present sources of anxiety in the world of parenting today. Practicing skills and making use of tools (such as the CALM technique, page 42) can help us enormously as we endeavor to do our best, accept our shortcomings (just as we accept those of our loved ones), and strive to improve.

Parenting is not for the faint of heart. It can bring even the savviest parents to their knees with a sense of vulnerability, terror, failure, and frustration. But it can also yield satisfaction, pride, and joy like nothing else. With a little practice, effective skills become second nature, so you can handle the hard stuff of parenting while moving the dial toward the positive for both you and your child, regardless of your temperaments, circumstances, and challenges.

At the heart of this book lies a very important concept for all to embrace: We do not have to be perfect parents, only good enough. We want to embrace change while accepting ourselves and our children completely. How can we do this? By engaging our wise mind and considering what's right for us, right now.

As Fred Rogers ("Mister Rogers") once said, "Love is an active noun, like struggle." And indeed, at times, love is a struggle. But it's also a powerful motivator for parents to be nurturing, vigilant, patient, and wise, growing ever more skillful, and evolving along with their children in the glorious chaos of these early years. Welcome to my idea manual, and get ready to tap into your wise mind as you chart the path that works best for you, your child, and your family.

CHAPTER 1

Secure attachment: Staying connected while mastering separation (and getting some sleep!)

We begin at the beginning, with the single most important thing you can do to help your child reach his or her full potential of happiness, success, and independence: build a secure attachment. Secure attachment refers to the trusting bond your child has with you and other loving caregivers. You've been busily creating this attachment since your child was born, in many, many ways, big and small, and often without realizing it.

Secure attachment predicts a vast range of social, emotional, and academic benefits throughout your child's life, well into adulthood. When your child is securely attached, she can draw on that sense of security as she learns to manage separation. Security allows her to explore, learn, and become capable of independence, enjoying preschool and other new experiences. The ability to handle separation — and all the fear, anxiety, and frustration that can go along with it — is a crucial competency, not only for your child's development, but for the harmony of your entire household.

Helping your child cope with separation is the key to easing many of the challenges of parenting throughout the early years, including one of the most exhausting and pervasive of those challenges: sleep deprivation. Because sleep issues are so common — and because they have such a major, negative impact on the functioning of families — I am going to begin with effective techniques for solving them. However, you can use these same skills to help your child separate in many other situations, from preschool drop-off to basketball practice to a weekend at Grandma's.

Scene: Mom and Dad's bedroom, 3 a.m.

> *Mackenzie: Mommy, I had a bad dream! I need to sleep in the big bed! (She pulls at her mom's outstretched arm, yanking hard.)*

> *Dad (groaning): No, Mary, please don't. Don't let her. We promised each other. She's five years old! We agreed we need to stop this!*

> *Mom: Just for a few minutes.*

Dad: You know we'll just fall asleep with her in our bed again! It's almost every night these days. Why can't we get our sleep routine nailed down? I'm going crazy from exhaustion!

Mom: She needs us. She's scared. We need to reassure her.

Mackenzie: I'm scared. I need you, Mommy. Let me into the big bed now!

Dad (to Mackenzie): Hey, sweets, go to bed. Go hug your teddy like we talked about earlier.

Mom: I can't stand it! Mackenzie, stop yanking my arm! Just get in here!

Was Mom right to cave, or should she have held firm (despite her exhaustion), as her husband wished? Isn't helping a child when she is in distress the way a parent helps her feel secure and establishes a secure attachment? Isn't building trust all about being nurturing, attuned, and responsive to a child's needs?

The answer to both of these questions is "yes": These qualities are practiced by parents who want to build their child's sense of security. And wise-minded parents can do this while also pursuing other goals at the same time, encouraging self-soothing and self-reliance, and coping with challenging situations. The trick is to know how to handle the highly emotional moments of parenting in a way that accomplishes both goals. Mackenzie's mom isn't doing that yet. Her handling of that all too common situation reflects a common process that plays out in many homes every day (or night):

Child is distressed → Parent gives child what he wants →
Child feels relieved and rewarded

And what happens next? Parents may feel gratified to see their child relieved and happy, but also may feel ambivalent, because they know they've just rewarded their child for whining, throwing tantrums, or avoidance. And the parents are probably also well aware that they've just reinforced a process that is more than likely to continue into a fourth step:

Child is distressed → Parent gives child what he wants →
Child feels relieved and rewarded → *Behavior is reinforced and repeated*

Your child may want to sleep with you, eat another cookie, or get different crayons while you are making dinner. Your child may scream for your attention while you are tending to a sibling, on the phone, or paying for groceries. Your child may want to get out of sports practice or a classmate's birthday party. Addressing all of these situations requires you to cope with distress, skillfully negotiate, and potentially set limits — all the while maintaining your child's sense of security. These are complicated scenarios that require you to make many discerning decisions every day (and probably on many nights), in moments of exhaustion, frustration, and possibly even embarrassment. Practicing wise-minded parenting and the CALM technique (discussed on page 42), and learning to use a few tools, can help you (and your coparent) greatly ease these moments now — and improve or even prevent them in the future.

BALANCING SECURITY AND SKILLS

Many sleep problems stem from a child's need to build the competency (or skill) of separation: He needs to be able to physically separate from you in order to sleep independently. If sleep is not an issue for you, you may be seeing separation problems in other situations, such as summer camps, babysitter nights, or school. Your child needs to learn how to manage his emotions in order to cope with your absence. Secure attachment requires that you balance your child's need for your emotional support and connection with increasing opportunities to learn self-soothing. This practice requires you to be attuned to your child's particular cues and abilities, so that you neither underestimate nor overtax his capacity for coping with challenges, separation, and independence.

Anxiety about separation can generate a great deal of distress for parents and children. It's important (and often difficult) for sleep-deprived parents to remember that when kids have tears, fears, and fits, there is a good chance those behaviors are caused by anxiety, not willfulness. Understanding and managing emotions (yours and theirs) and behaviors (yours and theirs) are central themes of this book. In the coming pages, you will learn about tools and skills you need to produce much better results than you'd ever get from reacting negatively or caving to an emotional child's demands (as Mackenzie's mom did), or ignoring them altogether.

Embracing the dual values of security and competency building
It's important for parents to simultaneously embrace the dual goals of secure attachment and competency building — even though they may sometimes seem to be at odds.

While it is imperative that we create a secure attachment with our children, responding to every desire and distress call is not the best way to do it! Part of building inner security in children involves building competencies, such as coping with anxiety when parents are not present. Just as with any other skill, the best way to learn to cope with anxiety is to practice doing just that.

Parents have many reasons for complying with a child's demands and distress calls, and frankly, sometimes our "responsiveness" is more self-serving than we'd like to admit. We want the child to stop screaming, period. We want to put ourselves out of our misery (i.e., get back to sleep!), even though we say we are doing it for our kids.

A parent recently said to me, "I realized that I was a thief, robbing my son of the opportunity to learn." This very loving mom had nurtured her son ably, and certainly provided him with responsive, sensitive parenting. But she realized that through her efforts to keep his life wonderful every single minute, she was robbing him of the chance to learn to delay gratification, self-soothe, and cope with negative emotions. Now she had a ten-year-old who wasn't able to sleep in his own room alone.

What this mom needs now is a new way to achieve the dual agenda of maintaining a secure attachment (which she's doing well) while building competencies (which is her next challenge). To do this, she will ultimately have to experience her child's — and her own — strong emotions, such as frustration, resentment, fear, anger, guilt, and sadness. These emotions will arise as a natural result of saying "no," talking about negative emotions, negotiating plans for managing the separation, and sticking to plans to increase her child's inner competency. This mom and her spouse will want to employ "emotion coaching" skills (page 144) to help their son put his feelings into words, and then validate his feelings, and make it clear that they want to collaborate with him on this challenge, rather than imposing it unilaterally.

The power of acceptance

Throughout this book, you'll find many strategies that will help you through emotional moments, and a few techniques to help you reach for your skills during the extremely intense ones. Borrowing from the Buddhist tradition, I offer "mantras": easy-to-remember phrases you can call to mind (and possibly chant repeatedly) to keep you focused on your goal. The first of these is a reminder of a crucial underlying concept in parenting, one that enables all other strategies to work effectively:

The Acceptance Mantra:
I accept my child exactly as she is.

The concept is simple, but the practice is complex, because accepting your child as she is during messy, emotionally charged situations can be extremely difficult. However, copious research in the field of secure attachment has proven that acceptance of one's child is essential to the child's sense of security. Building on this body of research is the work of Myla and Jon Kabat-Zinn (Kabat-Zinn and Kabat-Zinn 2014), who have brought the practice of mindfulness to the world of parenting. They emphasize "mindful parenting," which involves being present with one's child in the moment, free of distraction and without passing judgment. This acceptance gives the child a sense of security, and from this base of security, that child can master new challenges and develop competencies.

Researcher Marsha Linehan (Linehan 2015) at the University of Washington extended the concept of acceptance when she created the principles of dialectical behavior therapy (DBT). A "dialectic" is a pair of opposing ideas that, when examined together, actually help you reach a better, fuller understanding of an issue. In Linehan's framework, our Acceptance Mantra evolves to include this dialectic: acceptance and desire for change. Although opposite concepts, they are not mutually exclusive: You can simultaneously accept your child exactly as he is *and* want him to do better. Building new competencies requires change, but change is most likely to occur in the context of complete acceptance. Here's another mantra to remind you of this crucial concept:

The Dialectic of Change Mantra:
I accept my child exactly as he is … and I want him to do better.

For parents, the process of acceptance begins the minute their babies emerge from the womb. We adore our children exactly as they are, but from early on, we also engage in a mutual dance of shaping each other's behavior. Our children will need us to change and adapt to their new needs as they mature, letting them run freely, choose their friends, and keep a secret — even though we're nervous about it. And we will nudge them to build new skills, dress themselves, and refrain from hitting — even though they are resistant to it.

It's a mutual process of acceptance and change for both parent and child.

Secure attachment: the holy grail of parenting

Before we discuss ways to balance this dialectic of accepting completely and encouraging change, we'll take a look at how secure attachment really works, and why the quest to create this attachment is the holy grail of parenting.

Up until the 1970s, most people did not appreciate the critical importance of developing secure attachments between parents and their babies. It wasn't until relatively recently that scientists demonstrated that positive parent-baby interactions actually affect the growth of a child's brain! Brain scans show how loving interactions with a responsive parent stimulates a baby's brain growth; this effect doesn't occur with an impassive, depressed parent (Schore 2001).

Longitudinal research has documented that secure attachment with a primary caregiver predicts healthy social, emotional, and academic functioning throughout a child's life and into adulthood (Cassidy and Shaver 1999). Children with secure histories have greater initiative, self-control abilities, and capacities to make and keep friends than those with histories of anxious and insecure attachments. These patterns hold up even after factoring in the effects of social class, IQ, and temperament.

Furthermore, secure attachment has been associated with an ability to form trusting romantic relationships in adulthood, greater resilience to stress, and lower levels of mental health problems. No wonder forging strong attachment bonds early in life is a parental holy grail!

From a base of secure attachment, babies begin to build trust, first with their parents and then within themselves as they explore their environment. This inner security, combined with the drive of innate curiosity, contribute to a child's zest for exploration.

Exploration pays off in the form of learning, with the aid of hands and mouths, and then by crawling and walking. Infants and toddlers are learning machines and brain-wiring engineers, and it all starts with secure attachment. The children who have received attuned and responsive parenting become secure explorers. They then learn skills for becoming competent in their ever-expanding social and physical worlds.

When one- and two-year-olds show developmental momentum to become more independent, explorative, and even oppositional, they are beginning to forge their parent-child separation (surges of such behavior occur and intensify again during adolescence). The dynamics of this developmental dance, which accelerate between ages three and seven, will be further discussed in Chapter 4, because so much of it is played out in interpersonal (social) ways. But the trajectory of maturation involves a lot of hurtling forward, then getting scared and pulling back (or just resting). Depending on your child's temperament, your child may be the type to "hurtle" or to "turtle" (pull back into the safety of his or her shell), or maybe a little bit of both. Mackenzie, with her drive to sleep with her parents, is the turtling type.

When emotions surface that make parents like Mackenzie's wonder whether they are endangering their child's security, it's easy to buckle. Distress can trigger a "must rescue!" response from the parent, but that's not often the best path to building competency. When parents wonder whether pushing their child toward independence is compromising the child's sense of security, it helps to have a few parameters in mind.

Parents who promote secure attachment:
- are empathetic
- offer support appropriate for the developmental needs of their child
- demonstrate sensitivity to their child's temperament and related needs
- accept the child exactly as he is, while also helping him to mature
- balance support and challenge

Parents who promote secure attachment **do not:**
- try to rid their child of negative emotions
- avoid setting limits just because it displeases their child
- rescue their child from all distress
- push their child to master challenges beyond his or her capability
- attempt to keep their child happy all the time

A rocky yet secure road
Secure attachment is the foundation for everything we want for our children at the end of the rocky road of childhood: high achievement, positive emotional adjustment, and stable relationships. Accepting the rocky part — in which kids scream at you for some of the limit setting you do along the road — takes patience, and a lot of practice.

One of my favorite phrases from neuroscience is "The neurons that fire together, wire together" (Hebb 1949). When we — adults and kids alike — process information from the internal or external world, neurons are firing in our brains. The process of learning new things literally wires neurons together, establishing new neural circuits in our brains that are reinforced with practice. This is how skills are mastered.

When our children are challenged to learn new things, they (like all humans) will need to practice, practice, practice, until these new skills can run on automatic pilot. When the child masters a challenge — whether it is going to sleep alone, overcoming the urge to hit his little brother, or memorizing math facts — he frees up new neural turf for learning other things.

The learning drive
The neurons that fire together, wire together. Learning experiences, secure attachment, and a rich environment enable brain growth. Challenge and even struggle are good! When learning is difficult (but not overwhelming), neurons are more likely to be firing — and wiring, creating new gray matter.

Children's temperaments are significantly determined by their DNA, and it has a lot to do with what they find challenging in learning situations. For instance, children who are predisposed toward anxiety will have a tougher time learning to self-soothe when faced with new social experiences and separation from their parents. Impulsive and high-energy children will have a tougher time learning self-control. I'll explain much more about temperaments in Chapter 2; for now, suffice it to say that our job as parents is to persevere, be patient, and work with these "challenges" (or, as they so often seem, "emotionally draining ordeals!").

Positive parenting

By the time children enter early toddlerhood, parents need to begin thinking about a lot more than providing their kids with love, security, and interesting play activities. Of course, toilet training has already become an agenda, but so has teaching children not to hit people or run into the street. To do this requires a measure of limit setting and discipline. Unfortunately, the whole concept of discipline has gotten mixed up with punishment (more about this in Chapter 6).

The word "discipline" comes from the Latin root word *discere* and means "to teach or facilitate learning." Punishment, which means to impose a negative consequence or hurtful experience for teaching purposes, is one form of teaching, but it is only effective if used very sparingly and in appropriate proportion to the child's infraction, without violence or threats.

Far more effective is a program of positive parenting (Sanders, Turner, and Markie-Dadds 2002; Hawkins et al. 2008; Webster-Stratton, Reid, and Stoolmiller 2008). This includes:

- maintaining a secure attachment
- engaging in play, empathic interactions, and attentive conversations
- emotion coaching, cooperative problem solving, and giving positive attention
- encouraging desirable behavior
- modeling and teaching new skills
- using calm and supportive guidance
- ignoring annoying but harmless behaviors
- implementing logical consequences for misbehavior

When you take a positive parenting approach, you have dozens of tools and strategies at your disposal, which I will cover as we proceed through the next chapters. The following chart shows the degree to which parents build their relationships with their children through play, nurturing experiences, listening, empathic interactions, and spending high-quality time together. It also shows how much we build skills through encouragement, positive attention, and guidance — before we ever need to impose negative consequences or punishment.

Positive Parenting

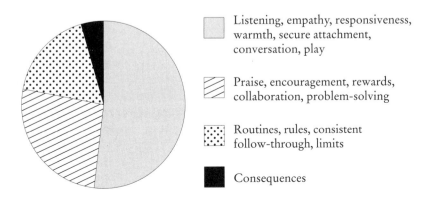

Listening, empathy, responsiveness, warmth, secure attachment, conversation, play

Praise, encouragement, rewards, collaboration, problem-solving

Routines, rules, consistent follow-through, limits

Consequences

Despite the emphasis on positive relating depicted in this chart, limit setting and consequences are inevitable, and so are the negative emotions that erupt as a result. Loving and sensitive parents can have a hard time accepting negative emotions in their children, and become weak-kneed at the daunting task of exercising discipline — even though they recognize the importance of teaching skills. But if parents dread tears and uncomfortable moments, they are going to have difficulty being effective at teaching new skills.

In fact, an aversion to negative emotions can make the transition from parenting an infant to parenting a child a tough one. As crucial as it is for kids to trust their parents, it's important for parents to trust their kids, too — trust them to handle challenging learning curves, frustrations, and disappointments. We need to accept that children will have negative emotions (even about us!) and that we don't need to "fix" them. We need to trust that these negative moments are temporary and know that they are an inevitable part of the learning process.

TEACHING SOLO SLEEPING

Many negative emotions can surface in families that struggle with sleep issues, which can also cause exhaustion, parental conflict, and confused notions of secure attachment. Sleep is integrally related to health and well-being, so it's especially painful when parents and children are deprived of it because of struggles at bedtime.

I'll address other versions of separation anxiety later in this chapter (e.g., aversion to new experiences such as sleepovers, preschool, and camp), but sleeping on their own can be especially difficult for kids, because their parents are right down the hall! The temptation to scream and terrorize the parent into staging a rescue is monumental.

Why do so many fabulous parents go through epic struggles over sleep routines? Most will say they're in a quandary about what's good for nurturing their kids; many others will say they just can't stand listening to their children cry or beg at the bedside. Sometimes it's just easier to crawl into their bed, or let them crawl into yours. And let's face it: It's pretty heavenly to wrap your arms around your beloved babe (and it's heaven for them, too).

Despite this bliss, there are downsides to co-sleeping. Co-sleeping children keep us awake, come between us and our partners (literally and figuratively), and can even learn to associate co-sleeping with safety. They are not actually safer in our beds — and babies are actually at risk of being smothered — but because they have learned to connect safety with co-sleeping, children also connect sleeping alone with distress. This same absolute mental connection between togetherness and safety can result in kids avoiding camps, school, sleepovers, and other challenges. One of our key responsibilities as parents is to help our children cope with the distress caused by normative challenges, and learn to cope with or overcome their fears.

The ages and stages of sleep challenges

Sleep is a major building block of health; sleeping through the night — ideally about 12 hours for a young child — contributes to overall physical health, mood stability, concentration, learning, memory, and well-being in both children and adults. Children spend as much as 40 percent of their childhoods sleeping.

Many toddlers slip into sleep problems, even if they had a successful sleep routine in infancy. Your one- or two-year-old may become distressed about sleeping solo because of mixed feelings about the greater independence that comes with crawling and walking. Most parents have also observed a very normal version of stranger anxiety in their children, which can also cause sleep disruptions; this may emerge at around eight months of age and run through about the end of year two.

Late in their third year and into their fourth, children usually have another burst of seeking autonomy. They push for more independence on many fronts, and their greater cognitive capacity results in expanded imaginative powers — which instigate greater fears. At this age and into year five, they often wonder if something dreadful will befall them, Mommy, or Daddy during the night. The darkness and the separation at bedtime can cause those fears to skyrocket.

The good news is that their newly capable minds can also be quite open to creative solutions. Your child may accept a prayer, a song, or an audiobook to dispel their fears. Don't expect logic and your explanations of reality to help much; if your reassurance about nonexistent monsters doesn't work the first or second time, stop talking and try another tack.

The family bed

Some parents don't mind midnight visits to the big bed. Others enjoy co-sleeping, and are comfortable postponing solo sleeping until the child (hopefully) chooses to sleep on his own. While health practitioners vary in their opinions about co-sleeping (Moon 2015), I take a qualified middle-of-the-road approach: Both children and parents need a routine that ensures that all parties get good sleep. The family bed can be fine for some, but if sleep is disrupted or either parent is dissatisfied with the arrangement, working toward solo sleeping for the child becomes a goal.

Many family-bed enthusiasts believe that co-sleeping enhances security; in actuality, it doesn't ensure secure attachment any more than holding hands all the time would. Maintaining proximity, such as having your child with you in bed, is an overly simplistic and reductionist way of understanding healthy attachment. And for many sleep-deprived couples — and couples that like to have sex spontaneously — co-sleeping with a child can be a major nuisance.

Since co-sleeping doesn't really enhance the mental health or security of the child, many parents will eventually choose to tackle the solo-sleeping challenge. And contrary to some parents' fears, security and the parent-child bond will not be harmed by a few nights of tears within an otherwise loving and responsive pattern of parenting.

Research backs this up. A recent study addressed the long-asked question of whether techniques to support solo sleeping caused stress in kids and led them to be less secure or well-adjusted in the long term (Price et al. 2012). A group of parents of seven-month-olds were taught certain sleep techniques (including "controlled crying" and "camping out," which I'll explain in a bit), and that group was compared to a group who did not receive training. Years later, when the children were 6, those who were taught to sleep in their own beds were no more likely to show emotional, behavioral, or attachment problems than those who were not trained. Since these babies were trained in sleeping solo at seven months of age, I hope this quells worries about negotiating it with a three- to seven-year-old, especially when using the stepwise, emotionally supportive framework outlined later in this chapter.

Many parents end up co-sleeping, not because they prefer the family bed, but because they dread the difficulties of their child's transition to solo sleeping. Establishing a program that builds the child's new skill of sleeping in her bed all night is accomplished in the same way that other skills are built. Before we tackle the specific program for sleep, I'll review the steps parents take to get any new behavior up and running. This is achieved through a program of positive reinforcement.

Positive reinforcement

More often than not, by the time parents realize they want to see more of a desired behavior, they are frustrated and upset by its undesired flip side. Whether these undesirable behaviors involve dawdling, tantrums, or aggression toward siblings, the family may have descended into a pattern of negative power struggles. Referring back to the chart on page 9, the first order of business is for parents to make sure the general level of positive feelings in their relationship with the child is high. If not, invest in more of the activities described in the section on play (page 115). As you consider behavioral charts and other deliberate ways to attend to positive behaviors, know that those efforts are always more effective in the context of lots of positive relating. Next, parents need to focus on supporting positive behaviors and ignoring small, negative provocations.

When children engage in certain behaviors, it's because those behaviors are rewarding in some way. While undesirable behaviors might be driving you batty, your own behavior may be reinforcing them, creating a negative feedback loop. Who among us doesn't pay attention when a child shrieks in the car? The problem is that when we scold that shrieking kid, *she is actually more likely to continue shrieking*. Any attention — even negative — can be reinforcing.

One of the most misunderstood facts in psychology is that negative approaches to discipline can actually be reinforcing, because even negative attention is rewarding. Kids may hate it when their parents yell and punish, but they are likely to continue the undesirable behaviors for two reasons: number one, they received attention; and number two, now they are really mad at their parents (more about punishment and ignoring is in Chapter 6).

Kids fight fire with fire, often reacting with more misbehavior in response to scolding and yelling. These power struggles invariably lead to a lose-lose outcome. Even if a harsh punishment scares the child into temporary submission, it does not encourage long-term compliance and good will. A win-win solution occurs when parents give their child incentive for positive behaviors by offering rewards, and keeping their attachment secure by being trust-worthy and understanding. If you always start with the assumption that your child's emotions are valid, you will be able to address both the "acceptance" and the "change" part of the challenging situation.

Strategic ignoring
By paying attention to undesirable behaviors — even simply telling your child to stop whining — you have just made it more likely that they will continue to occur. Try to ignore most low-level undesirable behaviors, praise the desired behavior, and consider what needs drive the behavior in the first place.

Let's take the example of whining. It is extremely easy to slip into telling your toddler to stop whining. You may even say that you'll give him what he wants if only he'll stop. But talking about whining and rewarding kids for stopping it are problematic; both reinforce the behavior. The reward gives him incentive to do it again to get another reward. A better solution is to ignore the whining until it stops. When your child starts talking normally, wait a minute or so, and then praise him, saying, "I love it when you use your big-boy voice!" Or you could simply engage with him again; that is reinforcement enough. More elaborate strategies for reaping the benefits of strategic ignoring are available in Chapter 6.

It's important to remember that although we can't always give children our immediate attention, they do need our attention! When we seek out the "why" behind behaviors (page 112), we are helping our children learn to put feelings into words and appreciating the developmental normalcy of emotionally fueled behaviors. It helps us keep our empathy high — even as we struggle against the urge to give into our children's demands or criticize them for normal and valid feelings and behaviors.

In some ways, parents are set up for failure; humans are wired to pay more attention to problems than to business as usual. In neuroscience, this tendency is called the "negative affectivity bias." Reacting to stressors, especially life-threatening ones, has been a survival mechanism for millions of years in our evolution. But most parents need to learn to override the instinct to react to every irritation, exercising willpower to ignore the little stuff and praise the positive efforts. In this way, we shape our children's behaviors as they progress toward goals.

First, we praise our toddler when she puts toothpaste on her toothbrush, then when she brushes all of her teeth without being coaxed, and then when she traipses off to the bathroom to do the routine independently. We try to ignore her lapses — or at least not yell about them — because attention can serve to reward those lapses!

HOW TO SET UP A BEHAVIORAL PROGRAM

Decades of research have demonstrated the effectiveness of behavioral programs, which are plans that help you and your child work toward a goal, tracking and celebrating progress along the way (Kaminski et al. 2008; Kumpfer and Alvarado 2003; Kazdin 2005). Does your family need a behavioral program? Maybe not. But if you are engaged in power struggles and are tired of pleading, nagging, and yelling — and your child is, too — you may find that a sticker chart is your new best friend.

Behavioral programs are effective, but they are also easy to goof up, so the details are important. For instance, if threats or scolding get mixed into the program, the potential for success gets scotched pretty quickly. Also, I always recommend that parents first spend a couple of weeks of increasing play and positive interactions with their children; some kids naturally become more cooperative when they're enjoying more time with their parents.

A key ingredient in setting up your own behavioral program is to create a chart that identifies goals and tracks progress. Points, checkmarks, and stickers indicate that the desirable behavior occurred. The chart reminds you and your child to celebrate positive achievements — new skills! It also reminds you that your job as a parent is to monitor progress and supply rewards.

Get a poster board or other big piece of paper, and use decorations and fun markers to make the project attractive. Put the days of the week at the top, three to six behaviors listed down the left-hand side, and record the occurrence of those "target" behaviors with stars, checkmarks, or stickers. Empty boxes show when the behavior did not occur. Note: If you have other children, create charts for them, too; otherwise, you may create a problem of sibling rivalry.

Here's an example of what your chart might look like:

	SUN	MON	TUE	WED	THU	FRI	SAT
Brush teeth							
Get ready for school on time							
Pick up toys							

A word about rewards

Some parents have a problem with reward systems. They may think, *Kids should do what they're asked. Why do we have to bribe our kids just to do the right thing?* This is where our third mantra, the Reason Mind Mantra, comes in:

The Reason Mind Mantra:
I might be right, but am I effective?

Sometimes, kids are naturally motivated to do the right thing (this is called "intrinsic motivation"). They put on their coats because it is cold, put their belongings in their cubbies at school because it feels good to conform with their peers, and take a nap because they are tired. But many, many other times, they don't want to do what we want them to do. They want to dawdle in the morning and stay up into the evening because there are so many other fun things to do. Parents supply "extrinsic" (external) reinforcement in the form of structure, incentives, and praise to support the development of skills. Kids internalize these rules and routines at some point and "get with the program," but until they do, parents will get better results with honey rather than vinegar.

Mountains of research have shown that kids learn most effectively with positive reinforcement than they do with punishments, yelling, or authoritarian approaches (Kazdin and Benjet 2003; Kiesner, Dishion, and Poulin 2004; McMahon and Forehand 2003). Although it would be nice if we could encourage desirable behaviors with nothing but praise and explanations, the truth is that sometimes we need to resort to incentives to prevent those power struggles.

Rewards and learning
The research is overwhelming: Rewards help us learn and accomplish minor and major goals. As incentives, they serve to enhance motivation.

Once the new habit becomes automatic, external rewards can be phased out, and so can charts. Consider rewards as "jump starts" for new habits, which, once firmly established, are powered by their own motivational fuel.

To establish a positive reinforcement program for desired behaviors, follow this basic plan:

Ten guidelines for behavioral programs

1. Decide on the target behavior. Identify the desired behavior you want to reward (e.g., brushing teeth, dressing, getting out of bed when asked, one hour spent peacefully with little brother).

2. Involve your child in a positive way as you create a chart. "We're building a new skill!" you can say. "You will receive a goody for your efforts! I'm excited because I know you can do this big-kid job, and then we will celebrate." Explain that you are going to create a chart to keep track of progress.

3. Decide on an attractive reward. Make sure the reward is something your child is excited about and that will motivate him.

4. Reward as quickly as possible, and be specific: The child exhibits X behavior, and he will receive Y reward.

5. Remember, for older children with more challenging target goals, provide points that earn bigger rewards. For a child five or older, consider using a point system in which a certain number of points earn bigger treats. More powerful reward systems engender more motivation to engage in target behaviors. Younger kids can't understand delayed gratification, so stick with stickers or goodies you give immediately.

6. Treat the chart as a cheerleading opportunity. If you are using stickers, keep them secret so that they are surprising. Hang the chart in a prominent place. Remember that your approval is a primary motivator, not just the reward.

7. Give minimal prompts to remind your child about target behaviors, such as:

- "It's time to do your morning routine."
- "Let's look at the chart so you know what to do next."
- "Let's see what you need to do to earn points toward that teddy bear."

8. Stay polite, positive, and attentive to your child. Young children need shepherds to help them stay on task, without nagging or negativity. Inattention and distractibility are built-in characteristics of their immature brains. Don't blame them for those characteristics any more than you would for their height or hair color.

9. Remember that your approval and praise need to be maintained after you phase out the program. Your positive attention represents a huge part of the reinforcement, even though you dole out rewards initially to entice your child to work hard on new skills. You'll phase out the program after the target behavior becomes automatic, but you'll still want to keep showing appreciation for your child's self-management in genuine, loving ways.

10. When your child has failed to exhibit the target behavior, say nothing and make sure you initiate no punitive responses. If anything, just say, "I'll bet you can earn a sticker next time." It's important to be neutral and make this failure a non-event. If the program becomes negative, it will tank.

Creating a behavioral program for sleep

The biggest challenge of creating a behavioral program to build sleep skills is the intense hardship on both the parents and the child, who must master the child's fear of separation while in a state of absolute exhaustion. You may have to listen to bloodcurdling screams, being called "bad mommy" and "mean daddy," or really dramatic statements ("You're killing me!"). With aversive stuff like this coming at you, how can you persevere?

Better nights in the long run
Many people don't like the idea of a sleep program, since it may be associated with some upsets while solo sleeping skills are being established. However, parents who adopt such a program may experience fewer tirades and charged emotional exchanges with their children than those parents who do not, the latter instead hoping that their children will sleep on their own naturally (someday), but ending up with prolonged and disturbing negative nocturnal interactions with their kids.

Maybe you aren't ready for a solo-sleeper program. That's understandable, given the effort involved in implementing one with minimal emotional hardship on your family. It's critical that you and your co-parent carefully choose the right time to begin; you both need to be willing to endure the learning curve for establishing this new skill. You also need to be extremely consistent with your program. If either parent isn't ready for a couple of nights of potential hell on earth, she or he can sabotage the whole effort with a single rescue that teaches the child more about upping the ante than about self-soothing. Unity is mandatory.

If parents are divorced and have different policies (or grandparents do), you can still be successful with your program. Why? Children can adapt to situation-specific programs — one for travel, one for Dad's house, and another for Grandma's. But in your own home, follow the same routine every night and keep it consistent.

Programs that ease infants and children into sleeping alone, when carried out responsibly, have never been shown to harm children or cause long-term negative effects. In fact, such programs often improve life, especially for kids who have depressed parents. Successful sleeping programs have been shown to diminish maternal depression, a condition that is associated with negative behavioral and emotional consequences for kids. For specific sleep disturbances, such as sleep walking or night terrors, consult your pediatrician or a sleep specialist.

A crucible in the sleep-separation challenge

When kids are crying about sleeping solo, remember that both child and parent need to master their fear of separation. Fetching children into your bed is not necessarily a proof of your attachment; it just means you can't stand the screaming, don't feel like you have the right plan in place, or you simply aren't ready.

The Successful Sleeper program

By the time kids are two or three, parents have usually established some kind of bedtime ritual. Physical play should wind down about an hour before bedtime, as should socializing and screen time for older children. Optimally, parents follow the same drill every night, which prepares the brain and body for "classical conditioning," linking the routine to the sleep response. Typical bedtime rituals include bath, snack, glass of water, hugging the pet, brushing teeth, bedtime story, toilet visit, and a tuck-in with a kiss and a snuggle with the teddy bear or blanket.

The Successful Sleeper program is a behavioral program, and it assumes you already have a bedtime ritual that you follow every night. If you don't, establishing one is your first step, because the program builds on top of that strong platform.

The way you present the Successful Sleeper program to your child will depend on his age and stage. With a younger child (ages three or four), you can explain it by drawing pictures. With an older child, you will discuss the program in more elaborate terms, giving him some power in deciding details and creating the chart and pictures. You are setting the goal of the child sleeping solo, but giving your child choices about his program helps with buy-in and cooperation.

Here are the steps to building your Successful Sleeper program:

1. **Present the new program.** Say something like this: "I'm sorry that I haven't helped you become successful with sleeping through the night in your own bed. We are going to help you learn to do that now! Do you remember how it was hard to learn how to ride a tricycle [or some other mastered challenge], but when you did, you felt really good about it? When you become a successful sleeper in your own room, you will feel good about this achievement, too."

Make sure you have this meeting during the day, and, with younger children, start that very night. With older ones, use your judgment as to whether your child needs to first prepare a toolkit (see number 5, next page).

2. **The chart.** Create a chart or calendar with a schedule of your goals and the rewards earned for successes, similar to that on page 16. For a young child, the chart can include a picture of him sleeping in his bed as one goal, a picture of him waking up and staying in the bed as another, and a picture of him getting up in the morning with a smile on his face as a third. You can also have a picture of the reward he will earn for a successful night of staying in bed.

3. **Defining success.** Success for a younger child is either staying in bed all night, or cooperating without protest when you escort her back to bed. For an older child, a major success is staying in bed all night; a minor success is cooperating with the parent's escort back to her own room. The reward for

the major success should be twice what it is for a minor one.

4. A "pass" occurs when a child fails to stay in bed all night, and then fails to return to bed in a cooperative manner; in other words, he throws a fit or won't stay in his room after being returned there. No reward is earned. He is taking a pass on receiving a reward.

On "pass" nights for all kids, as well as on "minor" reward nights for older children (they've gotten up but they are cooperative about returning to their beds), parents should attempt to be as boring and neutral as possible. If the child reacts to not getting a sticker the next day, assume a "let's hope for the best next time" attitude; avoid anger, threats, or lecturing. If the child takes passes on a nightly basis, parents should return to the drawing board, and make sure that they are not being inconsistent (this is usually the problem) and that the rewards are adequately motivating. Also, you can consider using the "camping out," "controlled comforting," and "door duty" methods (discussed late in this chapter).

5. Rewards. Rewards serve as incentives for kids who dread sleeping alone. They can be sweet treats, stamps, stickers, or small trinkets, but they should be given and recorded on the chart first thing in the morning, since young children are not motivated by delayed gratification.

As explained on page 17, older children may be intrigued (and motivated) by a point system, perhaps used during visits to your "store." Points are earned for minor and major successful sleeper nights, marked brightly on the chart, and are exchanged for goods from a little store you establish — which is really a box that can be opened only at pre-arranged times. You will categorize items valued at various point levels (five, ten, twenty), and your child "purchases" items with her accumulated points. This system has the advantage of getting children excited by visits to the store (and hopefully sleeping successfully in their beds!), because it is an unexpected, fun, and rewarding game. Occasionally adding items to the store keeps the store visits fun and surprising.

Younger children (three- to four-year-olds) will only have one level of a reward (not "major" or "minor"), which they will earn by staying in bed all night or by cooperating with the escort back to bed. Young children can't handle too much complexity, and if they handle the walk back to their room without a squall, they deserve a reward! If they are consistently emotionally distraught while being returned to bed, consider an interim program like the "camping out" or "controlled comforting" options described later in this chapter.

6. The self-soothing toolkit. Most young children use a blanket, stuffed animal, or other prized item for self-soothing and coping when parents aren't around. These items are called "transitional objects," because children hold on to these objects to bridge the transition between being with the parent and being alone. These security objects serve to reassure them during the going-to-sleep phase and at times when they wake up and need additional self-soothing. Have you heard stories about a well-adjusted youth taking her teddy bear to college? It happens!

The self-soothing toolkit is a collection of things your child will use as sleep aids to help her stay in bed and self-soothe, instead of begging for you at bedtime. If she's been returned to bed by your (boring) escort service, she'll engage with her toolkit instead of protesting or begging. A partial reward for cooperating with this minor success makes sense, because she has accomplished a lot by exerting the self-discipline involved in using the toolkit instead of pitching a fit.

Talk with your child in detail about how she will self-soothe in the middle of the night. You want to prepare her for those anxious feelings by making a plan and a toolkit. How will she calm herself instead of coming to your bed? Does she want to pretend to feed her doll a bottle? Sing a song to her teddy? Tie five blankets around five stuffed animals? Practice breathing exercises together (page 158) and encourage their use during bedtime.

If your child has a recurring bad dream, have her finish it with a funny or empowering ending. One child I worked with had the recurring nightmare of a boogeyman with a gun. When she woke up, she would "play her mind story" that the boogeyman turned into a clown with a banana. In this way, she mastered her nightmare.

Consider creating and recording a "guided imagery" story (page 170) that she can use every night to fill her head with pleasant thoughts instead of scary ones. All humans need techniques for self-calming when anxious, and little ones need help and encouragement from parents to identify what will work for them.

An extra-special addition to a child's toolkit may be a favorite story recording on a device (not a smartphone or any other device that allows her to access stimulating games or media). Make sure your child only has access to a couple of recordings, preferably ones that aren't novel and arousing to the brain. Listening to these recordings is something your child can do instead of waking you, which gives her control of her own self-soothing. You are conditioning her to connect the toolkit with sleep; her brain registers "This cue means sleep."

The self-soothing toolkit is made extra-special when it is only available at bedtime. The iPod loaded with favorite lullabies or a sweet story may be hard to keep in the kit, but it becomes extra-special if she only gets access to this enticing pleasure at night.

Buying new items for the toolkit is OK because it sweetens the deal; just don't expect new items to equate with perfect compliance. Any challenging new habit means steps forward and backward along the learning curve.

7. Play practice. Make a game out of practicing the program. In the light of day, playact the program with your child. He can pretend to wake up in the middle of the night and use his toolkit. He can come to your bed, and you can sleepily and boringly walk him back to bed, after which he will choose a calming strategy for going back to sleep without you. He can pitch a fit, earn a "pass," and you can practice saying, "Better luck next time." Kids even get a goody as part of the practice! They enjoy this technique, because they get to see their parents being silly, and they even get rewards for it. They love to play practice — even though they may hate your expectation that they follow the program consistently at night.

8. Start date. For children younger than age five who don't have a good sense of time, start the program the same day you introduce it. Have the self-soothing toolkit organized with your best guess of stuff they'll use for middle-of-the-night soothing rituals. For older children who may need more ownership of the program and time to select their own soothing tools, choose a date together and decorate that date on your chart.

9. Innovation. Your child probably knows what she likes best for rewards and soothing techniques, but most programs need tweaking along the way. Your child may upgrade her toolkit from stuffed animals to books, or maybe a mindfulness recording on an iPod. You may discover that your wee one will do absolutely anything, including sleep through the night, for a Pop-Tart. You may hate the junk, love the sleep, and worry about morning nutrition another time.

10. Backsliding and caving. Forgive and recommit! Backsliding should be expected. Illness, travel, houseguests, and other stressors can screw up anyone's sleep program. If both parents are getting enough sleep and want to continue the family bed for a while longer, that may be a perfectly fine decision (just like postponing summer camps and team sports). But when you're ready for a new start, have a summit meeting with your co-parent and child, and recommit. Start fresh with a new chart. Try your hardest to persist and persevere for two weeks.

Remember that if you cave on day ten and allow your yelling child back in the big bed, you have just reinforced your child's screaming fits. *It worked!* the child thinks. *I cracked the code!* And he may try other strategies for getting his parents to cave: One night, screaming works; another night, crying about a horrific dream; yet another, describing tummy aches ... whatever it takes. And don't forget, even while implementing a sleep program, you'll be doing lots of validating, helping him master sleep fears with guided imagery and explaining how distress can turn into stomachaches. Self-calming is the goal.

Children (especially older ones) who fail to cope with fears and instead escape challenges by pitching fits are probably swimming in stress hormones, so they truly are experiencing tummy aches and need calming. Even though Pop-Tarts, iPods, and stickers sounded great at that successful-sleep meeting during the day, in the middle of the night, with anxiety flowing, the biggest reward is always sleeping with you.

Three techniques for easing sleep struggles

Some children are so unhinged emotionally when they are flooding with separation anxiety that you may want to employ some extra steps in your program. These extra steps make success at sleeping through the night longer to achieve, which can be frustrating for the parent who must endure more sleep loss. But for more anxiety-prone children — or the parents who has a hard time with child anxiety or protests — these steps can help get them through some of the tougher nights, with supports that keep them on track.

'Camping out'

The "camping out" technique can take several forms. You can let your child sleep in a sleeping bag on the floor of your room. Every night, you drag it a foot closer to her room, until she ends up there, sleeping alone. Rewards are given for staying in place all night. For an older child, you can mark the plan on the chart so that she is participating in the negotiation; with the younger child, you will just describe this plan and do it.

Another version of camping out involves your sitting by the child's bedside (or as far away as she can tolerate for step one) while she falls asleep. You move a foot farther away per night, until your child falls asleep without your being nearby. This approach is also called "gradual retreat." It's your time to read a book to yourself!

'Door duty'

The "door duty" method works well for children who won't stay in their beds after the bedtime ritual has been completed, perhaps unless their parents lie down with them for "just a minute" (which can turn into hours for exhausted parents). Pretty soon, your child is like an infant who has never learned that going to sleep alone is a safe experience; the very idea can throw these children into a frenzy.

For door duty, the parent leaves the child's room and comes back to the doorway at certain intervals, until the child is asleep. The deal you strike is that if he stays in his bed, you will agree to door duty. The agreement starts with five-minute intervals between visits on the first night, and stretches to ten, fifteen, or twenty minutes over time, until the child is successful at sleeping without this routine. Make an agreement during a daytime meeting to add five (or more) minutes to the interval of your door duty every week and put it on the chart. Your child gets a reward for staying in bed.

Since the child should have a much earlier bedtime than you, you can set a timer and do other things — but make it a sacred covenant to show up on time. If you don't, your child will learn to not trust you with agreements, and you will have opened up a can of psychological worms (in the form of your child's distrust, threats, and emotional tirades) that are hard to squish back into the can.

When you return to the doorway, the rule is that you do not go in. Sure, it's hard not to cuddle or be pulled into all manner of little requests. But remember that the Successful Sleeper program assumes you've already done your bedtime ritual and taken care of regular requests.

What do you say and do at the door? You can say, "Checking in, like I said I would. Good night. Sweet dreams. See you in the morning." Have your child come up with a jingle you repeat; the more your child "owns" the program, the more likely she is to cooperate. Heck, if she wants you to sing a verse of "The Ants Go Marching," do it! (Only one verse, though.) Do not engage in elaborate reassurances; they just focus the child on her anxiety.

When your child pleads with you to come into her room, refer to the rule. "The rule is that I'm only allowed to come to the door. The deal is that you try to quiet yourself in your bed and then I come back in five minutes. OK, here I go. I'll come back in five minutes!" This way, you are complying with the rule, and you are not the bad guy. Rewards are given for compliance with the agreement that the child to stay quiet and in her bed. A little judgment is required here; if she shrieks a bit but stays in her bed and makes an effort to self-calm, you will want to give her a reward. If she screams the whole time, the system is not working, and you will want to consider backing up to a shorter interval.

While you might be tempted to also offer to do door duty after escorting your child back to bed in the middle of the night, try not to; it's very hard on you to do this. It's better than getting into bed with them, but how many parents want to set timers and stand for door duty at 3 a.m.? Not me. We are not trying to be superhuman here. For children struggling with midnight freak-outs that can't be quelled with their own self-soothing, consider using camping out or "controlled comforting."

'Controlled comforting'

A very common technique that parents use when their child yells out from his bed is "controlled comforting." When your child cries for you, you respond — from your bed, and only after about a minute or two. Keep delaying your response more and more on subsequent nights. You muster your kindest and softest voice and say, "It's time to sleep. You can do it. I will see you in the morning." Avoid saying much more than that, because you want your child to know you are there but that it is time for sleep, not for a reunion and elaborate choruses of reassurance.

It can be incredibly difficult for parents not to reassure (or to delay reassuring) a child who is begging for it. But focusing on fears, even with reassurances, can create more anxiety. Think about it: Explaining that you are right there, loving her, and not letting anything bad happen to her puts the focus on you. But you do not want your child's goal to be engaging you; you want it to be sleep. You can say, "You might want to sing that lullaby you like. It's time to sleep. Nighty-night."

Start with a one- or two-minute delay before you speak up; then move to four, eight, or ten minutes. Your child is learning that you are indeed down the hall, but you are not coming to his bed. While waiting for longer and longer intervals (or screaming initially and then stopping to listen), he falls asleep.

Crafting what's right for you

Since the key to success is consistency, you need to tailor a program that you can stick to. Setting yourself up for success is important, so don't try a new program if your family is experiencing a big transition, illness, or other stressful situation. And if your intuition tells you that you don't have it in you to do anything about sleep (or some other big competency-building endeavor) right now, postpone it, because consistency is the name of the game when it comes to successful parenting.

As you review the options above for your anxious seven-year-old, your persistent three-year-old, or your own reluctant self, you will have a sense of what ingredients might be best for you and your family. You want "wins" and rewards to keep the child invested in the plan. If the program you initially devise isn't cutting it, add steps that allow your child mastery and rewards, as she scales the learning curve toward sleeping successfully alone. Innovate as needed to create a program that works for you.

Being a secure parent

Parents often tell me that they give in to their children's distress pleas even though they fully believe that their children need to learn more self-reliance and self-soothing. Two of the most common reasons parents have for caving relate to their perceptions of their child's security: They want to avoid "abandoning" their distressed child, and they want to offer comfort during their child's time of need. These motivations essentially trump the goal of enhancing self-reliance (and self-soothing) in the child. With their own anxiety triggered, these parents slip into believing that they must choose what they perceive is supporting security (caving to distress) over skill building (sticking with the program). Effective sleep programs can support both security and skill building at the same time, but to the anxious parent, it can seem like the two concepts can't coexist. Extreme emotions hijack our ability to think in complex and rational terms. (See more about the science of emotions in the Chapter 5.)

Do you find yourself caving to your child's distress calls over your better judgment? Do you worry about your child's security, and feel insecure about your parenting calls? The problem may lie in a miscalculation of what really hurts children. Your child's emotional reactions to reasonable challenges may translate in your mind to bad parenting or an interference with a secure attachment. It's hard to feel secure when you are faced with your child's bloodcurdling screams and overwrought words, especially when they are directed at you personally ("I need you!" "I'm scared!" "I hate you!"). The highly distressed child will use any words or actions he can think of that might end his misery.

The trick for dealing with your child's extreme anxiety is to avoid absorbing her words as truth. Yes, your child feels terror in the moment ... and it is a moment that will pass. How can you help? First, you need to understand the emotions behind separation anxiety.

DEALING WITH SEPARATION ANXIETY

You may not have a sleep problem with your child, but your child might be facing fears about separation from you in other contexts. If your child experiences extreme anxiety when separated from you, in many situations, you should seek a professional consultation; treating a full-blown case of separation anxiety is outside of the scope of this book. Excessive anxiety may surface as inconsolable crying, sweating, diarrhea, and other physical problems.

There are evidence-based therapies for separation anxiety that involve cognitive-behavioral and exposure therapy and teaching the child coping techniques similar to the self-soothing toolkit on page 22 (Compton and March et al. 2004; In-Albon and Schneider 2007; Velting, Setzer, and Albano 2004). The most effective programs introduce children to their fears in a stepwise fashion, so they can experience distress and then calming.

Children who are triggered by a fear when separated from a parent will not feel safe just because their parent tells them they are. They must learn it by experiencing the rise and fall of anxiety without the parent acting as the "safety zone" (the thing that makes them calm and feel safe). If parents respond to their children's fear by rescuing them, children will believe that the only reason for their reduced anxiety was their parent's presence. Lesson learned? "I am only safe when my parent is with me."

Anxious children need to face whatever triggers their anxiety, use self-soothing methods, and experience the success of reducing their anxiety by using their coping skills. They learn to ride the wave of anxiety to its natural reduction. In treatment circles, this procedure is called "exposure and response prevention," which basically means such children are exposed to the scary thing (e.g., sleeping alone, a swim lesson, a new school) and they do not use escape to deal with the fear. Anxiety is like gravity: What goes up (the heart rate) always comes down. Essentially, the children learn that the solution is coping skills, not avoidance or escape.

Don't argue over emotions
Whatever your child is afraid of — sleeping alone, a new school, or a swim lesson — can be considered a fear trigger. Acknowledge that he feels fear; don't try to talk him out of it! He won't feel safe just because you say he is. It is remarkable how ineffective reassurances are in dousing the fires of extreme emotion.

Constant reassurances only exasperate both you and your child, because when your efforts fail to reassure, you will most likely become frustrated, angry, or intensely anxious. Now both of you are basket cases!

The importance of learning how to deal with fears and anxiety is wildly under-estimated. If a child learns that the solution to reducing anxiety is proximity to parents, she doesn't learn that anxiety abates naturally within a certain time frame. She also does not learn self-calming. Many techniques can be employed to deal with waves of anxiety. A common refrain in my field (from Jon Kabat-Zinn) is: "You can't stop the waves, but you can learn to surf," which is an excellent mantra for self-soothing:

The Soothing Mantra:
You can't stop the waves, but you can learn to surf.

Self-soothing skills

When we last saw Mackenzie and her parents, they were sharing a bad moment in the middle of the night. Now, let's visit Mackenzie and her mom at a good moment the next day, when Mom demonstrates both her sensitivity to Mackenzie and her desire to support her coping skills.

Content (what is said)	**Process** (the underlying dynamic)
Mom: Do you want to talk about that dream last night? You were scared!	Mom is not avoiding this difficult subject, which shows that she wants to help her daughter face her fears.
Mackenzie: I hate it when I dream that coyotes are chasing me. That's why I want to sleep with you, Mommy!	Mackenzie sees seeking proximity to Mommy as the solution to her fear trigger.
Mom: What did you do the night that you slept at Grandma's and had that same dream? You did a really good job of dealing with your fear.	Mom has directed the conversation to a time that she knows her daughter coped well with her fear and did not require co-sleeping.
Mackenzie: I woke up and did that thing where I finished the dream the way you taught me; you know, I made up a good ending. A unicorn came by and picked me up and carried me home to my safe bed in my purple room.	Mackenzie demonstrates her ability to use a coping technique from her toolkit. Mom has helped her "finish" her bad dream in a good way and be empowered to face her fear trigger.
Mom: I'm really sorry that I didn't take you back to your bed last night. You could have practiced being the brave girl who rides a unicorn! What a cool ending to that dream!	Mom lets her daughter know that she regrets her harshness at the bedside. Even though they had a setback in their sleep routine, Mom admires Mackenzie for her earlier coping capacity for self-soothing.

Children can manage their distress in some settings when Mom isn't around (like at Grandma's house), but that doesn't mean they won't reach for the ideal comforter when they have the opportunity. Remember: Practicing new skills is really hard. Why not try to get out of it if you can? Don't we adults have a hard time keeping our exercise habits going? Or persevering through strife? I'll admit that I'm quick to call my tech guy when I'm freaking out about a computer problem, instead of figuring it out for myself.

TIPPING THE SCALE TOWARD SELF-RELIANCE

If constant rescuing is at one end of the scale and abandonment or neglectful treatment is at the other, the happy medium is secure attachment while promoting skill building. Some parents, afraid that they will seem detached or unavailable to their child, feel compelled to seek solutions for every distressful moment. Some of these parents suffered abuse or deprivation in their own childhoods, so they seek to compensate for what happened to them. But, as we've established, responding to every moment of distress with a rescue operation is counterproductive for parent and child alike.

Mackenzie's mom has mixed feelings about the successful sleep routine. Mackenzie has bad dreams, tummy aches, dry mouth, coyote fantasies, and all kinds of ways of hooking mom in the middle of the night. Her mom wants to be a really good comforter, but she also wants Mackenzie to get good sleep and learn the skills to cope with distress. She wants both secure attachment and self-reliance for her daughter. She knows she has to deal with her own distress about seeing and feeling her daughter's distress.

When parents are tuned into the signals sent by their child, and then attend to the child's needs, it's referred to as "attunement." Attuned parents are sensitive to their children's behavioral cues and emotions, feel empathy for them, and then *decide* how to respond, rather than just reacting emotionally.

Sometimes, parents have difficulty separating their own feelings or needs from those of their child. When we absorb our children's emotions, it's difficult to think clearly enough to figure out what they really needs and what is best for them. For instance, if you are feeling 100 percent of your child's panic, you may not be able to think or act effectively when your child melts down with the babysitter, neighbor's dog, or boisterous friend.

When psychologists talk about "psychological boundaries," they are referring to the imaginary line that separates us from others. Ideally, we don't have boundaries that are "permeable" (letting all feelings in) or "rigid" (not allowing feelings to affect us), but instead we have "firm" boundaries, such that we can empathize with others, but still organize our thoughts and make judicious responses.

The critical importance of psychological boundaries
We parents need to strike a balance in which we are empathetic and attuned to our children's feelings, but have firm enough boundaries that we can think for ourselves, figure out what they need from us, and do what is truly in their best interest.

Parents who have permeable boundaries often have a hard time setting limits, because they can be overwhelmed with the feelings they absorb from their children. Parents with rigid boundaries lack empathy and may neglect their children's emotional needs because they are cut off from feelings. Firm boundaries allow parents to use their hearts and minds to make tough and wise decisions.

Most parents will have moments of doubt, wondering whether they should tilt the balance toward comforting or instead nudge their child toward building a new skill. If we decide on skill building, using a behavioral program is an effective way to avoid lectures, punishments, threats, and power struggles.

Are you ready for a behavior management program?
You are ready when you believe your child has the capacity to both maintain secure attachment and tolerate distress from some of your parenting decisions. You also believe you can encourage your child's coping, even though there will be moments of anger directed at you for challenging her with this goal.

Mackenzie's mom is facing a dilemma: She values being nurturing and responsive, but she also values supporting her daughter's capacity to cope with distress. She can't always be her daughter's comforter, and she doesn't want to be, because that would impede her daughter's ability to self-soothe, become independent, and competently manage stress as she explores the world. This mom is also ready to stop the bedside fights late at night, when everyone is being deprived of sleep and at their wits' end.

In the light of day, Mom knows she wants to recommit to helping her daughter with those skills. She likes the idea of the Successful Sleeper program, but she has to resolve her ambivalence and work through the jumble of her complicated thoughts, feelings, and actions in order to commit to it.

Wise-minded parenting

Throughout our parenting lives, we are faced with the dilemma of whether or not to take action on a problem. Should we enforce rules, or let things ride a bit because our child is overstressed by other matters? Should we "pick this battle," or step back because we are asking too much of our child, given his age or temperament? The wise-minded framework can help parents think through their values and the needs of their children so they can feel wise, grounded, and good about their decision making. Let's use Mackenzie's mom as a model case.

How can Mackenzie's mom resolve her dilemma in a way that is best for her daughter, her husband, and herself (not to mention her marriage)? How can she overcome her own personal distress when her daughter is distressed?

This mom needs to find a way to balance both sides of her mental equation: her rational thoughts *(My daughter needs to learn to self-soothe)* with her emotions *(My daughter needs me!)*. In dialectical behavior therapy (DBT; introduced on page 5), this is called balancing "reason mind" with "emotion mind." When you achieve that balance, according to DBT, you are using your "wise mind," combining the power of thinking with a keen understanding of emotions to come up with thoughtful and effective ways of handling difficult and emotionally complex situations. This concept has powerful implications for parenting — so much so that I cowrote a whole book about it *(Wise-Minded Parenting)*. I'll outline its essence here.

Our emotions allow us to feel empathy and love — but in extreme forms, they also lead us to react intensely to fears and threats. In DBT, "emotion mind" is the term used for what's in control when we're flooding with emotion.

Our cognitive skills help us use logic, information, and analysis — but alone, they can also lead us to be exceedingly judgmental and lose sight of the emotions that truly motivate people. "Reason mind" is the term used for judgmental and overly rational reactions.

The wise mind integrates emotional and cognitive skills, and reaches deep for intuition about what is personally right for us, right now. Both emotion mind and reason mind alone can mislead us, but when we put the best of our emotional and cognitive insights together, we have the opportunity to understand what is realistic and effective for solving our problems. People often use the term "gut check" for that intuitive sense that something feels right or wrong.

Let's take a look at Mackenzie's mom's thoughts and feelings in her emotion, reason, and wise minds — and some mantras that can help calm the extremes.

Emotion mind

- I feel extremely distressed when I see Mackenzie's suffering at night.
- I feel afraid that she will hate me or feel abandoned by me.
- I worry that she will be emotionally scarred if I leave her crying in her bed alone.
- I resent that I have to rescue her (and myself!) from these terrible feelings.
- I hate her in the middle of the night and then, in the morning, I hate myself!

The Emotion Mind Mantra:
My child is doing the best she can (given her emotional state), and so am I.

Reason mind

- If we had mastered a sleep routine at age two, we wouldn't have this problem at age five.
- Mackenzie's hysteria shouldn't put our whole family into a tailspin!
- This amount of obsession about a sleep program is irrational.
- Mackenzie is way too old to be co-sleeping. I have been indulgent with her in the middle of the night. I just need to get over it.
- This anxiety I have about separate sleeping is ridiculous.

The Reason Mind Mantra:
I may be right, but am I effective?

Wise mind

- In the big picture of Mackenzie's development, I want her to develop coping skills and independence. It's a high priority.
- I believe that she can be resilient as we challenge her with the task of learning to self-soothe in the middle of the night.

- I have the ability to self-soothe, and so does my daughter. I want to model those skills and be strong for her and with her.
- My intuition tells me that encouraging self-reliance is the right thing to do. She will thrive by mastering this skill.
- Deep down, I trust that she is secure in my love and the love of her father, and that inner security will support her as she faces this challenge.

The Wise Mind Mantra:
My intuition will lead me to the right path.

Looking at this list, you can see the problems that arise when either emotion mind or reason mind are given free rein. Without the tempering influence of wise mind, Mackenzie's mom would never have arrived at her successful outcome: a wise integration of her thoughts and feelings.

Mackenzie's parents did finally use the Successful Sleeper program, to great success. After a few weeks of effort, everyone ended up sleeping through the night, and feeling good about it. It worked because they were ready, but it could also have gone the other way; the parents' wise-minded conclusion might have been to embrace the family bed for a while longer, while they developed more resolve about reaching for the solo-sleep challenge. In that case, postponing would have been the best decision for them at that time.

Often, parents are in conflict about decisions like this one; when that happens, they need to enter into negotiations (much more on this in Chapter 7). With emotionally charged parenting decisions, it is common to have one parent get stuck in emotion mind and the other, in reason mind. Ideally, polarized parents calmly pull back from the extremes, come together in a caucus, and come up with mutually agreeable and wise-minded solutions that they both can implement for the benefit of their child.

Gut check
A "gut check" is pausing to discern one's courage or resolve in a matter. As parents, we know more than we think we do. We have all experienced quiet reflective moments when we reach clarity about some matter that has previously befuddled us. When you use your wise mind, you can achieve that clarity and sense of what is true for you.

Why do parents know they shouldn't give in, but do it anyway? Why do some parents mistake indulgence for love? Why do some parents lecture and judge their emotionally reactive children, even though it doesn't result in change? Moreover, how do they miss the signs that their judgmental stance is harming their child?

Dealing with kids' intense emotions requires that both parents have strong psychological boundaries, so that they can be calm and resolved (or at least strong enough to hold the line) about policies, even as their children say such things as "I hate you! I'll never forgive you! You're the worst parent on the planet!"

Like Mackenzie's mom, parents who tend to fuse with their kids' emotional states and lose conviction in emotional moments need to realize that they can be empathic and follow through on policies. Parents need to have faith that negative feelings can be tolerated until they pass. Parents and child alike will benefit from the use of techniques discussed in detail in Chapter 5, because these techniques help parents validate those extreme feelings, help the child verbalize them, decide on coping methods, and convey acceptance. These heart-to-heart talks won't take place in the middle of the night, but rather when parent and child can share a calm moment.

Secure attachment does not require a blissful parent-child connection 24/7. The concept of the "good-enough parent" helps parents tolerate the upheavals. We cannot make every minute perfect for children, nor should we, because that does not prepare them for the real world. Children learn to self-soothe even as infants, when they suck their thumbs or entertain themselves when a parent isn't around. Our goal is to nudge them toward self-care, slowly but surely, at a pace that matches their developmental abilities.

The good-enough parent
The goal is to be a good-enough parent — not a "perfect" parent. You are preparing your children for a world that won't always be perfect, provide comfort, or respond to their every desire.

The lovely concept of the "good-enough parent" does not mean we get to be lazy or cavalier about learning good parenting skills (Winnicott 1960). It means that when we inevitably anger and upset our kids with our disagreeable routines, limits, and policies, we don't have to worry that we are necessarily scarring them. They won't love us any more for caving; in fact, their lives won't be as rich and productive without the opportunity to develop competencies. The paradoxical truth is that by developing health-promoting routines and building competencies — which result in moments of their "hating" us — our children will become happier, healthier adults, who are more likely to love us evermore.

Overemphasizing self-reliance

Just as parents can become embroiled in their children's emotions and struggle with building self-reliance, the opposite can also be true: Parents can push for independence with inadequate concern for secure attachment. It is common that if one parent takes up the exclusive cause of promoting security, the other parent might become polarized and promote only self-reliance. These parents may be insensitive to the child's feelings and more motivated to teach independence than to be attuned to the child's emotional state. These parents need to study up on emotions (and read Chapter 5 — maybe twice!).

Overly enthusiastic promoters of self-reliance may tell children like Mackenzie that sleeping alone is "normal" for five-year-olds. They may tell their seven-year-old child who freaks out at the mere thought of summer day camp that she is silly to be scared. They may lecture their shy three-year-old about how inappropriate it is to cower and run away when Grandma tries to hug him. These parents lack sensitivity to their child's readiness to handle these challenges.

They are also suffering from the delusion that children can comprehend "shoulds," especially when overwhelmed with fear. These parents are overloaded with reason mind and would do well to remember the Reason Mind Mantra: *You might be right, but are you effective?* They also need to call up some empathy for the child's feelings, rather than dismissing them.

Parents are often quite reasonable in their assessment that skills need to be learned for their child's own good, but wrong in their assessment that kids, or even co-parents, can use reason while under the influence of emotion. By summoning the Reason Mind Mantra, you can often pull back from lecturing or telling kids how they should feel or act differently in moments when they are clearly not benefiting from that approach.

Are you angry about your child's lack of self-reliance?
Parents who are angry about their child's lack of independence may be compromising their child's security. While change may be needed, the first step is unconditional acceptance.

Knowing how to balance the dual values of security and self-reliance requires tuning into your child, his history, and what he needs from you right now in his development. This attunement requires that you slow down enough to reflect and connect with your child. Being present for this type of awareness is one of the most important parts of parenting.

Mindful parenting

Myla and Jon Kabat-Zinn describe mindfulness as "in-the-moment, nonjudgmental awareness" (Kabat-Zinn and Kabat-Zinn 2014). As I first described on page 5, these longtime researchers have applied their understanding of the benefits of mindfulness to the world of child rearing. They suggest that we learn to look beyond our habitual judgments and reactions so that we can thoroughly appreciate the innate goodness in children. Mindful parenting means that we accept our children as they are, not as we wish they were.

In unconscious moments, when we are whipping around getting things done, we are often not thinking about how we are relating to our children. At times, this mode of "doing" rather than "being" is inevitable, but if it becomes predominant, we can lose sight of our children's needs. It's easy to fall into this habit; after all, there are jobs to do, grocery stops to make, car pools to manage, food to cook, routines to maintain, and an onslaught of external agendas to respond to and dispense with.

As understandable as this hyperproductive mode is, it leaves us disconnected from our loved ones, unaware of what they need from us, and abandoning our best intentions to parent well. We claim that children are the most precious things in our lives, but it is far easier to ricochet around dealing with the "doing" agenda than to prioritize being in the present moment, and bringing mindfulness and empathy to our everyday parenting.

I truly feel that the only way we can implement skillful parenting is to practice mindfulness as a core value. Only by cultivating the awareness of the present moment — without distraction or preoccupation — can we really understand what we and our children are feeling. Only then can we be deeply attuned.

Mindful parenting is the process by which you can embrace the Acceptance Mantra, "I accept my child exactly as she is" and its corollary mantra, "I accept myself exactly as I am." You can pause, breathe, and focus on the present moment. If you are upset, use the methods described on page 158 to free your mind of judgmental and reactive thoughts, and focus on slowing your heart rate. Only then can you can strive for acceptance of your child in difficult moments. Being present and calm allows you to examine the big picture of what is going on in your family.

Socialization: preparing your child for the world

In the process of teaching good habits, new skills, and problem solving — all in the context of a secure attachment — parents also accomplish something else: socialization. It's a long haul, because it involves teaching children to behave well, follow rules, do chores, try hard at school, care about others, handle hardships, develop resilience, cooperate with routines, and deal with distress. Don't worry – you have a couple of decades to pull it off! It's how we prepare our children to meet the demands of living in society. And, as luck would have it, the same virtues and competencies kids need for this agenda are the ones that lead to living a good and purposeful life.

We need to accept that carrying out these responsibilities can sometimes result in parental hell on earth, with our kids hating us (or vice versa!), and us wishing that we were anywhere but in our homes working at the job called parenthood. Too strongly stated? I think not.

If there is one thing I've learned from my decades-long practice, my teaching, and my own parenting experience, it is that the hardships incurred during socialization (sleep problems, tantrums, disobedience) cause us to suffer greatly, even as we relish the loving part of parenting. From a moral perspective, we owe it to society and our children to socialize them, and that means we can't expect parenting to be a full-time love fest.

A lot of parents set out thinking that the loving and happy moments will far outweigh the difficult and even hellacious ones. Obviously, the balance depends on a zillion biological, social, and economic family factors. But even those of us with advantaged lives are sobered by the number of parenting situations that bring us to our knees and practically cripple us with humility.

The balanced approach is hard. Staying positive and accepting while also building competencies is exhausting. It's easier to let our kids crawl into our beds, opt out of chores, or weasel out of routines — and then say we're doing it out of love and tenderness.

Summary

Accepting our children exactly as they are is the most important gift we can give them. Our unconditional acceptance, patience, and empathy give them the security to explore the world. Mindful parenting teaches us to focus on the present moment without passing judgment, so that we can connect optimally with our children.

Parenting a three- to seven-year-old can be tricky terrain, because it involves setting limits, building competencies, and managing behavior. Parents begin this process during toddlerhood with toilet training and other self-management efforts, but the agenda for competency building grows by leaps and bounds during the five years that follow. While it is still critically important to cuddle and play with children, parents now need to add the promotion of self-management, discipline, and mastery of new routines to their job description.

The parenting road is rocky, but there are glorious vistas along the way. There is no better a feeling than watching a child grow increasingly competent and take pride in their achievements. As a society, we tend to talk a lot about academic successes, but equally sweet are successes such as learning to tie a shoe, sleep through the night, make new friends and keep them, ride a bike, save for the purchase of the next bike, and bike to school.

Given the hardships, these sweet moments make our parenting job more tolerable. Most parents will tell you that parenting is the toughest job they've ever had. But here is the silver lining: For all the work it takes to build competent and secure children who are ready to take on the developmental tasks of their tweens and teens, it can also be the most gratifying job we'll ever have. It produces the gift that truly does keep giving, because secure and competent children are more likely to become secure and competent teens and adults. And as adults, they become people whom you can enjoy forever.

CHAPTER 2

When your child needs more self-control
(and you do, too)

Many parents believe that a high IQ is the best indicator of how successful their children will be at realizing ambitious goals. But research shows that to be truly successful in life, what your child really needs is good self-control. In fact, researchers who followed groups of children for three decades have found that self-control is a more powerful predictor of overall success in life than either their IQ scores or their parents' education and income levels!

For three- to seven-year-olds, self-control issues come in all kinds of developmentally appropriate shapes and sizes. Whether she's clobbering that kid who grabbed her dolly, or he's throwing an epic tantrum over Cocoa Puffs in the grocery aisle, young kids' gaps in self-control can translate into stressful and embarrassing situations for parents. In this chapter, I'll share tools and strategies for coping with meltdowns and show you ways to build on your child's skills for self-control in all kinds of situations. We begin with an all-too-familiar scene for many parents.

Scene: At the grocery checkout counter with a three-year-old.

Liam: Daddy, Daddy, that guy has a beard just like yours! (Liam lunges for the magazine rack.)

Dad: Liam, don't touch the magazines. Stop it right now. People don't want to buy them if they've been mashed up. Sit down in the cart.

Liam: Wow, look at the cover. He has a beard just like you do! (Liam grabs and wrinkles the magazine.)

Dad: (irate, voice raised to a bark) Sit down! Look what you've done! Now I have to buy it. What did I tell you one second ago?

Liam: (starting to cry) You told me to sit down.

Dad: (angry and raising his voice further) What else? What else did I tell you about the magazines?

Liam: (crying and yelling now) You are yelling, Daddy. You tell me not to yell. You are yelling! (Liam starts to flop around in the cart and knocks a candy display off the checkout counter.)

Dad: Now look what you've done! I told your mom you couldn't keep your hands to yourself at the grocery store. You are out of control. No video for you tonight, or dessert. I'm not taking you out until you learn to control yourself!

What parent among us has not experienced some version of the scenario above? When we review this episode in detail and consider some alternative techniques for managing the situation, a central truth becomes clear: So much of what works in parenting just doesn't come naturally. Wouldn't it be wonderful if we were all given training before we embarked on the journey of parenting (or even just the journey to the grocery store)? Thinking ahead and planning for problems is not how most parents prepare for a simple trip to the grocery store. But, as it turns out, it sure does help.

Because Liam's dad lost his temper in the grocery store, he wasn't able to avert his son's tantrum, or deftly deal with it once it was unleashed. Information on techniques for helping tykes with tantrums will come later in the book, but as this vignette illustrates, before the child's need for self-control can be addressed, a parent's own self-control needs to be fully engaged. It's like the airplane oxygen-mask rule: You put on your own mask first so you can be in good enough shape to help others.

Getting to CALM

When you are flooding with emotions, it's nearly impossible to cope effectively with a young child. Here's a simple but important technique to help you rein in your emotions so you can make the best decisions possible:

C   **Cool down.** Breathe deeply and quiet your mind; do not think about the bad interaction or you will stay agitated; get your heart rate down with a distraction or deep breathing.

A   **Assess your options.** What are the strengths and weaknesses of various approaches you might take for solving the problem? This evaluative step automatically engages the part of the brain associated with reason, facilitating good judgment.

L   **Listen with empathy.** When reengaging your child, acknowledge your child's feelings first, without any "buts." Empathy doesn't mean approval or agreement, but it does open up communication channels.

M   **Make a plan.** Use your calm and wise mind to figure out realistic goals and how to reach them.

The following are some basic behavioral management skills that could benefit this father. You will recognize themes of positive reinforcement and parental approval from Chapter 1. You'll also notice how helpful it can be for parents to understand the basics of child development, so they can be prepared for typical defiance among young children. It's perfectly normal for little kids to want what they want, *when* they want it — especially when they are in challenging situations! Parents need to build skills for overriding their own natural inclinations to "go negative" with kids when they are being oppositional.

Let's review a list of the errors that Dad made in this classic meltdown scene, along with a few strategies that can help in the future.

Easy-to-make error: having unrealistic expectations. Children want to explore interesting stimuli around them. It is unlikely that a child will be passive and sit still in a grocery cart, since the grocery store is a treasure trove of engaging visual, tactile, and sensual delights.

Better strategy: preparing for challenging situations. It's important to know what's normal for your child's age, stage, and temperament. Three-year-olds are interested in everything around them and are driven to explore, so grocery stores should be considered inherently challenging situations. Moreover, if you have a high-energy, novelty-seeking child, you need to double your efforts to keep him engaged in desirable activities, such as talking about grocery shopping, playing guessing games, and helping you.

The best way to keep a child from misbehaving in a store is to engage him in conversation and give him things to do. He can count the lemons, put them in a bag, and estimate their weight. Waiting in line can be boring, so you can be ready with games: "Hey, can you show me a letter L on this package?" "Do you want to hold this tissue box for me?" "I spy something green. Guess where!" In this way, you can avoid the natural slide into the dreaded track of grabbing, begging, or yelling.

Easy-to-make error: giving attention to undesirable behavior. All kinds of attention are rewarding; Dad rewarded the wrong behavior by saying, "Stop it!" His response only served to keep Liam focused on that magazine, which is already very engrossing *(It's glossy! George Clooney's beard looks like Daddy's! How cool it will be to look inside!)*. The idea of "stop" is just not registering.

Better strategy: acknowledging desirable behaviors only. Better to keep chatter going about how well your kid is staying in the cart without fidgeting than to pay attention when he doesn't. What else is your kid doing right? Pay attention to that. Approval from a parent is very reinforcing, but it's easy for us to go on autopilot when doing a task with a child and forget to say things like "I want to count with my fingers all the things I appreciate about your help" as you describe what he is doing right: not grabbing at tempting items, putting items you request in the cart for you, crossing off items on your grocery list.

Easy-to-make error: missing a chance for early intervention. When Dad saw Liam initially lunging for the magazines, he might have engaged him in something that distracted his focus on that fascinating target.

Better strategy: redirecting. When your child becomes dangerously attracted to the stuff in a store, the goal should be to engage her in another activity. Since the array of attractive stimuli is everywhere at the grocery store, you need to be ready to practice this parenting skill, especially while waiting in line. Keep a fun guessing game going with stuff in your cart; after all, there are endless things to discuss about groceries. Stores are a lot like swimming pools — attractive, yet dangerous. Unlike pools, you can't put a fence around a store, but you should probably be ready to swerve your cart out of range of any grab.

Easy-to-make error: talking and lecturing while angry. When Liam initially grabbed the magazine, Dad barked orders and scolded him. Liam is too young to comprehend Dad's points about compliance, self-control, and product destruction. All of us — even the most even-tempered adult — are unable to utilize our brains optimally when we are overwhelmed with emotion and being yelled at for some wrongdoing. However, it's easy for parents to fall into the trap of talking too much when their emotional buttons are pushed (and this situation would do that to most of us).

Better strategy: engaging the wise mind. The first step is exercising your own emotional self-control (self-calming); the second step is avoiding unhelpful judgments (*A three-year-old should know better!*); and the third is figuring out a realistic way to manage the challenging situation. It is important that you shut your mouth and focus on getting to a calm state, because only then can you reflect and assess how best to proceed effectively.

From a brain-science perspective, your emotional brain is triggered at times like these and you are probably "flooding," your heart rate soaring to well more than 100 beats a minute. In order to activate your best decision-making capacities, you must first quiet the neural circuits in your limbic system. These circuits are quick to activate and can overpower your rational brain when you are in an anger-provoking situation. Once calm, your neural circuits will give you the potential to make good choices about how to manage an impending fiasco in a grocery store.

Your child just wrinkled a magazine. Now what? Considering the developmental phase of your child (He's three years old!), the emotional stress for both of you (He's sensitive to your scolding!), and your emotional tolerance (You're already at your wit's end, and your child knows it!), I vote for modest goals. Avoid making the situation worse: Direct your cart so that your child can't do more damage, accept the reassurance of the grocer (even if it seems insincere), and don't talk until you know you are saying something truly helpful, or at least benign. Anything you say at this moment could reflect your distress and make things worse.

Easy-to-make error: trying to make a teachable moment out of an unteachable moment. Liam was extremely upset by the time Dad tried to get him to "learn his lesson" ("What did I just tell you?"). There was no way his little brain could have come up with the right answer.

Better strategy: teaching through play instead of lectures. From the land of crumpled magazines, we need to proceed to the land of damage control. If you want to teach a lesson about wrecking products (or any other debacle), it will best be learned through a calm discussion later, when you can be respectful, accepting, and savvy about the comprehension level of your child. Shaming doesn't work, but reflection together does. That said, the developmental stage of your child, his temperament, and the quality of your parent-child relationship will determine how receptive your child is to learning this lesson.

With a younger child, gaining deep "insights" about wrongdoing is a ludicrous goal, but play practice might nudge a neuron or two. Here's an example we can use from Liam's situation: At home later, crumple up an old magazine and place it beside a few others for a game of "store," in which Liam plays the part of a shopper. (You can also do the same with some other item — such as bruising one apple and leaving one picture-perfect.) Ask your child to choose from the selection of items. When he chooses the intact ones, you can ask him why. See if he understands why you didn't want him to tamper with the items at the grocer's. A young child's learning will be limited, since he is ruled largely by impulses, and he may not be able to associate the store game with the next store visit. Also, the game will only be fun if you avoid shaming and maintain realistic expectations for a toddler. Even if it seems like your kiddo isn't making a connection between the real and play grocery situations, you never know!

Easy-to-make error: pushing an upset into a tantrum. By scolding Liam in a harsh tone about matters that he couldn't comprehend at that moment, Dad probably incited the next level of Liam's emotional arousal, which included flopping around and pushing over the candy display. Sometimes, when we angrily describe our children's bad behaviors to them and try to teach them a lesson, we cause the child's emotional storm to spin into a full-blown tornado.

Negative emotions in situations like these are understandable. When our buttons are pushed and we are angry, frustrated, embarrassed, ashamed, disappointed, and resentful, we can easily end up yelling at our children. If we play back an imaginary video, we may realize that if we had shut our mouths, practiced the CALM technique on page 42, and exercised a little self-control, there is a good chance the child's behavior would not have escalated to the next level of emotional tirade.

Better strategy: doing damage control. Tantrum management involves true damage control; in other words, just trying to avoid making things worse. Although your heart rate is zooming into the extreme range, all your efforts need to be directed to self-calming. The only thing that will prevent the next error is lowering your heart rate, biting your tongue, and breathing deeply. To reiterate the first step of wise-mindedness: First, you must calm your own physiological arousal level. Only after getting your heart rate down can you even begin to decide that damage control is a better move than lecturing or rebuking your child.

Pick up the candy, move your cart, and pay the grocer. Figure out if there are lessons to be learned *later*, when everyone has a better capacity for reflection. (By the way, you can use this tool throughout the adolescent and college years, too.)

Easy-to-make error: dumping verbally. Dad was so frustrated with this experience that he discharged blame to Mom, and punishments and threats to Liam.

Better strategy: reciting the Emotion Mind Mantra. *My child is doing the best he can (given his emotional state), and so am I.* When your child is in full tantrum mode, you need to staunch the flow of verbal outpouring of negative emotions as much as possible. If you can, pull yourself back from the precipice and remember that some grocery visits just wind up this way! Sure, there may be some "take-home lessons" for you and your child about how the visit could have been more successful. But despite any and all lessons learned, some trips to the grocery store (or preschool or the restaurant) will still go south. There are too many factors playing out with messy development and messy emotions.

When you've calmed down, apologize to your child and to the grocer, and try to meditate on acceptance. Forgive yourself and your child, and tell yourself, "These things happen. I'll do better next time. And so will my child." You can retract the threats and make amends later, but now is the time to just get home. Drive carefully!

> **Strategies for preventing toddlers' tantrums**
> *1. Prepare for challenging situations and plan ways to divert and distract.*
> *2. Acknowledge only desirable behaviors.*
> *3. Redirect attention away from attractive dangers.*
> *4. Get to calm and engage your wise mind.*
> *5. Teach through play, not through lectures.*
> *6. Practice damage control.*
> *7. Recite the Emotion Mind Mantra.*

How is tantrum management different for five- to seven-year-olds? You add a slight variation to step one, above: When you know what triggers your older child's tantrums, plan ahead and "pre-coach." Tell him what you expect and then get his feedback about what he thinks would help him cope and avert upsets. Whether it's a birthday party, a shopping trip, or a brother's basketball game, agree on your mutual plans for success at the outing. Engage your child to get his ideas about what will help make it successful, such as snack time, agreements on time limits for things your child finds boring or distressing, and favorite aids in the day pack for distraction and self-calming (consider touchscreens to be a last resort). Together, run an imaginary video in your minds of the successful experience, which will make it more likely to happen.

As discussed in Chapter 1, socialization of a child involves providing her with external controls and gradually removing them as she develops self-control (also known as "scaffolding"). The child is dependent and pretty helpless until she develops her own self-control. Supporting self-management in children is a long and tedious process for adults, who have lives that are already crammed full of demands, responsibilities, and emotionally trying challenges. Still, parental self-control is a necessary precondition for building the child's capacity for self-control. If we can't control ourselves, how can we help our children do the same?

Most parents would admit that at some point in their parenting lives, they've committed many of the errors in our grocery-store vignette (count me in). But here's the crazy thing about parenting: All of Dad's reactions were perfectly natural. It is natural for Dad to react negatively to his son's wrongdoing, noncompliance, impulsivity, crying, and yelling. It's natural — but it isn't optimal. And it certainly isn't effective.

When parents remember to employ any of the strategies I've just outlined, they are demonstrating their own self-control. Furthermore, if Dad had been proactive and prepared for the situation, he would have engaged Liam actively and positively throughout the trips down the aisles. His tolerance level might not have been as maxed out by the time he hit the magazine display at the checkout.

Think proactively about challenging situations
Our capacity for self-control becomes depleted when we are under stress, so we should think proactively about how to set situations up for success. With young children, it will always include keeping them positively engaged.

Even those of us who practice the skills on a regular basis will still make mistakes. Getting it right during every single trip to the grocer's would be a tall order. However, we should resist the urge to harshly judge a kiddo for being a very normal three-year-old fascinated by a magazine cover that looks like Dad. And even if we slip and yell at a child for normal behavior, we can still practice acceptance, which includes an apology and forgiveness (of yourself, too!)

SELF-CONTROL AND MINDFULNESS

Asking yourself the question "What will help make my trip to the store with my toddler a pleasant experience?" primes your brain for self-control, because you are cueing it to develop a plan. The best plan is to stay mindful — fully engaged and present with your child, not just focused on getting the shopping done. Staying mindful while shopping is an ambitious goal and one that will probably require you to sacrifice efficiency, but it boosts your self-control, because you are staying conscious of your feelings, interactions, and actions.

The Mindful Mantra:
I will stay in the present moment with my child, without passing judgment.

You are being a mindful parent when you are focused on this moment right now, and not passing judgment on yourself, your child, or other people. If you focus quietly on your breath, you'll be surprised at how much less likely you are to talk, react, and express criticisms outwardly to your child. "Mindful shopping?" you're asking? Yes! Shopping, carpooling, and transitioning between daily routines are all challenging experiences for children. When you decide to invest creative energy in staying present and fully engaged during challenging moments, you will be raising the likelihood of smooth interactions.

Obviously, a three-year-old has limited self-control, despite a parent's vigilance, warnings, and directives. If the goody in front of your child is fascinating enough, or the unpleasant thing (e.g., seat belt compliance, sibling nastiness) is bad enough, you are going to have a tougher time avoiding the downward slide into negative interactions. Maintaining self-control will be much more likely if you keep our strategies in mind.

Even with our strategies front and center, and you make every attempt to be present and engaged with your child, you can still have an outing from hell! Parenting is like that. A tantrum could result from you saying "no" to a third cookie. Perhaps you paused to talk to a friend and couldn't give your child your undivided attention. Maybe you sent a text when your child wanted you to listen to her. Numerous things trigger tantrums in children (even those with the best parents in the world!). Exiting the tantrum superhighway doesn't require you to give in to your child's demands or avoid setting limits. And you can reduce the potential for tantrums by practicing the skills discussed in this chapter.

> **Accepting tantrums**
> *We need to accept that tantrums and emotional outbursts will happen, regardless of our best efforts, for a variety of reasons related to our child's age, temperament, situation, and a zillion little provocations of the day (ours and theirs).*

Our goal is not to vanquish negative moments or emotions; it's to minimize the percentage of them that happen because of our own preventable actions or misguided expectations. When they do happen, our goal is to manage them effectively. Given how ambitious this goal is, we need to practice acceptance in our parenting, because otherwise, we might actually slip into thinking that if we become mindful, skilled, and evolved enough, our children will always be free of tantrums and well-behaved. Ridiculous! They are children!

Emotional intelligence

For the most part, children learn to increase control over their explosive feelings which erupt into tantrums during the first decade of life. Called "emotional regulation," the skill of controlling emotions is a building block of both effective executive functioning (an extremely important brain-science concept discussed farther on in this chapter) and what is known as "emotional intelligence."

Emotional intelligence can be described as the ability to accurately perceive emotions in oneself and others, use emotions to facilitate thinking, understand the cause of emotions, express emotions appropriately, and regulate emotions (Brackett, Rivers, and Salovey 2011). Emotional intelligence is a cornerstone of all the emotional and social skills discussed in Chapters 4 and 5. Utilizing and controlling our emotions help us accomplish just about every single important thing we do.

Just like adults (on good days), children learn to calm themselves instead of blowing up, use words for expressing emotions, and cope with frustration in healthy ways. But that's a twenty-five-year project. How is it achieved? Mostly through maturation and practice, practice, practice. Learning to control and express emotions constructively evolves with the help of parents and other adults who encourage, guide, and model these skills. Big deterrents in the project are harsh punishment for tantrums and other naturally occurring lapses, as well as unreasonable expectations that children develop self-control more rapidly than they are developmentally capable of doing. We will discuss emotional regulation more in Chapter 5.

Since our innate emotional systems are so powerful, our efforts at self-control are always being challenged. When we adults have our buttons pushed, our mature brains help us inhibit our impulses. But little children have very immature frontal lobes (the place in the brain where rational, conscious processing occurs), so we need to cut them a lot of slack. Again, this doesn't mean giving up on the project; on the contrary, it means we need to help kids exercise that self-control "muscle" so they can increase its capacity. And it also means that parents need to exercise extraordinary patience for this long haul.

Strengthening the self-control muscle
It's helpful to think of self-control as a muscle that we want to help our kids (and ourselves!) develop, condition, and exercise regularly — but not overload.

Self-control is a major topic. For adults and children alike, it can encompass inhibiting impulses, enhancing rule compliance, increasing cooperation with routines, and finding effective ways of expressing feelings. It takes self-control to follow directions, get along with others, and just make it through the day without major havoc.

You may have already seen great breakthroughs of self-control in your child's toilet training, cooperation with morning and evening routines, and complying with rules. But in other arenas, she still may have work to do to avoid hitting her little sister and lying when confronted with infractions. In your own life, you may have nailed your exercise regimen and cut down on desserts, but might be struggling to overcome your urges to yell when frustrated or check your smartphone too frequently. Everyone's self-control is challenged in one arena or another, because the emotional systems in the brain can be so overpowering. It's helpful to remember this fact so that we don't judge children (and ourselves) too harshly.

There are enormous differences between children in their ability to control their impulses and emotions, even within age groups. Because temperament has such a strong influence on behavior, some three-year-olds can display more self-control than a highly impulsive six-year-old. Our mission should be to figure out what capacity our child *currently* has for self-control in various situations and build skills from there.

The second marshmallow

Walter Mischel's famous marshmallow experiment, conducted in his child psychology lab at Stanford University in the late 1960s, has become the stuff of legend (Mischel, Shoda, and Rodriguez 1989). More than 600 children around the age of four participated in a study aimed at understanding the mental processes kids use to help them defer gratification. Each child in the study was left alone in a room with one marshmallow (or another treat of their choice). They were told by the researcher that he would return at the ring of a bell at any point, whereupon they could either eat the one treat, or wait a few minutes (fifteen) and have the opportunity to eat two. One-third of the children were able to wait the fifteen minutes.

Mischel videotaped the children because he was interested in examining the strategies kids used for self-control. They might pet the marshmallow and pretend it was a furry animal, play with their hair, or turn around so they wouldn't be tempted. Distracting themselves seemed to help with the waiting.

A few years later, Mischel's daughter, who participated in the study, shared her observation that the kids who couldn't wait and ate the one marshmallow were still the ones who seemed impulsive. The way the story goes, her comment gave him the idea to look at self-control as a predictor of future behavior.

In follow-up studies years later, Mischel found that the ability to delay eating the marshmallow was a meaningful psychological measure (Shoda, Mischel, and Peake 1990). It turned out that this measure of self-control was twice as predictive of SAT scores as were IQ scores! The children who could delay the reward (the "waiters") scored an average of 210 points higher on their SAT tests than the "instant gratifiers." The children who couldn't wait were also more likely to have conduct problems, peer difficulties, poor teacher evaluations, and substance-abuse problems by the time they were thirty years old.

Another study of 1,000 subjects in New Zealand followed children from birth to age 32 (Moffitt and Arseneault et al. 2011), and found the same strong relationship between self-control and adult measures of health, income, and safety (fewer traffic accidents and less criminal activity). The researchers were able to disentangle the effects of intelligence and social class and demonstrate the benefits of self-control.

These studies emphasize the importance of self-control for children's long-term successes regarding health, educational attainment, income, and relationship stability. In fact, self-control has been incorporated into the important concepts of grit, resilience, persistence, and character. But before you sink into depression, certain that your child is an eater and not a waiter, take heart: It turns out that self-control is teachable.

Self-control is a powerful predictor of success — and it's teachable! *Self-control measured in four-year-olds is a more powerful predictor of success in young adults than IQ measurements and SAT scores, regardless of parental income and education. The good news is that methods of improving self-control can be taught.*

Remember, Mischel was interested in the strategies that helped kids cope with waiting. After learning what some of the kids did to distract themselves, he was able to teach the "eaters" how to wait by distracting themselves (Mischel and Ayduck 2004). Yes, waiting is a skill that can be taught! When the treats were covered up so that temptation was out of view, 75 percent of the kids were able to wait the full fifteen minutes. Helping children avoid distraction aids them in self-control and task success, too (you'll read about the "guardrails principle" later in this chapter).

Training your child to be able to wait is important; think about how many good things spring from the capacity to delay gratification. Children need to wait their turn, do their homework before they play games online, and learn how to save for a purchase. They need to do chores before they go on play dates, write thank-you notes instead of texting friends, and avoid taking an extra cookie before dinner, even though Mom isn't looking. An individual child's intrinsic ability to wait is somewhat bundled into his or her genetic makeup, but all children benefit from lots of opportunities to build their self-control muscle.

Not only should parents give their children chances to learn how to wait, but they should consistently celebrate and reward waiting. If a dad rewards a three-year-old by swinging her in the air (her favorite thing) after she successfully waits three minutes while the baby was put to bed, then the child is learning that waiting is really valued and important.

What happens when parents make promises they don't keep? Critics of the original marshmallow study questioned whether some of those four-year-olds might have grabbed the goody because waiting had not paid off for them in the past. Was the grabbing a reflection of genetic impulsivity, or of a home environment that didn't make waiting worth their while? It only takes children a few experiences with disappointed expectations to figure out that waiting is a sucker's game.

How many of us have told our child, "Wait a minute" only to make it ten minutes? How many of us do not reward the minute they waited, and instead yell at them for the fit they pitched at minute number five? Count me in.

Remember the good-enough parent concept (page 36) as you contemplate the error of your ways. Then vow to do better by consistently setting up situations in which your child can be praised for waiting, rewarded for delayed gratification, and celebrated for long-term projects that they have planned, executed, and completed.

When my daughter was ten, she bought her first used bicycle with money she earned from lemonade-stand and brownie sales, and you've never seen a prouder girl. When you encourage your kids to save their allowance and birthday money for a big-ticket item, you are helping them build skills that enable them to delay gratification, and increase their self-control and self-esteem.

Routines and good habits

Self-control grows by leaps and bounds between the ages of three and seven. Starting when their child is three, parents can begin to help build good habits by establishing routines, which teach skills and independence and build self-control. I'm a huge fan of routines, because they make behavioral compliance so much easier. A lot of parents who consult me about various problems with their kids groan when I say this, because they may be the carefree type who finds routines to be a drag, or are just overwhelmed by the logistics of life. However, like all good things that come from hard work at the front end, routine builders end up saving themselves and their family a lot time, energy, and suffering. Prioritizing routines that teach kids how to delay gratification and cope with not getting what they want earns a spectacular return on your investment.

METHODS TO ENHANCE SELF-CONTROL

Taking turns. Taking turns with a sibling or playmate to play with a toy is a good way for children to learn how to wait. Make it explicit; explain that you have a timer and your child is to wait a certain number of minutes (perhaps the same number as his age) before he gets to play with the toy again. Help him choose ways he can enjoy himself, perhaps with another toy or by drawing, until the bell rings. Then praise him — "You are good at waiting!" — and make sure he gets that toy he waited for!

Free play. Cooperative free play requires self-control, because peers or siblings will have ideas your child won't like, whether it's about building a fort, creating a play, or dressing a doll. If you have a younger child (or a frisky older one), you may need to supervise the play to make sure the child understands the behavior you are expecting and rewarding. Explain that cooperating successfully includes coping with not getting her way. You can ask her, "When you are frustrated, what are some ways you can direct your attention to other things?" Take the time to observe the play and praise her for waiting, sharing, stepping back from insisting on her way, incorporating her playmate's ideas, and expressing her preferences politely without domination. Celebrate afterward with treats and a review of the ways she practiced social skills that involve self-control.

Saving. Teach your child how to wait for a purchase. You can help him keep a ledger system for tracking birthday cash and money earned by doing little jobs. Let him experience the thrill of anticipation as he waits for something he really wants.

Work = fun. Another trick to motivate children (and adults) is to turn "have to" tasks into "want to" or "get to" tasks. It takes some creativity. Try raking leaves into piles and letting your child jump on them before they're put into bags. Math can be so much fun when done with Skittles, and doing dishes is more fun with dancing breaks.

Games. Games have rules, and following them requires self-control. Consider Freeze Tag, Musical Chairs, Simon Says, and Red Light, Green Light. The harder you have to work to control your impulses, the more you are working that muscle. What if you reverse the Red Light, Green Light game — go on red, and stop on green? You are helping your child "self-regulate" with effortful control and doubly working that muscle.

Self-talk. Encourage your child to talk out loud while she plays or performs a task; it's a way of reinforcing her ability to regulate her behavior. You could also have her plan and practice a skit or a play, which requires her to remember her part, inhibit her impulses, cope with others' distracting behaviors, and act in pleasant ways so that her ideas might be accepted.

Chores. Do chores with your toddler, and add complexity and difficulty as you see mastery achieved. Delayed gratification comes in because your child will do chores before he gets to do what he wants. Screen time? First, he does his chores.

Age-appropriate chores

Here's a list of age-appropriate chores for you to consider:

• 3-year-old: Pulls bedspread up and over pillow and "makes the bed," picks up toys, and puts away silverware.
• 4-year-old: Helps to fold laundry and put it away, sets the table, and wipes surfaces.
• 5-year-old: Empties dishwasher, helps to clean garage or closets, and cleans sinks.
• 6-year-old: Helps to load dishwasher, sweep kitchen, and vacuum.
• 7-year-old: Helps with yard work, all aspects of housework, and meal preparation.

Don't take this chore list literally. You might have a four-year-old who loves to vacuum and a 7-year-old who is a master at laundry. It's important to teach skills and have some nonnegotiable chores (especially related to self-care), but also to be attuned to your child's strong preferences.

Having your children do chores (or at least help with chores) takes more time initially than to just do the chores yourself. Did you notice how many times my list included the word "helps"? Children need your guidance, and a lot of it. Of course, there will be bad attitudes, poor work ethics, and fights over who did or didn't do their share. Don't be discouraged! These obstacles are par for the course when it comes to establishing routines for chores.

First work, then play

One of the most valuable rules is "First we work and then we play" (alternatively, first the child does what the parent wants, and then the child does what she wants). Getting that reward of play motivates kids to participate in responsible routines. Isn't that the way life is supposed to work? Adults get to do what they want — after they work. Our job as parents is to get our little tykes ready to be responsible for customs practiced in the real world.

> **Getting ready for the real world**
> *Enforcing the routines that build skills, get chores done, and exercise the self-control muscle is a major undertaking. Remember, you aren't just working toward the day that your child does chores automatically, you are teaching children that in the real world, first you do your work and then you get to play.*

Obviously, age and temperament have a profound influence on your child's ability to practice self-control and emotional regulation in classrooms and social situations. The key is to see what your child's capacity is right now (called a baseline) and take steps to build the muscle, little by little. Don't be too ambitious or it will lead to frustration, shame, and resignation for everyone. Remember: This is a twenty- to twenty-five-year project, because the adolescent brain's self-regulation system is not fully mature until around the age of twenty-five.

The importance of realistic expectations

The self-control muscle gets tired, especially by the end of the day (Baumeister and Tierney 2012). Inevitably, when we have two difficult tasks to do, we do the second one less capably. Research on adults has found that whatever we have a weakness for (e.g., chocolates, cocktails, shopping) is likely to tax our self-control capacity more by the time we reach the evening. Our self-control muscle just poops out. And think about our children! While they might have held it together and practiced self-control all day, all of us (especially wee ones!) run out of gas sometimes.

The good news is that you can fill your self-control gas tank with some R & R and nourishment. Isn't it amazing how much better we all behave (usually) after dinner? Snacks get kids through carpools, and they do magic for kids who are working their brains to the max during homework time. Kids need lots of breaks when they are working that self-control muscle. The harder the child is working at self-control, the more her parent should consider reducing demands and offering snacks, jokes, breaks, naps, and jumping jacks to cut the fatigue with rejuvenation. This is especially true for children who have learning and attentional disabilities; they expend much more self-control energy performing academic tasks than do other kids, so it's critical to cut them some slack.

It's essential to have realistic expectations with regard to our child's age and temperament. We can plan activities that help him practice using this muscle but do not overwhelm his ability. When demands exceed ability, stress occurs. Once again, we have one of the dual agendas of parenting — challenging children to grow their abilities and exercising sensitivity about their limited capacities. Staying attuned to children is the solution.

The key to helping kids build self-control capacity is to establish a baseline: What can your child do right now regarding behavioral self-control, and what would be an incremental improvement? You are going to have problems if you utter statements like "A three-year-old should be able to ... " Even if your child is behind on some skill — sitting at the table, doing homework independently, or behaving well at Grandma's — it doesn't help to judge yourself or your child harshly. If you find yourself seething with "shoulds," it's time for the Reason Mantra (page 34) to keep judgments under control. Kids will feel (or hear) this critical judgment, stress out, and usually perform more poorly. Wouldn't you?

> **Demands > ability = stress**
> *As much as we want to challenge children to stretch their capacity for self-control, we don't want to overload them with expectations they can't meet. When the various demands of a situation exceed one's ability to perform, stress occurs.*

Implementing a plan to enhance self-control

Let's go back to Liam and his dad. Dad wants to help Liam learn how to wait and cope with frustration. Here, we'll see Dad do this by redirecting Liam's attention to alternative engaging activities, encouraging him to entertain himself while he waits.

Dad: I need to do some work at my computer for about five minutes. How do you feel about that?

Liam: Bad! You're always at your computer. I want to play Gladiator with you. Let's put those helmets on!

Dad: It's hard to wait for Gladiator games when you are thinking about how much you want to do it right now, isn't it?

Liam: Yes, I want to play Gladiator right now, right now, right now!

Dad: Let's walk over here to your toy shelf. How can you have a fun time with something here while you wait until I'm finished with my work? Gee, I don't know what you'll choose, but you'll do it, because you are the expert on you.

Liam: I know! I can blow bubbles.

Dad: What a great idea! What else?

Liam: I can build some block towers and then we can knock them down when we play Gladiator.

Dad: Fabulous. I can't wait to come back and see what you've done while I'm doing my boring computer job. OK, here's the timer. Come get me in five minutes. Don't be late!

Instead of focusing on thwarting the child's goal — "You have to wait, because you are not going to get my attention right now" — Dad focused on the goal of having Liam engage himself in something so he can learn to cope. When five minutes are up, Dad can praise Liam for waiting. And the other big reward for Liam: playing Gladiator and knocking down the blocks!

Coping with waiting

Children need strategies for coping with uncomfortable feelings and redirecting their attention when they are not getting what they want. Younger children will need help on these ideas from their parents.

Aids for waiting and coping with distress can include toys, stuffed animals, breathing exercises, art supplies, books, and songs. Many parents choose instead the most powerful distracters and engagers of all time: electronic games on little smart gadgets. The problem with electronics, as we will explore in depth in Chapter 7, is that they possess such strong reward-delivery systems, with their vast potential for sensory stimulation, that your child will become less capable of developing other methods for self-soothing. For as long as is possible with children, we should encourage other methods of self-soothing and engaging in creative play before we resort to screens.

When screen use is excessive, children will find many other play avenues boring, and even playmates will prove lacking in fun potential. After all, those games stimulate the brain's release of dopamine (the neurochemical associated with pleasure) at much more regular intervals than contact with a measly playmate can. And forget dinner conversations, board games, or hanging out with parents! They represent weak competition in the dopamine department.

On the other hand, games on those handy little devices do make life easier for parents. If the electronic game genie is already out of the bottle at your house, just make sure you are also using the gadget as an opportunity to teach self-control. Make rules, withdraw gadget access for infractions, and be realistic about their power over our better judgment. Put them away (often) so that you and your child don't use up all your self-control stamina just resisting, fighting about, and yearning for the gadget.

TEMPERAMENT AND SELF-CONTROL

Temperament is based in our DNA and is responsible for a lot of our behavioral characteristics from very early in life (Rothbart, Ahadi, and Evans 2000). It plays a major role in influencing what kids (and adults) will find challenging in the self-control department.

Some kids are born with a strong drive for novelty, and they love new experiences, exciting activities, and arousing play. In contexts that are not highly stimulating, these kids will be very challenged to wait, delay gratification, and cope with what they may experience as boredom. At the other end of the continuum, some children will be highly reactive to new things, and want to avoid novelty and unfamiliar people and places. Their self-control challenge will lie in facing their fears, making an effort to ride the wave of anxiety that spikes with new experiences, and tolerating exposure to things that make them uncomfortable.

Here is a list of characteristics that make up temperament types. See if you recognize some of your child's (and your own) traits at the low or high end of the continuum.

Temperament types

Characteristic	Low end of the continuum	High end of the continuum
Novelty tolerance	Prefers familiar people, quieter settings, and risk avoidance; becomes anxious when faced with new endeavors	Likes new activities, stimulating situations, and adventure; seeks thrills to reach preferred level of arousal
Activity level	Likes quieter settings, can sit quietly and is slow to get going	Likes to move around a lot, gets restless with sitting, and has a high energy capacity
Adaptability	Finds it difficult to adjust to changes or new routines and can become rigid and inflexible when expected to shift gears	Resilient to changes in routine and schedule and can tolerate the unexpected; bounces back from mild stressors
Tolerance of physical sensation	Reactive to physical sensations, textures, touching, temperature changes, and noise	Doesn't seem bothered by touch, bright lights, or noises
Sociability	Prefers own company and may find people irritating and/or social situations trying	Loves to be with people, enjoys peers, and seeks social situations; wants to be accepted by others
Aggression	Does not attack or strike out when upset, disappointed, or offended	Strong urge to strike out at others when offended, quick to display anger, and has intense reactions to frustrating events
Moodiness	Maintains a positive and stable mood, is easygoing, and doesn't get bothered by little things	Tends to be negative, see things with a "glass half empty" view, and become irritable easily
Impulsivity	Can wait and control urges, temptations, and desires	Struggles with the impulse to act on every whim, whether in reaction to rewards or negative emotions

As you read down the list, do you have a feel for where your child's characteristic style lies on the temperament continuum? Maybe somewhere in the middle, but if at the low or high end, you will immediately recognize some of the challenges you have had (and will continue to have) with raising your child. Remember, though, that personalities are not set in stone. Parents can play a big role in helping the rigid child become more adaptable, the less sociable child learn to enjoy relationships, and the aggressive child become more self-controlled during conflicts.

But the first and most vital step in the process is to accept our children exactly as they are. Every parent raising a child who has a challenging temperament will want to practice the Acceptance Mantra a lot. If temperamental tendencies are inborn, how can we blame our children for these characteristics?

The Change/Acceptance Paradox

It's natural to want more self-control for children who suffer from problems resulting from their temperamental excesses or deficits. However, change will occur best in the context of acceptance. It's a paradox: Do you want to see change in a loved one or yourself? Start with unconditional acceptance.

The challenges of certain temperament characteristics

All you have to do is glance at the temperament grid to figure out that some kids are a lot harder to rear than others. You've probably heard of "difficult," "spirited," and "challenging" children. Maybe you find labels off-putting, or maybe you find them validating. If you have a child who is open to new experiences, adaptable, conscientious, sociable, and positive most the time, you — and more importantly, your child — have won the genetic lottery. Add a calm and stable home environment, some socioeconomic advantages, and a solid IQ (it doesn't even have to be superhigh!) to the mix, and you can throw away this book. (But I hope you don't, because by reading it, you can develop empathy for the rest of us!)

If your child is a novelty seeker, negative, aggressive, and impulsive, you will naturally be concerned that these traits will compromise his ability to do well in school and in relationships. If your child is avoidant, negative, and unsociable, you will be concerned that he may lack the social experiences he needs to develop friendships and all manner of new skills. Your fears are justified, but the Acceptance Mantra stands. Everything you do to "help" expand your child's opportunities and build his skills must start with unconditional acceptance.

It's completely natural for the parent of the impulsive five-year-old who steals stuff, breaks rules, and says foul-mouthed things to think, *You must learn to control yourself!* The thought will be the same for the parent of the avoidant child who throws tantrums when Dad takes her to her new day care or Mom informs her of tomorrow's school field trip.

The problem is that they can't control themselves. Their intense emotions are trumping their reason, and they are incapable of reining in those emotional forces — in spite of all the reasons you give for why they should behave, think, and feel differently. If you are tempted to lecture in these situations, the Reason Mind Mantra might be helpful: *You might be right, but are you effective?*

Taming a brain on fire with emotions is like taming a wild elephant. Trying to reason with a child who can't comprehend abstract concepts is like pontificating to your dog. And repeating your logic to try to get through to someone who can't comprehend makes you more upset. Better that you stand back, get calm, and try to resurrect your wise mind. What will help in this situation?

In temperament taming, you will want to exercise the strategies below. Lecturing a child about the need for self-control is not going to do the trick. Coping with the challenges of certain temperaments is a long-term project, especially the development of effortful control over the strong emotions associated with biological leanings.

Your understanding of your child's temperament can truly steer your parenting style. You can adjust your expectations for your child based on her temperament as much as you do for her age — and sometimes more.

Parenting to your child's temperament

If you have a child who is high-energy, impulsive and seeks thrills constantly to rev up and enjoy life, you have perhaps considered the diagnosis of attention deficit disorder with hyperactivity. Whether your child meets the criteria for the diagnosis or not, if you identify with these characteristics, then you know you need to take action (a lot) to harness his powerhouse energy for the good and avoid the fallout of the not so good (e.g., damage to property or persons, your good will, and that of others). You will want to sign your child up for a lot of physical activities so he can let off steam and have a place to excel at physical skills. You will also want to monitor his whereabouts all the way through high school, since he's more likely to go off track without guardrails in place.

If you have a child who is avoidant, anxious, or slow to warm up, you will want to take lots of extra steps to approach new activities, but always insist on progression toward new challenges. She will want to avoid day camps and sleepovers, but you can negotiate and reward stretches into new frontiers. Steps for nudging, not pushing, your child toward scary stuff are on page 169.

If you have a child who is moody, you will work especially hard on validating his feelings while modeling a "glass half full" attitude yourself. With growing self-awareness (over the next decade) and your support, he will hopefully learn to override his "Eeyore" stance on things and avoid negative self-talk, which can forecast his life. In the meantime, it's up to you to model optimism, place him in positive surroundings, and keep him engaged in activities that give him positive feedback and experiences.

> **Nobel Prize for parents?**
> *The parent of the child with a challenging temperament must exercise more patience, skill, tenacity, and acceptance than the parents of easy kids. There are no Nobel Prizes for this undertaking — but there should be.*

The parent-child mismatch

What if you are high-energy and social, and your child begs to stay home, can't look people in the eye, and dreads doing anything new and different? Not only is it difficult, but you are bound to think there is something wrong with your child. You will create a story in your head (not completely unfounded) that your child will not develop optimally if you give into his shy and avoidant nature. But responding to his avoidance as if there were something wrong with him, or expressing your judgment and negative forecasting, will not help him improve. While your sense that he will benefit from a nudge toward the big world is accurate, that nudge should not be a push, and it should be carried out with empathy. He may be experiencing the same tsunamis of anxiety over T-ball that you would feel singing solo in your underwear in Carnegie Hall, and you may be dismissing his painful experience with constant refrains of "Just try it!"

That word "just" needs to be struck from your vocabulary; it discounts the force of those tsunami waves. They can be crushing and overwhelming.

Temperament tango
Empathy for your child's challenges will be especially vital if your temperament differs from your child's. It's critical that you practice acceptance of your child's innate temperament — even the challenging parts — otherwise, you risk triggering a negative, self-perpetuating cycle.

If you are thinking in judgmental terms, you can bet your kiddo knows it. Don't fool yourself; your kids have been living with you for a while, and they have finely tuned instincts for picking up on your thoughts, judgments, and negative emotions. Certain parental behaviors, such as using a harsh, exasperated tone, reveal emotions, which reflect thoughts. You may think your kids are just seeing that you are fuming and frustrated, but they also perceive the associated judgments and criticisms (they remember them from other times you have leaked them). See if you recognize yourself below.

Accepting your child's temperament (or not so much)

PARENTAL BEHAVIOR	THOUGHTS	FEELINGS

The low-energy child with the high-energy mom:

Mom gives him a little shove to the shoulder and a loud command, "C'mon, we're going be late to preschool!"	*He is always dawdling! He must learn to hurry up. He ends up controlling the whole household with his lazy ways.*	*He'll be the death of me! I can't take it anymore! I wish I could just throw him into the car.*

The reactive mom with the anxious, risk-averse child:

Mom says, "You can't back out of the birthday party now! It's a commitment! This is embarrassing!"	*She isn't normal. She is so wimpy! If I let her out of this, she'll be spoiled rotten! She already is!*	*I am humiliated and so frustrated. I feel controlled by her. I wish I had a "go-getter" kid!*

The mild-mannered dad with the aggressive child:

After his son hits his friend (again), Dad says, "You'll never have friends if you act that way! You need to learn to control your impulses, young man."	*He is five years old. I'm practically giving up. He should have learned by now how to use his words. He is like his granny, always lashing out.*	*I am at the end of my rope. I'm afraid that he will never have friends, get expelled and end up in juvie. How can he be my son?*

Your kids know your thoughts and feelings because of the emotional experiences they have already had with you. Are you thinking, "But my child is only three, so how much can they know and remember?"

> **Emotional mind reading**
> *Our kids "read" our minds. Kids learn to associate facial and emotional expressions with judgment and criticism. Learning begins to take place from the minute your child is born — especially with respect to you.*

We all have reactions to our children because of temperamental differences. The goal is to be mindful, which means catching those thoughts and feelings before they become behaviors that actually push our children into negative behaviors.

Self-control and grit

Self-control is a major building block of what psychologists call "executive functioning," which allows us humans to plan ahead and make goals. Our "CEO" functioning also helps us figure out steps to reach our goals, rejigger the steps when we have setbacks, evaluate costs and benefits, and regulate our emotions as we face frustrations and obstacles in our path toward those goals. Self-control is involved in accomplishing every one of these functions.

Executive functioning is not fully up and running until we reach our mid-twenties. The prefrontal cortex, which houses this executive suite of skills and self-control, undergoes significant remodeling during the teen years. While brain scans document this slow maturation, this fact won't keep you from wanting and praying for more executive functioning in your child. The many painful messes that occur because of that slow-growing frontal lobe leave the average parent yearning for more, and sooner, and right now, please.

> **Grit-mania**
> *Just as parents in the past wanted the recipe for building IQs and self-esteem, parents now want the magical stimulus program for self-control and grit. While there is no formula, we do know that kids benefit from achievable but continual challenges, fulfilling commitments, support for things they feel passionate about (even if it's not fancy stuff like chess and physics), and opportunities to practice coping with boredom and setbacks.*

"Grit" is perseverance and passion for long-term goals. Its operating system involves executive functioning, resilience, and tenacity. Gritty individuals would probably have excelled at that marshmallow test of self-control at age four. However, grit is a tricky concept, because as much as research has documented that high achievers and spectacularly accomplished individuals demonstrate grit on their path to success (Duckworth and Peterson et al. 2007), these are "retrospective studies." This kind of research identifies successful individuals and looks back on their lives; it does not follow a group of children, examining their behaviors and parenting over time in a way that can specify causal effects. Therefore, it is not clear how much we can zero in on parenting styles to figure out what parenting methods may have contributed to gritty greatness.

However, there is a strong relationship between authoritative parenting and self-control, which is clearly a component of grit. When parents provide nurturing home lives, establish limits, and practice positive parenting (see page 8), their children will develop better self-control and achieve more. It will require more research to tease out the "nature versus nurture" elements in grit and self-control, but there is concern that if parents (or teachers) become overzealous about producing gritty kids, they might overdo it.

Hard work and perseverance are virtuous, but too much of a good thing can be bad; kids can be pressured beyond their developmental and temperamental capacities. Unfortunately, the "hurried child syndrome" is alive and well; some parents still will want to hurry development and brain maturation, along with emotional, cognitive, and physical maturation. But optimal development doesn't work that way. In fact, the attempt to "hurry" development backfires, because the child loses the security and acceptance that underpins good mental health and healthy development.

THE AUTHORITATIVE-PARENTING PLAYBOOK

Throughout this book, you will be reading about how authoritative parenting (as opposed to permissive, neglectful, and authoritarian parenting), predicts positive outcomes in children, adolescents, and young adults (Larzelere, Morris, and Harris 2013). Not only does it engender self-control, but it also appears to, in part, explain success in other arenas, such as higher academic achievement, lower levels of risk taking, and higher-quality and more stable relationships.

Your child needs self-control to study nightly and achieve academically. He needs self-control to filter his negative reactions to friends, bosses, and loved ones so that he can manage relationships. He needs self-control so that he can later moderate alcohol use, attend to his many responsibilities, and plan goals for the future. And you need your own strong self-control to build the qualities of authoritative parenting so that you can help him develop his self-control!

Parents who practice authoritative parenting demonstrate three main qualities in their relationships with their children:

Warmth: Love, affection, kindness, and the characteristics that support secure attachment

Authority: Boundaries (setting limits), monitoring, rule enforcement, routines, consistency, and structure in the home, which supports compliance with behavioral expectations

Psychological autonomy: Respect and acceptance of a child's own feelings and thoughts, while keeping behavioral expectations intact

Doesn't it make sense that if parents focus on establishing routines and setting reasonable limits, their children will learn to self-govern? That if they encourage their children to express their thoughts and feelings, those kids will learn the skills of emotional intelligence? The secret to authoritative parenting is blending authority with warmth, and allowing space for all those messy feelings and thoughts that get thrown at parents while rearing their children. Parents lay down the law, adapting for the child's age, temperament, and specific circumstances, but they are also trusted and trusting, kind and loving, and accepting of their children's thoughts and feelings. We'll get to the "emotion coaching" section later in Chapter 5 (don't miss it!), but suffice it to say that it's all about accepting kids' negative emotions and their many negative and offensive thoughts, while keeping the authority ingredient firmly in the mix.

All other parental disciplinary styles lack at least one special and important quality. The "authoritarian" parent rules by "command and control," but lacks warmth and respect for a child's individual thoughts and feelings. The "permissive" parent may be warm and respectful of feelings, but does not practice strong authority or consistent limits. The "neglectful" and indulgent parent falls down on many fronts, but even so, may feel love for the child.

Authoritative parenting
The enduring qualities of authoritative parenting include warmth, authority, and autonomy for negative feelings and thoughts. Children of authoritative parents do better in school, are emotionally healthier, demonstrate more self-control, and are less likely to have behavior problems, including drug and alcohol abuse.

Every time I review the list of good outcomes related to authoritative parenting, I'm impressed. Fifty years of research on parenting styles keep pointing in this direction, so why don't parents hunker down and focus on enhancing this constellation of qualities, trusting that there is a science basis for what predicts good parenting, just as there is for other parts of human health? The fact is that many parents do.

Some people like the way their parents raised them and mimic it, some people want to throw out their parents' playbook and start over, and some parents retire parts of the old book — techniques such as shaming and lecturing — and cherry-pick for the new one. But whichever playbook you choose, make sure it's built on authoritative parenting.

Cultural differences play a role. Traditional families may include heavy doses of authority, and other families may verbalize more praise, but it's remarkable how universal these key ingredients are in the winning combination. It makes sense, of course: Despite the strong messaging around achievement and respectful behavior in some cultures, parents with well-adjusted children are still communicating love and appreciation in their own ways. And some of the parents you might consider on the liberal or somewhat permissive end of parenting are still probably offering structure and imposing behavioral expectations if their kids are turning out with strong character and a drive for achievement.

And what about those parents you feel are permissive, neglectful slouches who still manage to rear self-disciplined achievers? It can happen. When research demonstrates strong patterns, like it does with the benefits of authoritative parenting, there are always many individual differences amongst the thousands of families studied. When diamonds in the rough spring from homes riddled with deficiencies, there's a good chance that kid won the genetic lottery of adaptability, positive mood, and sociability, and also has smarts and some supportive adults around her, too.

Authoritative parents reinforce their behavioral expectations with methods that support compliance and self-control. Parents routinely ask, "How can I get my kids to do what I want them to do without punishment and threats?" Along with this comes the question, "I know nagging doesn't work, but what's the alternative?" What a bonus if you use an alternative that helps the self-control agenda at the same time!

The counting method

The counting method can work wonders in motivating your child to comply with requests (Bradley and Jadaa et al. 2003). However, as with time-outs, this method can win awards for the most detested method in the books on behavioral management. I understand this controversy, having counseled hundreds of families. What works for one family doesn't work for another. Personalities, belief systems, and emotions often make a big difference as to whether this method becomes a coercive, harmful hammer for behavioral control or a well-executed, helpful lever for increasing compliance and in- stilling self-control.

First, let's discuss what it looks like when the counting method — in which a child must comply before the count of three — works well. We hear a parent say, "Please get in the car right now." The child ignores the parent. The parent says, "OK, here's your reminder. That's two … " And then you see the child jump into the car seat. What happens if the parent gets to three? Does the child get yelled at or spanked? Not if the parent is using the counting method correctly.

On a different day, when this child is too tired to comply with that second reminder to get in the car, the parent would reach three and give a kindly ren- dered time-out (see Chapter 6) that lasts for one minute. (Since this example involves a family using the counting method correctly and successfully, the child will cooperate after the time-out.)

What is the incorrect, ineffective version of the counting method? The parent is angry, repeats the counting or draws it out, threatens, or yells. She may even spank the child on the count of three. Corporal punishment, yelling, and threats do not work as well as consistent routines and incentives. Fear of harsh punishment may result in compliance *in the moment*, but it also results in distrust and distance in the parent-child relationship. (See Chapter 6 for more reasons why harsh or excessive use of punishment is discouraged.)

Many parents end up misusing this method, so it is essential for parents to know as much about how to implement this method as how *not* to use it. I also provide extensive cautions about how *not* to use time-out; make sure you understand these warnings before you employ these methods.

Implementation of the counting method:

1. Set clear expectations and consequences. Tell your child you have a way to stop your nagging: You will only ask your child to do something two times! Yay! No more nagging. If your child does not comply after two requests, she will receive a one- to three-minute time-out of sitting quietly, removed from action and attention (but not banished or shamed).

You can say something like this: "I want to help you learn to put on the brakes when I'm asking you to do something. Your engine is going fast and you may want to keep driving, but sometimes I need you to stop, think, and follow my directions. Occasionally, I'm going to ask you do something, which counts as a first time. If you don't follow my direction the first time, I'll give you a second reminder. I will look you in the eye and say, 'That counts as two.' Then you can try to remember to put on your brakes and do as I've requested."

"My job is to speak clearly and kindly, so you can really hear my instructions. Your job is to understand and cooperate. If you don't, I'll give you to the count of 'three' and then you'll have a time-out to cool your engine."

2. Count gradually, at regular intervals of no more than five seconds, in a neutral and calm tone. Do not threaten. It's important that you do not draw the counting out, especially the "three." The child needs to expect the exact same procedure every time or she won't take you seriously about your intent to follow through with a time-out.

3. When the child fails to comply and earns a time-out, do not talk about it anymore. The time-out is the consequence for noncompliance, so there's no need for more talk, which amounts to attention that reinforces the undesirable behavior. Rubbing in bad news is like shaking a red flag in front of a bull: You enrage, you don't teach. If your child does not cooperate with the time-out, she will have to go to bed 30 minutes early (or incur some other reasonable consequence).

4. Be sure to follow through every time you use the counting method. The procedure won't work without consistency. This procedure is conditioning a new "automatic pilot" system in the child's brain. It will take time, and kids respond to the program better if parents keep a neutral attitude.

If your child does not cooperate with the time-out, you can choose the earlier bedtime or another alternative, but remember that young children learn best with immediate consequences. Since their resistance to your directives is usually related to their engine going at full speed, a time-out is a logical consequence for noncompliance, because they get to cool off. Over time, they will learn to associate your directives with "serious business," and that a one- to three-minute consequence is a better deal than an earlier bedtime or loss of another privilege. Without consequences for noncompliance, many revved-up children will not take parents seriously about the need for cooperation.

A technique I use to get the system off to a good start, especially with a young child, is "play practice" – practicing the routine as play. When you introduce the new system, choose three scenarios together for practice. Maybe the child will be throwing the ball at the bedroom wall and you ask him to take the ball outside. Maybe the child will be playing at the park and you ask him leave the jungle gym and walk with you to the car. Maybe he is playing and you ask him to set the table. Make sure he occasionally practices noncompliance at the count of "two" and cooperates with the time-out, so that he can see how benign the consequence can be. Commend him for cooperating with the time-out.

Each time you act out these little vignettes, with your child complying after the first or second count, you should praise your child's ability to do as you asked. If you want to celebrate a successful play practice with an ice cream cone, it will help send your child the message that building self-control is a positive mission.

Kids understand and take the counting system more seriously if they've run through the drill a few times. If your older child is too old to enjoy play practice, just discuss various scenarios so that he understands the process.

The reason that this system works better with time-outs than with reward systems is that noncompliance results in an immediate consequence. Charts often are not readily available, nor do you want to incentivize noncompliance. More importantly, this process is a natural way for children to learn to stop on a regular basis and strengthen that self-control muscle when they are revved up.

The counting method should be used to encourage cooperation and to slow down the child's engine. It should never be about exacting revenge on perfectly normal child behavior. Children need to learn to follow directions. The alternative to the counting method is usually the talky, talky parent who begs, pleads, and explains (which inadvertently rewards noncompliance with attention) or the angry, punitive parent. (Sometimes, they are the same parent!)

Parents who love this method and use it successfully report that they almost never get to "three" (after a couple of times early on before the child learned they meant business). They also report that it all but eliminates noncompliance and power struggles.

Parents who don't like this method report that they don't approve of the time-out procedure, and that it is training their children to fear them. Although struggles with getting their children to follow directions may be frustrating for them and even reinforced by the tussle, they prefer to try to use reason and explanations.

I think parents should consult their wise mind when considering whether to try this method. Perhaps they will weigh the negative fallout from power struggles (maybe they have very few) against the concerns or hassles (maybe they have a lot) of using this method, and punt. Other parents may reflect on their situation differently and give it a try.

The counting method seems easy, but many parents goof it up by waiting too long before they count. They chide and threaten to count, and then they start to count in such a hostile way that the child is challenged to meet anger with anger and rebellion. Also, parents may pile scolding on top of counting, which can inspire a power struggle. In addition, they need to be sure their kids respond well to time-outs, which I measure by how easily they cooperate, seem resilient, and benefit from a "reset, reboot."

Parents should use the method calmly, without emotion. Here is an easy way to remember:

Do not TALK:

Threaten

Argue

Lecture

Keep nagging

Preservation of self-control

Kids work really hard to comply with expectations all day long. It can be one long, enormous slog of compliance with morning routines, school expectations, and evening routines. That self-control muscle gets exhausted. In addition to the breaks, nourishment, and realistic expectations discussed earlier, there are other ways of removing unnecessary strains on the self-control muscle.

If your child is using up energy to not look at the TV during homework, you can remove the TV. If your child is distracted by siblings during the evening chores, you can make sure he's by himself. If you are having a hard time being present for your child because of incoming texts on your smartphone, put the phone in a place where you can't see it. Consider these maneuvers to be guardrails. You are protecting yourself and your child from using up energy on self-control that could be directed to more important targets, such as homework, chores, and being present with loved ones.

The guardrails principle
You can protect yourself and your child from unnecessarily exhausting your capacity for self-control by placing temptations out of reach. These arrangements serve as guardrails that keep us on task and focus our attention on desired goals.

These arrangements are called "default" systems by the experts who study willpower (Baumeister and Tierney 2012). We can reach goals more effectively by using preset systems that keep us from wasting self-control on unnecessary distractions and caving to indulgences. Automatically preset thermostats help us save energy. Retirement plans help us set aside money so we don't spend it. And turning off the router at 9 p.m. helps the whole family get to sleep on time. The parts of the brain in charge of self-control get tired, and we are all susceptible to temptations.

Summary

When you find yourself dreading a situation, worried that your child won't control herself at the grocery store or preschool drop-off, it's time to employ your toolbox of parenting strategies. Dread is a cue from your intuitive brain that you need to address impending risks by using effective methods.

As a parent, you'll be more effective if you plan ahead and use behavioral management techniques that help you set limits, prevent problems, and avoid power struggles. Not all parent-child messes are preventable, but we do what we can. Tantrums will still happen. When your child is in full meltdown mode, your most important tool is the Acceptance Mantra (I accept my child exactly as he is), because your negative reactions make things worse. Your child picks up on your judgment of him.

Childhood is one long workout for parents' and children's self-control capabilities. We need to give children self-control practice with exercises in setting goals and delaying gratification. Because temperaments and abilities vary enormously across age ranges, assessing your child's baseline is critical. Knowing how long he can wait now allows you to know what kind of "workout" you want to give your child. The next step is to help him wait a little longer.

There is a circular nature to helping your child develop self-control: You need your own self-control to help your child develop hers. Your executive functioning (e.g., planning ahead, making sound decisions, regulating emotions) is required to help your child develop her own, because you assist your child with making and meeting her own goals and regulating her own emotions.

The authoritative parenting style is a top predictor of a child's self-control and all of the wonderful things that come with it, including successful academic performance, emotional adjustment, and healthy relationships. What's your own personal combination of the three qualities — warmth, authority, and acceptance of negative or offensive thoughts and feelings in your child — and which ones do you need to work on?

Self-control and willpower exist in a finite supply. We can rest up and fill the tank, and replenish it with fun in between workouts, but we must be realistic about our limits. Children ages three to seven are working on effortful control all day. Temperament and age play large roles in determining their capacities. We must know our kid and plan our expectations accordingly.

As parents living in a fast-paced world, we must be realistic about our own need to take breaks and rest our self-control muscles. Parental self-care is a necessary part of optimal child rearing. If we don't take care of ourselves, we won't have enough capacity for this gargantuan enterprise called parenting.

CHAPTER 3

Academic success:
When you worry about school performance

What is the biggest factor in determining your child's future success? If you're like most parents, you answered "academic success." It's an area of intense focus for parents with kids of all ages, including during the early years, when school habits and attitudes are first forming.

To many parents, a child's performance in elementary school seems like an enormously high-stakes window into the future. Frequently, parents nurture and prepare their young children in every way imaginable to get them "school ready," only to find them later giving short shrift to homework, or lacking in the kind of drive that seems necessary for future success. Many parents perceive that their kindergartners and first-graders lack persistence on academic tasks. Does that mean they don't have the grit needed to one day get into an Ivy League school? Does it mean that they are "lazy learners"? Or are they just being kids?

Scene: Dealing with a first-grader's disappointing report card

Mom: Tanesha, your dad and I are worried about your report card. Even though your grades are average, they could be better, given your intelligence. And the comments are disappointing. What do you have to say about your continued academic slump?

Tanesha: I'll try harder?

Mom: Why is that a question? Your last three report cards were all the same. They say that you don't pay attention, often distract the other children, and rush through your work. You are too social and don't apply yourself.

Tanesha: It's boring to sit in chairs all day, Mommy. It's always "Do this" and "Do that." Mrs. B. doesn't like me.

Mom: Honey, she is frustrated with you. Everybody is. We see that you have tons of potential, which you are not using. First grade is not supposed to be just about having fun. It's too valuable a year for you to be a lazy learner.

Tanesha: I don't like school. I'm trying to do better, but it's boring.

Mom: You always say that, but you need to show the same fire in your belly for schoolwork that you show for playing your wizards game. You are a very smart girl, but the only way you are going to succeed in life is if you develop some grit for hard work and high goals.

This mom has an extreme case of reason mind if she thinks this kind of talk is going to inspire a seven-year-old to buckle down and improve academics at school. Why? Because even though everything she says is accurate (except for the "lazy learner" part), there is virtually no way that this kind of talk will motivate better school performance.

While this self-described "tiger mom" feels entitled to complain about her daughter's lazy ways, she's concerned that her approach is resulting in snow-balling negative attitudes, as evidenced by Tanesha's statements, such as "I don't care," "My teachers don't like me," and "I hate school." Tanesha's dad is frustrated and increasingly distancing himself from school issues, because he feels like nothing he does or says helps his daughter become more invested in school.

PREPARING YOUNG MINDS FOR SCHOOL

There is no such thing as a lazy learner. All humans are born with tremen-dous curiosity and drive to explore, just as all animals are driven to forage for food, watch out for danger, and seek opportunities. The learning that results from these quests has allowed survival of our species over the mil-lennia. The drive to learn and to be a motivated learner is built into our DNA.

Most often, when we call our kids "lazy," it's because they are not motivat-ed to do what we want them to do. We get frustrated when our kids don't do their chores, drag their heels during routines, and — the biggest, hairiest bugaboo of all — fail to show sufficient enthusiasm for school. Do you ever refer to your child as "lazy" or "lacking passion"? Do you ever call her an "underperformer," or say she's not living up to her potential? Does that help to change her behavior? To quote the Reason Mantra again: You might be right, but are you effective?

The myth of the lazy learner
There is no such thing as a lazy learner. Babies are born curious, driven to explore, and ready to learn. When a young child is not interested in academic material, the question should not be "Why is he lazy?" It should be "What can adults do to ignite his built-in passion for learning?"

The big question for parents is "How do I motivate my child to do her best at school?" If there are already parent-child conflicts about school, another question must be "Are there issues I need to work on before I can promote academic achievement?" Any child who is already labeled as lazy in first grade needs his parent to give serious thought to that question, and to these: Is the school curriculum appropriate? Is it focused too much on academics and not enough on play, physical exercise, and social and emotional learning? Research has shown that young children's academic thriving depends on social, emotional, and physical wellness, not just cognitive strengths (Diamond 2010).

Every kid is an individual, with different factors influencing academic performance. Tanesha's case illustrates a classic tangled web of elements that has gotten her off to a rough start with school, despite her solid abilities. Parents of children who have any kind of special learning problem or disability should seek a professional assessment. But with all kids, there is a universal truth about addressing academic problems: Learning potential is promoted by positive emotion, and shriveled by stress and criticism.

Tanesha's situation is not unusual, especially for children with educated parents who get anxious about perceived patterns of underachievement, which they fear may persist and ultimately doom their children's future. To understand her level of motivation at school, we need to begin by understanding Tanesha's school context, temperament, and age. And we need to examine her parents' expectations for academic achievement, the backfire effect that negative messages have on school performance, and the potential curse of being labeled "smart."

Tanesha's parents consulted me because they felt her disengagement with school was getting worse. She is a high-energy and sociable kid, and although these traits can be advantageous for academic achievement, at this moment, they are seen as liabilities.

Lately, Tanesha has been saying that she hates school, and doesn't care about doing well. These declarations have driven her high-achieving parents bonkers. The high value they place on education — and their own experiences as excellent students — have made them extremely frustrated and worried about Tanesha, resulting in a negative downward spiral of constant arguing. They knew they needed a new approach.

Beware of labeling
Giving your child negative labels is always dangerous. Prophesizing bad outcomes for bad work habits may seem like a way to motivate, but it's more likely to result in the outcome you least want: lackluster academic performance.

Tanesha is not a lazy learner. She is driven to build complicated constructions with Legos, participate in year-round sports, and illustrate books she "writes" about wizards. She is interested in academic material, but mainly when it is in an interactive format, and when she isn't constrained by boring "Do this, do that" demands. She loves spelling bees, math games with her father ("ones that don't feel like math"), and reading with her parents.

Group education — otherwise known as school — pitches curricula to kids with a range of abilities, as it must. But with twenty–thirty students in a classroom, let's face it: There are limits to what teachers can do to keep any single student engaged, attending, curious, and on task. Keeping active sprites like Tanesha enthralled with learning at school is challenging, and even in the best of school settings, teachers' motivation and ability to do so will vary. And even though you might think Tanesha would thrive in classes with hands-on materials and nonstop interactive teaching, schools can't cater to every individual child's learning style. Furthermore, research has determined that attempts at such catering have not resulted in advantages for students (Pashler, McDaniel, Rohrer, and Bjork 2008). It turns out that improving school performance is more complicated than pitching curricula to children categorized as verbal, spatial, or kinesthetic learners.

Tanesha is taking a lot of heat about academic performance for a first-grader. Getting pigeonholed for anything at age seven is a dangerous trap. Many kids her age, especially rambunctious ones like Tanesha, have ants in their pants just by virtue of their age and temperament. They just don't demonstrate their full intellectual firepower with first-grade brains. (Many kids don't until they're 20!)

Especially with traditional curricula, kids are expected to sit for long periods of time. Some schools have omitted recess and gym to prioritize the Three R's (reading, writing and arithmetic), STEM (science, technology, engineering, math), and academic "rigor" at the expense of everything else that we know benefits child development, learning, and brain functioning.

Tanesha's parents know from standardized testing that she is "smart," and it only adds to their frustration that she doesn't apply herself more at school. While testing is important to identify kids who need special resources, sometimes testing — like report cards — results in parental distress and criticism, rather than helpful problem solving. In Tanesha's case, her parents have become so preoccupied with what they perceive to be her underachievement that they can only think of the glass as half empty. Indeed, she is not applying her full intellectual capacity to earn higher grades, and her report-card comments complain about a lack of engagement and overly social conduct. But there is a positive side: Her motivation to learn, explore, create, and build collaboratively is stupendous! And let's not forget that she has good grades (mostly B's) and above-average standardized test scores.

Applying oneself in first grade is important, but so is entering school with solid math and language skills, as Tanesha did, thanks to her parents and her preschool. In fact, recent research has demonstrated that math and language skills in kindergarten are predictive of long-term academic success, and surprisingly, more predictive than attention-related skills and behavior!

Math and language literacy

Research conducted by Greg Duncan of Northwestern University and colleagues studied 35,000 preschoolers to examine the key ingredients of academic success later in elementary school (Duncan and Dowsett et al. 2007). The researchers determined that beginning school with solid math and literacy skills is the single most important factor in predicting later academic achievement. Even attention-related skills, although important, were not as strong a predictor, and this was the case for boys and girls alike. Furthermore, kids who had solid math and language skills in kindergarten but were described as disruptive in the classroom still ended up learning as much as their better-behaved classmates! Also surprising is that these findings held true regardless of IQ, income level of the family, temperament, type of previous educational experience, and whether the students were from one- or two-parent families.

The importance of math and language literacy
Exposing young brains to math and language skills in the first five years of life is crucial. Research has shown that while many young children will still show behavioral immaturity, introducing some basic literacy concepts to young children sets them up for becoming successful students when they start school.

Duncan, a professor of education and social policy, emphasized that these findings do not mean preschools should reduce their programs to math and recitation drills; in fact, he noted that well-designed play-based programs can foster the development of academic and attention skills in ways that are engaging and fun.

Tanesha is fortunate to be above grade level in her abilities. But for her and probably most kids, curricula are optimal when they make learning the traditional subjects the exciting, motivating, and successful adventure it can be. It is imperative to set kids up for the enjoyment of learning. Once they start an "I hate school" refrain, it's time to be concerned. What happened to Tanesha to have her end up here?

Temperament and learning

Because her parents have high standards and know Tanesha is bright, they have been talking to her for two years about her intellectual ability, her potential for achievement, and their disappointments. This accounts for about one-third of her life! Her report-card comments have encouraged this negative framework, along with the "lazy learner" label.

When I read negative school reports about kindergartners' inattention, poor work habits, and being "too social" with friends, I want to tear them to shreds! Such reports often seem clueless about child development, given most children's limited self-control and capacity for formal methods of academic instruction in preschool, kindergarten, and the early grades. Plenty of students like Tanesha will not meet criteria for a diagnosis of attention deficit disorder, but will be talkative, disruptive, and inattentive enough to frustrate teachers with their amped-up personalities.

Reframing report cards
*Given the natural tendency for many young children to be spirited, shy, or otherwise challenging from a temperament standpoint, report-card comments would be best if framed like this: "Everything your child is doing is within normal limits for his age, **and** here are some goals we have for your child's academic progress."*

Like parents, teachers need to work with the temperaments of the students as they are, not as they wish them to be. From that place of acceptance can come efforts to expand academic competence. Children in kindergarten and the early grades need a lot of wiggle room for developing their academic skills at different rates. Temperament interacts with intellectual capacities, and influences the degree to which children can attend to and engage in academic material.

Children with shy, anxious, and avoidant temperaments might be reluctant to participate in class exercises, prompting comments on report cards that can be just as upsetting as those describing inattentive and disruptive behaviors. Techniques for managing these two ends of the temperament spectrum and everything in between are standard curricula for today's teachers, but again, twenty–thirty students are a lot to manage. Furthermore, agendas such as Common Core State Standards, No Child Left Behind, and other state and federal mandates for testing further burden teachers with responsibilities that compete with giving children individualized attention.

While figuring out how to educate dozens of kids who are all over the bell curve of normal, teachers need to be ready to screen and refer the children who are outside the curve, so that they can be assessed formally for potential intervention. Early childhood educators need to make the distinction between kids who need referrals to psychologists versus those who need acceptance and support for developing at different paces. With the professional training teachers need in psychological and cognitive development, they deserve at least double their salary!

Gender and academics

Brain researchers have documented differences between male and female brains, but no one knows how or if we should translate these findings into child-rearing or educational approaches. On average, boys are more physically active, impulsive, and immature than girls, so there is a hue and cry for more recess and gym classes (girls need these things, too!). Because girls can feel intimidated by boys' boisterousness and hang back from challenges, there has been a push for single-gender schooling, despite the fact that it doesn't result in better educational outcomes for girls.

Considering the fact that there is no empirical evidence that changing up curricula will help girls or boys, caution is advised (Halpern and Eliot et al. 2011).

There is a history of bandwagon mentality in educational reform. The single most concerning achievement gap is that for children growing up in poverty: Low-income children, especially boys of color who suffer many sociological disadvantages, are the ones who truly get shortchanged in education.

Just like controversies regarding homework, standardized testing, and support for the humanities in light of the push for STEM subjects, the focus on gender may be important, but it pales in comparison to the monumental significance of addressing the achievement gaps between low-, middle-, and high-income students.

IMPROVING ACADEMIC PERFORMANCE

Most parents have heard of "self-fulfilling prophecies," but that doesn't stop some of them from labeling or using judgmental terms when they perceive academic slumps. Actually, it's pretty incredible to use the term "academic slump" to describe the academic performance of a six- or seven-year-old, given the variability of maturation in that age group. But these days, kids are expected to do in first grade what students did in third grade not long ago.

Since Tanesha's performance was at grade level and her test scores indicated that she was above average, should Tanesha's parents ignore the report card's comments about her conduct and work habits? Heck no! Her parents are right to want to work on her challenges related to temperament; they're just aiming for a lot higher than average (aren't we all?). The research discussed in this chapter may reassure them a bit about her academic future, but they still wonder how to tackle her lack of effort and conduct issues. Although their values are solid, their approach is a problem; they consistently show concern by nagging and lecturing, and they can see it's only making her defensive, critical of school, and less invested in trying.

Another typical pitfall in Tanesha's mom's approach is the reference to Tanesha as "smart." The word is not being delivered as a compliment: "You are a very smart girl, but the only way you are going to succeed in life is if you develop some grit for hard work and high goals." What do you think Tanesha hears in this statement? And what's the problem with calling your daughter smart when you consider praise of intelligence a good and reinforcing practice? Isn't it a compliment, and therefore encouraging?

Praising your child

Praising kids is an art and also a science (as you're about to find out), and far more complicated than once thought. Contemporary parents, more child-centered than previous generations, demonstrate their investment by providing resources, close scrutiny, and generous praise. Parents can be all over the map when it comes to philosophies about praise. As it turns out, kids don't benefit from "the more, the better" approach any more than a stingier approach.

Until about the 1970s, child-rearing practices prioritized obedience and strict discipline over sensitivity to the emotional functioning of the child. As with many trends that overcompensate for a previous phase, a focus on praise and self-esteem took off at the end of the last century. While emotional and social learning are profoundly important aspects of academic success, we've learned that supporting such learning is not as simple as pouring copious compliments all over kids.

Over the last half-century, the labor economy, once based on service industries, has shifted to jobs that require emotional intelligence as well as knowledge and talent. Academics have become more competitive than ever, and every aspect of academic performance and motivation is analyzed and optimized for progress and success. Benchmarks, testing, and new curricula are all on the table, and praise in the classroom and at home is justifiably perceived as one more lever. Praise can indeed motivate both academic performance and other desirable behaviors, but it depends on a few key factors.

Praising effort, not smarts

Since the 1960s, Carol Dweck, an eminent psychologist and researcher of motivation and perseverance, has been documenting the importance of focusing on children's effort rather than ability (Dweck 2007). Her research has indicated that there are huge advantages for children who have a "growth mind-set" instead of a "fixed mind-set." Kids with a growth mind-set believe that their successes are the result of their hard work; those with a fixed mind-set believe that their successes are the result of innate talent or inborn intelligence.

Children with a fixed mind-set agree with this statement: "If you have to work hard, you don't have ability. If you have ability, things come naturally to you." When these kids encounter failure — as we all will at some point, no matter how bright we are — they give up, thinking it's just proof that they aren't that smart after all! Throwing the high-stakes word "smart" around makes kids think it's a zero-sum game, and once they start to struggle, the only other alternative in their internal logic toggle is "not smart."

By contrast, children with a growth mind-set believe that they can get smarter by learning. They understand that even highly accomplished geniuses work hard. They also know that if they have a disappointing slump, they can commit themselves to more hard work and improve their performance. Without their smarts on the line every minute, they can choose challenge without it endangering their overall self-concept. How liberating!

> **Growing the growth mind-set**
> *Rather than focusing on innate intellectual ability, focus on intelligence as a muscle that must be exercised, developed, and maintained. The message should be "The more you challenge yourself and the harder you work, the smarter you become!"*

What determines mind-sets in kids? Dweck has examined various samples of children to answer just this question and identified a key factor: the way that praise is given. In one study, Dweck and her colleagues randomly assigned fifth-graders, evenly matched for cognitive ability, to two groups. After they completed some problems from a cognitive test, she gave them one of two different kinds of praise. Subjects in the first group were praised for their intelligence: "Wow, that's a really good score. You must be smart at this." Subjects in the second group were praised for their effort: "Wow, that's a really good score. You must have tried really hard."

After a first round of testing, Dweck rigged the second test so that all the children would fail. Then she gave them the original test a second time. The children praised for smarts performed significantly worse the second time around, and worse than the second group, which was complimented for its efforts. On the third test, after that rigged failure, the children praised for effort actually outperformed themselves on the original test as well as outperforming the other group. Challenge primed their intellectual pumps!

At another juncture, Dweck also presented the children with a choice between an easy or a more difficult task. The children praised for effort tended to choose the challenging task, demonstrated more motivation to learn, and showed more confidence as the problems became more difficult. However, the children praised for their intelligence more often wanted the easier task, presumably knowing that they'd have a surer chance at success. As the problems became more difficult, they lost their confidence, even inflating their scores when asked to report them later. Apparently, they were so discouraged that they were moved to hide their shame with untruths.

In another study that followed one-year-olds until they were seven or eight years old, Dweck and her colleagues observed the kind of praise moms gave in their homes. They also examined the kids' fixed versus growth mind-sets and their attitudes toward challenge. You guessed it: The children who were praised for effort were more likely to have an appetite for challenge and effort. The way you praise your toddlers makes a difference!

And what about unfixing a fixed mind-set? Dweck and her team conducted a study with underachieving seventh-graders and gave one group a "growth mind-set" course, and the second group some training in memory. The growth mind-set course was devised to teach them that their brain was a muscle, and that if they were behind in math, they just needed the math-brain workout. The kids who took the course improved their grades significantly more than the students who just received memory training. The takeaway for parents? Drop the word "smart" from your vocabulary and praise effort.

Encouraging and praising your child's academic work
- *Praise effort and hard work, not smarts.*
- *Avoid focusing on "potential." Kids hear this as criticism.*
- *Emphasize the positive whenever possible.*
- *Don't follow a compliment with a "but" — it nullifies the compliment.*
- *Praise thoughtfully, so that you don't slip into negatives.*

Principals of parental praise

Parents at either end of the praise spectrum — praise misers and praise gushers — have their reasons and philosophies. The parents in the deficit category believe that if their kids receive praise, they will relax into a lassitude that will impede effort. The parents in the effusive camp believe that copious praise will raise self-esteem, generate motivation, and maybe even raise the all-around, feel-good quotient of the parent-child relationship. In actuality, both extremes are problematic. Like a balanced diet, praise is crucial to the optimal nourishment of the child, but it motivates a child best when given in the right dose, in the right way.

Research has demonstrated that praising two-year-olds for independent exploration and problem solving is associated with later persistence and independence (Kelley, Brownell, and Campbell 2000). Sue Kelley and her colleagues observed interaction patterns among two-year-olds and their mothers, and assessed them again a year later. The three-year-olds who were most likely to tackle challenges and persist at problem solving were the ones whose mothers had praised and encouraged their independence at 24 months.

Although sometimes it's frustrating to watch a toddler struggle with a task (I admit it: I often straightened the tower of blocks so it wouldn't topple), it pays to encourage, rather than rescue. And though praise feels good all around, we need to praise their actual accomplishments. Also, older kids may figure out there is a motive to certain kinds of parental praise; they can detect subtleties that may feel like pressure, pity, insincerity, or even manipulation.

The GOLD standard for giving praise:

Genuine

Occasional

Limited and specific

Decent effort

Research has shown that praise, like many things, is best when you don't overdo or underdo it (Lepper and Henderlong 2000). Use the "GOLD standard" for remembering how to deliver praise for the best results. It's important to use descriptive language that conveys accurate information and attainable standards. For example, it's better to praise your five-year-old's progress in learning to dribble a basketball than to tell him he is ready for the NBA (which might make him think you expect him to be superhuman).

Also, save your praise for things kids can change — rather than for traits they can't — or for pursuits they already love. After all, if we want to motivate kids and keep praise meaningful and special, why not conserve it for times it can be appreciated, and help generate some incentive to keep going in the face of challenge?

The GOLD standard in action:

Instead of excessive and extreme praise:
"This picture belongs in a museum!"

Try "Genuine":
"I love the way the blue of the sky meets the green of the hill right at the horizon."

Instead of frequent praise:
"Great play!" "Good boy!" "Brilliant!"

Try "Occasional":
"I was impressed by how well you listened to the coach and passed a lot during the game."

Instead of general praise:
"Good job!" "Amazing kid!"

Try "Limited and specific":
"I appreciate that you cleared every dish off the table tonight."

Instead of comparing to others:
"You made the highest score on the Spanish test in your class!"

Try "Decent effort":
"Your effort to learn your vocabulary words is paying off."

It's clear from the examples above that the GOLD standard of praise requires more effort, and that's the point: When parents use such precise praise, it feels more genuine and trustworthy. Excessive praise can make kids uncomfortable and get them thinking about all the ways the superlative references aren't true, rather than making them feel good about themselves. Don't you feel uncomfortable when someone refers to you as the best, the most wonderful, or perfect?

Upon receiving the GOLD standard praise, the child thinks, *My parent was really paying attention.* Especially for young children, praise given immediately after a desired behavior is reinforcing: "You did a good job brushing your teeth tonight." Another valuable kind of praise is the "saved up" sort, when parents reflect back on the day and praise special efforts. It implies that the parents' recollections of their children's skillful behaviors are so special, they can remember them all day and comment on them during snuggle time.

Theodore Roosevelt once said, "Comparison is the thief of joy." You may not think of this when you are making a positive comparison, but you can only outperform others for so long. When kids are compared to others, we are teaching them that we value their relative standing, not their mastery of a goal. It also can make them insecure; while it's great when they're on top, what happens when they slip?

The "occasional" part of the GOLD formula may be a bit nonintuitive, since many parents think that more praise results in more reinforcement and more good behavior. But the brain's attentional system is not always on high alert; it rests when not activated and perks up and takes note when a reward (like praise) is delivered. It needs to rest; it can't be vigilant every minute, or we would wear it out pretty quickly. A steady patter of praise can become background noise, easily ignored.

By contrast, unexpected rewards make an impression. When praise happens only occasionally, the brain retains that information, because we're wired to pay attention to rewards (back in the caveman days, this was key to survival, when rewards were food, water, warmth, and safety). The brain registers "Bingo! I'm having that great feeling I get when I experience something really special and surprising!" When you hear "good job" every other minute, it is neither.

The boom and bust of the self-esteem movement

Back in the 1970s and '80s, the concepts of self-esteem and thriving child health got mixed up in the cause-and-effect mill, as such concepts often do. Teenagers who were high academic achievers, avoided substance abuse, and had lots of good friends tended to have high self-esteem. Those with problems had low self-esteem. It was assumed that praise would encourage those with low self-esteem to improve behaviors; give everyone a trophy, have special "Me!" days in preschool, shower kids with compliments, and zap! They'll feel good and behave differently. Not true; in fact, almost the opposite can occur. And generic, positive sunniness can feel phony to a kid who feels bad and struggles with a lot of problems. The higher self-esteem of students with higher grades is the result — not the cause — of doing well in school, as we now know from painstaking longitudinal studies.

In retrospect, it sounds kind of silly, doesn't it? What happens to children after their feel-good "You are special" days, if everybody gets the same special day? Does the trophy represent a big accomplishment if everyone gets an identical trophy on the soccer team? Although boosting confidence by offering praise for decent effort is a great idea, the "genuine" part of the GOLD standard is a key ingredient. Even young children can detect a sham.

Recently, a study conducted by researchers in The Netherlands examined this connection (Brummelmann and Thomaes et al. 2014). They showed that adults tended to give eight- to thirteen-year-olds with low self-esteem more "person" praise (praise for personal qualities) but less "process" praise (praise for behavior) than they gave children with high self-esteem. Apparently, this well-intentioned inclination to boost self-esteem backfires; the tendency to praise personal qualities among children who feel crummy about themselves results in their feeling even worse when they fail. That's because these kids attribute failure to their shortcomings as people. It is far more effective to praise effort and those "process" behaviors, focusing on specific things the child does to make strides toward mastery in any real, detectable ways.

It's a rare parent who isn't interested in grades, IQ scores, and standardized test results. Of course they matter. Of course they are predictive of academic success (although not as much as self-control is, as you read in the last chapter). But ironically, focusing on them too much can turn parents into critical, lecturing, overzealous helicopter parents who snuff out academic motivation instead of encouraging it.

Tunnel vision on IQ and grades

Since IQs and grades can be measures of intelligence and academic promise, parents often focus on them more than virtues, character, social skills, and emotional competence. Most people would say they want their kids to be "good," not just smart, but there is no measure for "goodness" any more than there is for character. With all the anxiety generated by cutthroat college admissions, competition in the global economy, and the loss of the American dream, it's the rare parent who doesn't worry about academic performance, even as early as preschool and elementary school.

As understandable as this stress on academics is, it has a dark side: Excessive preoccupation with academics can hurt kids. Suniya Luthar's research has demonstrated a link between academic pressure and depression, anxiety, and substance use among affluent high school students (Luthar 2003). The biggest predictor of academic pressure was a distanced relationship with parents. Given the number of times I've heard from teens, "All my parents care about is grades," I'm not surprised by this association. I also empathize with parents who are worried about college prospects. However, when that future focus damages the child's trust in unconditional love, then academic prospects are already at risk.

As crucial a part of their lives as it is, school is still only one part. We parents can suffer from tunnel vision with our focus on academic futures. We need to open the wide-angled (and wise-angled) lens and appreciate all the other things that are so critical to a child's development. Whether they are seven or seventeen, their optimal learning and academic performance occur in the context of a thriving life, one filled with friends, dreams, interests, responsibilities, hobbies, play, and rest.

As extensive research on social and emotional learning has documented, children's academic careers blossom when it is integrated with academics. (Zins, Bloodworth, Weissberg, and Walberg 2007). What does social and emotional learning mean exactly? It means focusing on recognizing and managing emotions, caring about others, making good decisions, behaving ethically and responsibly, developing positive relationships, and avoiding negative behaviors. No wonder it helps academic performance!

A balanced learning diet
Academic performance should always be considered in the context of the child's overall life. Like a healthy, balanced diet, a child's optimal achievement requires that cognitive, emotional, and social nutrients be in balance. Academic pressure can be a toxin.

A thriving childhood balances academic endeavors with social, emotional, and other elements of a child's life. When the child is not flourishing, faltering academic performance is often one of the first ways it shows up. If there is conflict at home, bullying, or other stressors, it's harder for the young child's brain to be in top working order. Even in the best of circumstances, the cognitive demands made on a child to stay focused and engaged in school all day are daunting.

Building blocks of learning

To appreciate how emotional turmoil can derail academics, we must acknowledge the central role emotions play in learning. You'll see this reflected in the key elements of an effective learning process:

1. Supply opportunities for learning that involve play and fun.
2. Set achievable goals.
3. Ensure that learning is rewarding.
4. Protect against excessive stress.
5. Inspire the drive for mastery by staying positive.
6. Spawn yearning for more learning by maintaining this cycle.

When kids start to turn off to a learning situation or academic material, it is crucial to figure out which one of these elements went amiss. Setting achievable goals (number two on the list) is often miscalculated, due to strong parental desire to see greater maturity in children before they're capable, and to reach impressive but unrealistic goals. You might want your five-year-old to master addition, but first he must be cognitively, emotionally, and socially ready to pay attention in math class. And that class needs to be fun, interactive, and taught at the appropriate level so as not to overwhelm and destroy motivation.

When we are exposed to learning situations that pitch the material way below our level of ability, we become bored and disengage. When the material is over our heads, we get stressed and worried. Stress occurs when the demands of the situation exceed our ability to cope. When our emotional brains detect "Danger!" and stress hormones are released, our heart rate soars (more on this in Chapter 5). The emotional part of our brain, when triggered by stressors, makes learning and thinking nearly impossible until calming occurs. In reality, a student who experiences "Danger!" alarms in class may be learning only one thing: She wants to avoid that class.

As a psychologist, I sometimes hear a parent say that a child should be able to handle a class "at her age." What I focus in on is the "should." From what perspective is the person making that judgment — from test scores, age, or grade standards? Even if that child has great test scores, she might be emotionally overwhelmed by the demands of the situation. Adults may think the math lesson, circle time, and gym class are benign, but the child's brain may be flooding with emotion, knocking her cognitive system offline. There are things we can do to help her cope, but throwing dismissive "shoulds" at her is not one of them. Likewise, comparing her to the other kids who are enjoying the class can be crushing.

Better to focus on setting achievable goals, rather than react to a child's failure to meet expectations. Figuring out small steps toward mastery becomes the central objective, and the "steps" may be emotional ones, not academic ones. Dialing back the math lessons to more reachable goals may help one child experience the gratification that comes with achievement. For another child, being allowed to participate partially in gym class at first may help quell her anxiety about performance, allowing her to gradually move to full participation.

When we talk of "rewards" in learning contexts, we aren't necessarily speaking about providing goodies for educational triumphs. In optimal circumstances, there is a good feeling that comes with learning, which is called an "intrinsic" reward. In fact, dopamine (the neurochemical associated with pleasure) is released in anticipation of a rewarding experience. When we are about to complete a math problem or hard assignment, there is a delight that can rival other pleasures, such as eating a favorite food, winning a game, or receiving a gift.

But children who struggle with learning may have already developed dread from previous failures and have a hard time moving toward challenges. Extrinsic rewards — any external goody that might motivate effort toward goals — can be helpful to jump-start the mission. Similar to the Successful Sleeper program discussed in Chapter 1, once the intrinsic rewards of mastery kick in, the extrinsic rewards can be phased out.

The 'sweet spot' for learning

The sweet spot for learning is reached when enough challenge is provided to keep the child engaged, enough reward is experienced to motivate the child to try again, and enough opportunities are generated for the child to reach ever higher goals.

This concept is actually at work in many of the computer games that kids play; it's what keeps them trying to move up to higher levels. "Gamification" is the word used by the gaming industry to refer to these well-established principles that make learning more engaging and rewarding. Although school reform is beyond the scope of this book, it's compelling to muse about which of these factors might be used in education innovation to help get kids motivated.

Finessing a turnaround

Tanesha's parents realized that they needed to infuse more positivity and joy into their parenting, because worrying about her school performance was destroying their overall relationship with her. Months into my consultations with Tanesha's parents, her mom described the following exchange, which characterized their new approach.

Mom: What did you enjoy the most at school today?

Tanesha: Math lab! Mrs. B. let me write the problems in different colors of pencil. You should see my workbook. It is so pretty because when I finish the problems, I decorate the borders. I even did the extra problems.

Mom: It sounds like you were really working hard. You put your own special touch on your paper with those colors, didn't you?

Tanesha: Yeah! And since I finished all of the problems, Mrs. B. let me write three of them on the blackboard. And then I got to use different colors of chalk.

Mom: Wow, so Mrs. B. got to see you work hard, help her at the board, and pay attention to the math lab all at the same time.

Tanesha: She said she'd give me extra math puzzles for fun. I told her that wizards need math for their potions, like you and I do with measuring stuff in the kitchen.

Mom: You are really working that math muscle in your brain, aren't you?

Tanesha: You aren't kidding, Mom. So let's make those wizard muffins, quick. My muscles are starving!

Notice that Mom is not talking about grades or performance. Both parents are committed to the wise-minded goal of focusing on their own attitude and behavior, instead of trying to control Tanesha's academic performance directly. Their new goals included showing Tanesha that they value learning, engagement, and effort. Since Tanesha's self-regulation and staying on task at school is a long-term project, they also committed to working on self-control with the exercises described in the Chapter 2.

How did Tanesha's parents manage to settle for less than straight A's? Most educational experts think first-graders shouldn't even receive grades, because parents can overfocus on them and become critical. After putting their inner perfectionist tendencies in check and doing some soul searching, Tanesha's parents backed down on grades. They understood that they were doing their job and feeding her academic potential already with the rich environment they supplied at home: extensive conversations at the dinner table, trips to museums, and gobs and gobs of reading. They knew that nagging was not only discouraging her motivation to learn, but harming her overall attitude about school.

Tanesha's mom committed to filtering her own critical messages by remembering to focus on the positive with the "glass half full" metaphor. Tanesha's dad filtered his critical messages by repeating to himself: "You catch more flies with honey than vinegar." Both adages are profound reminders of the decades of research supporting the benefits of positive reinforcement. Tanesha's parents also switched from talking about her "potential" and how "smart" she is to praising her efforts.

Talking to Tanesha's teachers about ways to keep her engaged helped, too. (Luckily, they were open to colored pencils and wizard illustrations!) Tanesha showed steady improvement in all of the areas addressed on the school report card over the next year. The teachers noticed Tanesha's increased self-control, which gave her parents encouragement that their positive approaches were helping across the board.

Due in large part to her parents' valiant determination to overhaul their approach to her academic performance, Tanesha became a motivated and engaged student by fourth grade. Even though she still didn't make straight A's, her parents figured out, in their wise-minded, big-picture analysis, that Tanesha's highest academic potential would be achieved when she enjoyed learning, improved her self-control, and developed a love for school. They realized that Tanesha would not improve at school by hearing that she should make straight A's because her IQ score shows that she can. Tanesha's mom shared her insight into the great restraint she needed to master — and to know when to keep her mouth shut: "I need to practice the duct-tape school of parenting."

Try, try, try not to lecture about academics
When parents are worried about academic motivation, it is incredibly hard not to talk about the importance of educational achievement. But young children can't process that long-term perspective; they hear the lecture as criticism.

Along with Tanesha's natural passion for learning when it hit her "sweet spot," her zest for art, imagination, sports, and friendships synergized to make her one of the class leaders by the end of elementary school. Teachers commented on her strong personality, but by then, instead of distracting peers, she was leading them. She was excelling in all the ways that result in one of the most important goals of early childhood: to develop a lasting love for learning.

PREPARING YOUR TODDLER FOR SCHOOL

The toddler's brain grows exponentially during the first five years, reaching about 90 percent of its maturation by kindergarten. During all of childhood (and after), the brain sculpts itself in response to learning experiences. Everything a parent does to nurture the secure parent-child bond enhances the brain's wiring for learning. Furthermore, when parents help their child to learn to delay gratification and organize routines, they are helping him build self-control.

Self-control expands learning potential because it allows children to participate in more varied social settings by giving them a greater capacity to follow instructions, wait their turn, and get along well with others. Besides secure attachment and self-control skills, there are a few other things you can do to prime your toddler for optimal learning.

The magic trio: talking, listening, and reading

Researchers at the University of Washington coined the term "parentese" to describe the way parents speak in a high-pitched tone and stretch out the vowels when they talk to babies (Ramirez-Esparza, Garcia-Sierra, and Kuhl 2014). Patricia Kuhl and her colleagues have shown how the rich timbre of a parent's voice, the quality of conversation, and mutual engagement enhance language development in a growing child. Your delightful and delighted talk from the beginning primes your child for language; talk coming out of screens won't do the trick (Roseberry, Hirsh-Pasek, and Golinkoff 2013).

A couple of decades ago, a seminal research study documented that by age three, children from low-income families had heard 30 million fewer words than more affluent children (Hart and Risley 1995). This "word gap" was later linked with being behind in school from the very beginning. The study kicked off a public-health campaign to get parents talking more to their children, as if parents needed to log more words, like steps on a Fitbit. Since that time, researchers have refined their understanding of the word gap, and determined that it is the quality of communication that is most predictive of later educational success, not the number of words the child has heard.

When parents talk more to their child, they naturally elaborate on details and nuances of an experience. They don't just repeat a word like "apple" over and over. They talk about the color, the shape, the taste, and its category as a fruit. Even in the original "word gap" study, the report emphasized that parent tone and sensitivity to child cues were significant predictors of IQ. Conversations that build upon a child's interests, comprehension level, and a mutual delight in talking seem to be the ticket.

Old-fashioned conversation
Children's brains are hungry for words, meaning making, and the dance of conversation. Nothing takes the place of conversation built on the here-and-now interests of the child to exponentially expand their understanding of the world.

The importance of nurturing young children and preparing their brains for learning and school has become an international health campaign. For immigrant children from low-income countries and other children from impoverished backgrounds, disseminating this message is as crucial as any other part of health promotion. Even though many kids become cognitively stunted by experiencing trauma or poverty early in life, the remarkable "neuroplasticity" of the brain means that nurturing relationships and learning opportunities can enable deprived children to catch up. Neural connections are created by emotionally gratifying and positive learning experiences.

For the more affluent, the concept of neuroplasticity can be taken the wrong way. For some parents, neuroplasticity means the race is on to create gray matter while the time is ripe. Sensationalistic media stories describe classes for babies and toddlers that range from yoga to foreign language training to math drills. But this "cramming" approach to learning can hurt children.

Just as with vitamins and supplements, too much academic enrichment can become toxic. Furthermore, if these activities involve stressful trips in traffic, negative impacts on the family, burdensome outlays of cash, loss of dinners and other family time together, and less time for reading and sleep, they have to clear a high bar to be worth it.

While just about everybody knows there is value in reading to children, some parents stop this fabulous habit as soon their kids can read to themselves independently. Scholastic Books, which has surveyed children's reading habits since 2006, and YouGov, a market research firm, teamed up to figure out what predicted avid reading in elementary school. Children ages six–eleven who were regularly read to aloud and had limited screen time were more likely to read for pleasure than were children who lacked these practices. In this 2014 survey of more than 1,000 children, only 31 percent said they read a book for fun almost daily, which was down from 37 percent found in the previous survey four years before.

> **Bedtime bliss: reading aloud**
> *Throughout elementary school, read aloud to your child at snuggle time, if your child allows it. By consulting your librarian, you can find books that both you and your child will find enthralling. What a deal — creating an avid reader, extra closeness, and a break from screens!*

Reading aloud to children allows more conversation, parent-child closeness, and the reading of more complex plots and vocabulary. It's not like we don't want to encourage reading independently, it's just that by reading aloud to them, we can travel with our children to uncharted territory of literary richness they can't travel to alone. And with a little help from your local librarian, you can find some amazing books that can delight both you and your child.

Making decisions about education

Whether it's preschool, sports teams, or art, music, or foreign language classes, kids can benefit as long as instruction is aimed at their developmental level. Translation? The child understands and enjoys the encounter without experiencing excessive stress. Modern-day parents can be duped by marketing pitches or "buzz" about educational programs that claim all sorts of magic powers to help your child excel, and that have no empirical evidence to back those claims. Fear of missing out — "FOMO" — is a marketing ploy that is alive and well and working its bad juju on well-meaning and worried parents.

Do you remember the trendy campaigns (some even supported by tax dollars) that promoted Mozart for pregnant moms, "Baby Einstein" tapes for babies, and flash cards for toddlers? Don't fall for it! Read the research in this and other evidence-based parenting books, and then defer to your wise mind for what's best for your child and your family. Especially for the first five years, the best academic plan involves interactive play, and lots of it. (See Chapter 5 for more on this.)

Falling for the designer kid lie
Parents love their children intensely and know how valuable the first five years of life are for learning. This can make them vulnerable to the "designer school of parenting" — believing they need to pay for fancy camps, high-octane classes, educational toys, and tutors to create a fabulous kid. Parent buzz or marketers will try to convince you that there are newfangled formulas for boosting IQs, academic skills, and school-admission potential. Don't you believe it!

How do you know if your child is benefiting from early childhood educational experiences? Assuming the school has sound educational resources, you can make a judgment call based on your child's social and emotional adjustment to the experience. If they are thriving in those two arenas, chances are that they are gaining cognitively as well. Is your child enjoying the experience?

Assessing the benefits of educational experiences for your preschool-age child requires consideration of your child's temperament. If your child is shy, you may need to wait for her anxiety to abate before you make a judgment call on whether your particular school is a good fit for her, since she'll balk at almost any new experience. That said, it's not necessary to continue a stress-inducing experience just because you were told that this is "the school, if only your kid can get in."

On the other end of the temperament spectrum, you may have a super-active, novelty-loving kid who's bouncing off the walls. He may thrive on preschool, extended care time, and sports activities. You may have to put on your Teflon shield when other parents (or your mother-in-law) tell you that you are guilty of overscheduling your child because you let him participate in lots of activities. Let his temperament and your assessment of what helps your child thrive inform your decision.

If you travel in upscale circles, you will hear that attending a certain preschool can help your child get admitted to certain elementary, middle, and high schools, with the implication that this trajectory sets you up for the jackpot admission to prestigious colleges. And even in middle-income cadres, you will be subjected to lots of theorizing about public versus private education. Given how individualistic a child's thriving is, and given the fact that rarified and competitive environments can have many drawbacks, it is important to resist the notion that some schools are inherently superior for all kids.

School Choice Mantra:
I'm not looking for a status brand; I want a thriving place
for my child to land.

After writing a book on launching kids to college, I was deluged by requests to consult on school choices. Even attending an elite, competitive, name-brand college does not prove to be advantageous to students unless they are from disadvantaged and low-income backgrounds (Kastner and Wyatt 2002). And the causal link between attending certain preschools and educational achievement is supported even less by empirical evidence.

I am now more convinced than ever that parents suffer as a result of the daunting array of school choices, anxiety promulgated by marketers, and the competitive academic climate. And if parents are suffering, so are their children. Even if academic performance is one of your top values, the fact is that you may get more intellectual mileage out of enjoying fun and games with your kids than with special tutoring or extra classes.

Worrying about college prospects when kids are preschoolers is the tail wagging the dog. Nurturing that puppy in the present is the most important way you can encourage cognitive development. In the next chapter, you'll read about the extensive research on how play primes toddlers for learning.

If you start to feel anxious as you contemplate preschool (and other school choices), you may have been pulled into the vortex of tunnel vision about school. Back up and gain perspective with your wise mind, and trust that if your child does not grow and thrive in the setting you choose, you are resourceful enough to find another.

You as a natural educator

Language ushers your child into an ever-expanding universe of experience and meaning making. Although listening to the parent next to you in the coffee shop chat it up with his toddler can be irritating, there is a point to it! When parents comment about (or "mediate") the toddler's world, show interest, and expound on what the child is curious about, that world is made more understandable. It stimulates the creation of complex neural circuitry in the child's brain. This kind of learning is preparing the child for language literacy in school.

Mediational learning
Parents help children decode the world and learn the medium of language by asking questions, showing interest, and offering words for the connections. Through attuned conversation, they "mediate" the expanding world of children, which eventually prepares their brains for schooling.

Your attuned conversation with your child helps her brain neurons wire together, and this helps her become coordinated socially, emotionally, and cognitively. Is your child pleased with the way the exchange is going? Is she over-stimulated and in need of a rest? Is he bored and in need of more attention? Does she like the alphabet song? Does he like playing "War" with cards, because he gets to compare numbers and acquire a bigger pile? While your interaction and play don't have to have an academic goal — and hopefully, they won't — they are far more sophisticated in creating the school-ready brain than ever imagined by earlier generations.

What about math? Bring it on! Like language, parents introduce math by using it in everyday activities, counting, and playing games. Since toddlers love to be the one with the answers, parents can create fun by coming up with guessing games involving math. Your child can count items in the grocery, learn subtraction with pennies, and enjoy engineering with blocks. Math is everywhere, just like language — if we are present enough as parents to see the opportunity.

Hitting the sweet spot for learning happens any time children are offered stimulating learning opportunities that provide fun and gratification. This also primes their brains for future education. The wonderful thing about enjoying the life of the mind with kids outside academic settings is that parents can aim at the joy part, instead of pushing an academic agenda.

Is your child ready?

A great deal of information is available online about school readiness. Parents can find checklists, guidelines, and recommendations, but in general, a parent should be comfortable with the setting they choose and confident that their child will thrive there. "Readiness" refers to the child having the emotional, behavioral, and cognitive skills needed to be successful in school.

States designate a specific cutoff date for starting school (usually age five for kindergarten and six for first grade), which creates consistency, but this does not necessarily mean all children are ready for the expectations of that grade. There has for some time been a trend of holding kids back, especially boys, to let them mature a bit more before starting school.

A comprehensive guide for readiness is beyond the scope of this book, but the list below gives you a flavor of the skills kids generally need upon entering kindergarten in order to be successful. Whether preschool is necessary for success in elementary school really depends on the alternative; what else would the child be doing in the way of enriched cognitive, social, and emotional development? Just as studies have indicated that quality is the key to whether day care compares favorably to home care for healthy child development, the same holds true for preschool.

School readiness involves the ability to:
- *Follow instructions*
- *Cooperate and play with other children*
- *Work somewhat independently with supervision*
- *Follow simple rules*
- *Listen and pay attention to what others are saying*
- *Write his or her own name*
- *Identify shapes and colors*
- *Count to twenty*
- *Recite the alphabet*
- *Use scissors, paints, pen, and pencils*

It bears repeating that self-control — which is reflected throughout this list — is the biggest cognitive predictor of future success in school and life. One study, conducted by researchers at Oregon State University, found that skill at the game "Heads, Shoulders, Knees, and Toes" among two-year-olds was associated with higher preschool academic performance, especially when kids were given new rules to make the game more cognitively demanding (Tominey and McClelland 2011). Imagine having to touch your head when the leader sings "toes," and touch your toes when the leader says "heads." Try it, and see how hard you have to work at it! You will be developing more effortful control when you work your brain that way, and so will your child!

Parental preschool work
Even though you'll want to build some basic language and math skills with your two- to five-year-old, routines related to following directions and building self-control also prepare your child for the academic and social expectations of school.

Preparing your child for kindergarten or preschool involves preparing yourself, too. An open "Wi-Fi system" exists between human brains — especially among loved ones — and emotions are contagious. If you are nervous about this transition, your child will be, too! And vice versa, causing parents and children to be fairly frazzled by the time they cross the threshold into the classroom.

Ideally, preparation for school, like any new activity, will match your child's needs. The child who loves novelty will bounce right into the fun new adventure. If your child is prone to anxiety, he will benefit from a drop-by visit, practicing the "get ready" routine, and hearing details about the pickup. Belaboring reassurance that he will be fine may reinforce obsessiveness, so if the child repeatedly asks the same questions over and over, name the problem as "worry," not school, and shift your focus to assisting your child with coping. Adaptive coping may include helping your child learn guided imagery (page 170), positive self-talk, and distraction. Notice the word "assisting" — instead of directing your child, ask him which coping techniques he wants to practice, and support him as he works to self-soothe.

The gift of preparation
Whether it's for you or your child (or both!), consider ahead of time what works best for adjusting to big transitions. If there is a strong worry factor, focus on familiarizing your child with the new school, and on self-soothing practices that will help ease the tension.

Good-bye rituals

Almost all young children appreciate a good-bye ritual at school, just as they enjoy the goodnight ritual at bedtime. Agree on this ahead of time, so that your child knows what to expect (and what not to expect, such as your caving to their efforts to extend the ritual). It may be as simple as a wave or a kiss. Or it may be as elaborate as a special handshake, a hug for their blankie-swathed teddy, and a butterfly kiss (eyelashes) to both cheeks. But I recommend a maximum of three gestures. Three are easy to remember, and keep the "on and on" extension from invading classroom time. If you teach your child that you are open to five or six added rituals, he may go for twelve or thirteen, to postpone the anxiety of taking leave. Pretty soon, your exasperation will really amp up his frenzy.

If your child does protest after finishing your ritual, tell him you trust that he will be able to calm herself using the techniques you've discussed, and that you have faith that he can be successful. Then tell him when you will see him again and what nice things you will enjoy together — briefly! After that, leave. If you feel anguished as you hear his wailing cry, practice your own self-soothing techniques (more on emotional regulation in Chapter 5).

The parent-teacher partnership

The buzzword for the school and family partnership is "collaboration." Your young child will benefit from the feedback you get from teachers and vice versa. Some parents are inhibited about giving teachers information on an impending divorce, learning disability, or psychiatric diagnosis, but teachers will understand how those factors may affect children's learning and can accommodate accordingly. You may want to schedule an extra conference to caucus on these matters and formulate a plan for helping your child through difficulties and adjustment. Better to examine your own taboos than to miss an opportunity for a trained professional, who spends many hours every day with your child, to comfort and help your child adapt to momentous changes in his life.

If you have a negative experience with your child's teacher, or hear complaints from your child, you may feel tempted to ask peer parents for their insights. I'd advise that you instead set up a face-to-face meeting with the teacher before a molehill becomes a mountain. It's easy for perceived slights to be misunderstood by your child. Also, small problems are easier to solve than bigger ones that grow over time, so don't be shy about asking for help. You are supposed to be an advocate for your kid!

As a consultant to preschools and elementary schools during major crises, I've seen my share of misunderstandings and mishandled problems that turn into disasters — which could have been prevented, if good communication had been initiated. In more than one incident, inadvertent tumbles on the playground became allegations of sexual abuse. A mimicked jumble of words picked up from a sibling by a preschooler became accusations of bullying. The violent death of a classmate's parent played a part in a student's school phobia that lasted for years. If for some reason your child's school doesn't take initiative when a problem has surfaced, you can initiate the communication process. After all, problem solving can start from either end of the partnership; that's what collaboration means!

Given how sensitive we all are when it comes to our dearly beloveds, parents and kids alike can easily magnify bad times with teachers and go off the deep end, making negative assumptions. If you aren't satisfied with the teacher's response to your concern, you can always go up the chain of command. But, as with all social mishaps, it's almost always best to start with a one-on-one with the person with whom you are experiencing the friction. Even if your child is only three or four years old, it's not too soon to practice and model effective conflict resolution skills, whether your child is observing the transaction or not. "I" statements and "sandwiching" your complaint are important interpersonal skills to practice with teachers, children, friends, and spouses.

"Sandwiching" your complaint means that you begin with appreciation and end with gratitude, and insert your concern in the middle in the most respectful way possible. Here is an example: "I appreciate that you have 25 students and work incredibly hard to meet the needs of all them as individuals. I hope we can work out an accommodation for my kindergartner, who is overwhelmed by the requirement to share at circle time. I would be grateful if we could do some problem solving on this matter." You can avoid sounding accusatory by starting every sentence with "I," which reduces your potential offensiveness and the teacher's potential defensiveness. Planning ahead and self-calming also help you meet these goals.

Respectful exchanges with teachers
If you perceive a problem at school, plan ahead so that you can organize a respectful presentation of the issue. "Sandwich" your concern with appreciation and gratitude, and remember to maximize your humility so that you can be open to the teacher's perspectives.

Summary

When parents think about optimizing the chances for future academic achievement in their toddlers, they often think of IQ scores, testing ability, and enrichment classes. But psychologists and educators think of enjoyable play, singing, talking, reading, and spending quality time in family settings. We also strongly encourage parents to minimize their use of electronics with and around their children, because learning is best conducted with face time, not with apps and marketing traps. Any "educational" toy for young children that interferes with face-to-face learning or reading with a loving parent should be considered more of a threat than an asset to early learning.

There will always be comments or grades on a report card that reflect areas that need improvement. Parents, anxious and caring about the futures of their babies, will naturally focus on these negatives, but it's crucial to keep the big picture of development in mind. Young children will naturally show uneven maturational progression in academic skills, attention, and behavioral self-control.

Attending to feedback from teachers and preschool staff is important, as is collaboration if there is a problem. Parents will want to use their wise-minded skills to set realistic goals, focus on the positive, and choose strategies that aim for their child's sweet spot for learning. Using the GOLD standard for praise will ensure that you are motivating your child, whether you are addressing academic or behavioral accomplishments.

School choices can be so perplexing for parents that sometimes having very little choice in your community (or your price range) can be a blessing in disguise. If you affiliate with a competitive crowd or are very focused on academics, it will be hard to remember that selective school admissions and elite academic institutions do not necessarily hold advantages for your child. While it sounds trite to say "Consider the individual needs of your child," decision making really should start and end there. The critical ingredients in your child's learning diet include cognitive, emotional, and social development, so look for school settings that optimize the development of your whole child, not just the academic aspect.

With three- to seven-year-olds, one of your most important parenting goals is making sure your child loves learning. Praising effort rather than ability and choosing positive approaches motivate young students and, more importantly, will create happy and competent learners.

Reading, talking, and playing with young children, and sharing fun and your mutual curiosity, are the ideal ways that parents prepare children for school. Enjoy your blossoming child — he'll be in full bloom before you know it!

CHAPTER 4

Social thriving:
When your child is bossy, mean, or wimpy

Your child's first social bond is with you. From there, it extends outward to a web of social ties that includes your extended family and friends. As your child comes to form relationships with more and more people, new and interesting social experiences are had, and new behaviors — not all of them desirable — are learned. For the very young child, these early social experiments within nurturing families provide an endless source of entertainment, fascination, and gratification.

Closely observing your toddler gives you a window into the ordinary magic of the world. A three-year-old drops his bread crust and discovers the marvels of ants. He fetches Dad to watch with him. An ant carries the crumb, then reverses course when the toddler places a stick as an obstacle. Then the ant recruits his band of brothers to navigate around the stick to make an assault on the crust. The dad and son squeal in delight as they witness this phenomenon together. But if Dad then picks up his son to prevent him from stepping on the anthill, the magic can quickly devolve into a tantrum. And since toddlers can't always understand adult reasoning — or explain what's upsetting them — both parties can end up distressed and befuddled as a beautiful outing goes wretchedly awry.

Such are the highs and lows of spending time with other people, especially very young people. For them, playing with friends and siblings can be challenging, because children are less flexible than adults and also have fledgling social skills. But parents, take heart: By about five years of age, your child will show some emerging capacities for cooperation, resilience, and even social graces.

Scene: Three six-year-olds are playing in the backyard. Mom is keeping an eye on them though an open window. Her son, Russell, can get a little bossy sometimes, so she has learned to intervene before things come to blows.

Russell: *Hey, let's drag this piece of wood up on top of the other two, and then we can take the tarp that Dad was using for leaves and make it into a lean-to!*

Ellen: Then we can put the leaves on the top and make it like a thatched roof!

Mark: No, that's stupid. Let's stick with the tarp roof.

Russell: (yelling) Hey, Ellen, stop raking those leaves. Stop it. Stop it, now! I'm warning you.

Ellen: Russell, you don't get to make all the decisions! How about we make a moat around the lean-to, fill it with the leaves, and use these sticks for the walls?

Russell: Well, OK. First, will you help me with this tarp?

Ellen: Sure! And then you can help me dig a ditch.

Russell's mother breathes a sigh of relief. She sees the mess they are making of the yard work she and her husband did this morning, but she knows that the afternoon is a big success (so far). Russell is cooperating with his friends, keeping his aggressive tendencies in check, and enjoying play outside. She is proud that she didn't intercede. She had considered it. During their six years with this rambunctious boy, she and her husband used a lot of the parenting tools referred to earlier in this book to avoid power struggles and excessive negativity with Russell.

Russell is a very amiable and sociable little guy. Friends like him in spite of his occasional zeal, because he is so exuberant and full of life. He loves to be with peers, and they like his positive energy, so he's motivated to try to cooperate. Russell's mom and dad use the guardrails principle (page 74), which curbs his aggressive impulses by removing the risk of those impulses running amok. His parents avoid overly exciting things such as toy weapons, extended playdates, or playdate invitations from wilder peers. These options would be fine for some six-year-olds, but Russell can't handle the stimulation without becoming too hyped up. Playing games with him in his earlier years was tough, so his parents worked hard on exercising his self-control muscle. If they overaccommodated Russell's strong-willed tendencies, they knew they would not be preparing him well for peer play.

Russell's mom played with him a lot, but setting necessary limits often provoked tantrums. She encountered more fits (and had to practice more self-calming skills) than the average mom, which was wearisome. She knew she wasn't always enjoying playtime as much as her friends who had more easygoing kids, but she kept telling herself that exuberant kids make some of the most passionate and accomplished adults (once they get socialized). Should I reveal here that I am Russell's mom? Are any of you?

UNDERSTANDING YOUR CHILD'S SOCIAL WORLD

Temperament makes a big difference in how young children forge their way into the social world (Sanson et al. 2004). Some extroverted three-year-olds run straight into the preschool and don't look back, relieved to have so much entertainment to whet their social appetites. Some seven-year-olds (and older!) will be reluctant, if not downright resistant, to start any new social activity, be it school, a sport, or camp of any kind. Introverts and shy kids enjoy the company of others, but they have narrower comfort zones regarding social variables, prompting them to ask questions like: "Who is the playmate?" "How many others will be there?" "What are we doing?" "Where?" "For how long?" And most importantly: "You'll be there, right?" Despite their differences, both shy and extroverted kids experience a natural progression of wanting, needing, and enjoying increased peer contact as they grow older.

As children develop, their expanding social world is both exciting and terrifying. The two-year-old takes the great leap toward independence — but then recoils, as if on a bungee cord, because that independence is scary. These dual drives of seeking first autonomy from you and then safety with you are worked out, again and again, between the ages of two and seven. The bungee-cord process continues into the elementary school years, but is more pronounced in what is called the "first autonomy" phase between the ages of two and six or seven. (You'll see it again during the second autonomy peak of adolescence.) The developmental thrust toward independence, sometimes smooth and sometimes bumpy, is ultimately the way children mature while experiencing their parents' supervision, support, and protection. The child says, "You are not the boss of me!" which reflects her growing individuation (becoming an individual). By saying "No!" in opposition to you, she is forming a self, with a separate will, motivations, and personality.

It's extremely important that we understand the feelings and thoughts of the toddler, because they determine how we interpret their behaviors and decide on our responses. If individuating toddlers could articulate their feelings about independence, they would say both, "I want to assert my new separate self!" and "I overwhelm myself and need to retreat and feel your protection." They would also say, "I love your protection when I want it, but I hate your limits when I don't." If the parent could send one vital message to be absorbed fully by the child, it would be "I still love you even when I set limits and get angry with you." This bungee process of independent investigation followed by reunion, with energy expended by both parent and child to influence the range and velocity of movement, comprises a large part of the young child's exploration into their ever-expanding social universe.

The 'why' behind behaviors

When children misbehave or throw fits, we need to appreciate the feelings or thoughts that might explain their behavior. Are they hungry, exhausted, sad, jealous, frustrated, or angry? Do they misunderstand some logic of the world that is inaccessible to them, given their age and cognitive limitations?

As the toddler's inner life becomes more accessible to the parent through language, there are still mysteries that surface daily. Why do they suddenly become afraid of the bathtub or the toilet? They reach their own personal conclusions about cause and effect, and it's up to the parent to decipher these meanings and help them interpret the world, so that they can feel secure. Your child may or may not be able to tell you that since they saw poo literally sucked down the toilet bowl, they fear they could be, too! But what about the sudden fear of bears when you live in a city? You may find out that the cause was a scary cartoon, but don't count on always getting to the bottom of every freak-out. If there is no specific trigger that can be identified, there is a good chance that the fears are related to that bungee cord — either perceived scary stuff in that vast social world or their developmental need to seek a temporary retreat from the scariness of the individuation process itself.

Little selfhood

The progression toward the forming of the separate self starts in early toddlerhood and advances, in ebbs and flows, through adolescence. You may see unbridled bursts of independence, followed by periods of quiescence, but the developmental process is nature's way of driving psychosocial maturity.

With toddlerhood, the parent-child relationship undergoes a transformation. The parent's goal is to support the development of new competencies and to tolerate the tantrums and tirades that arise when the toddler doesn't get his way. With confidence that the toddler has internalized security from those earlier attuned and loving years, parents can set appropriate limits, trusting that the bond will withstand occasional meltdowns. All those growing competencies — learning about the expectations of others, rules, and self-control — contribute to the ability of toddlers to increasingly "play nicely with others."

The social prep school of home

By the age of five or six, most children start formal education and want to be with other children. Most schoolchildren have the ability to restrain their impulses enough to play independently and enjoy it for some period of time. They like the natural rewards of surprise, collaboration, and pleasure they get from playing with others. However, they also prefer getting their way and imposing their own ideas. Furthermore, they are years away from accurately seeing things from the perspective of others. Herein lies the rub; actually, many rubs!

The limited social capacities of young children present an inherent problem in the attractive enterprise called play. A breakdown in the mutually gratifying interaction will inevitably occur with conflicts that amount to: "My will versus your will." Peer relations are rife with this dilemma (and parent-child ones are, too!).

A central dynamic in the vignettes of Mackenzie, Liam, and Tanesha from the last three chapters is "My will versus your will." Conflict takes up a large percentage of parenting time with three- to seven-year-olds. We are their chief socializing agents, and their immaturity requires us to set limits on their impulses when they are incapable of cooperating. Some parents avoid this responsibility and employ the "permissive" or "neglectful" disciplinary styles, allowing their children to run roughshod, with detrimental social outcomes for their children. The flip side of the continuum is just as lacking: the "authoritarian" style, which uses domination to force submission.

The middle-of-the-road approach is the "authoritative" style, which uses firm authority when necessary, but includes warmth, acceptance of negative emotions, and negotiation when possible. As discussed earlier (page 67), this parenting approach is associated with trusting and positive parent-child relationships, and good social adjustment in adolescence. Using tools such as the behavior management techniques in Chapter 1, emotion coaching (see Chapter 5), and other methods to enhance self-control (see Chapter 2), parents can avoid unnecessary power struggles while helping their children develop crucial social skills, such as waiting their turn, inhibiting impulses, and coping with upsets. These methods help children manage their negative feelings, so they can handle them when they naturally occur within peer relations and friendships.

The essence of being social is enjoying the company of others. However, enjoying and relating well to others on a sustained basis requires children to learn social norms and practice self-control. The parents' responsibility, from their children's infancy onward, is to prepare them for the skills they will need for successful peer relations by providing them with both security and limits.

Parent play as prep for friendships

Playing with parents is part of a child's preparation for becoming social and enjoying others. However, parents need to accept that, at times, play that's intended to be delightful will end up in conflict, with parents having to set limits. Social norms — such as not hitting, taking turns, and accepting others' ideas — are taught by parents. The authoritative parenting style has been shown to be most effective for teaching these crucial skills for social relations.

During a child's first five years of life, the parent-child relationship — the child's first and most important social experience — prepares the child for the huge social expansion that will include peers during the elementary school years. Of course, age, temperament, culture, and circumstances are influential, too, but they are all connected in elaborate social strands that weave together to create the fabric of a child's social competence.

'Miracle Grow' for social, emotional, and cognitive development

Our natural drives to explore, learn, and be with other people synergize in social interactions that are rewarded, repeated, and built upon in increasingly complex patterns. Play is the fun and intriguing platform upon which cognitive and emotional learning progresses in profound ways for young children. The trust and security experienced with parents in early life prepare children to enjoy relationships with others. Disappointments, hurt feelings, and frustrations about limits are experienced as well, but the delights of discovery usually trump the liabilities, especially in the good-enough home.

Play is defined as an activity engaged in for enjoyment, instead of for any practical utility. This qualification is a good rule of thumb for parents to remember, so they don't slip into an agenda to make play into "teachable moments." Teaching and correcting kids during play inevitably happens, especially when parents assist children in keeping play amicable and cooperative, but teaching shouldn't be the primary purpose of play. Amazing things happen during play.

THE MAGIC OF PLAY

Sometimes parents think that play is all about having a good time — hence the phrase (often uttered in a dismissive tone) "That's child's play." But play is nothing short of a miraculous process, one that takes mere DNA and brings its genetic potential to mighty fruition! Scientists analyze the elements of play and write scholarly books about its essential role in the building of brains, emotional intelligence, and success throughout life, but resistance to making it the core curriculum in preschools is as strong as ever. With so much anxiety about the Three R's, STEM, and test prep, it is hard for many parents and teachers to throw out the flash cards and play with finger puppets.

There are two kinds of parent-child play. In the first, your attention may be divided — perhaps with other children around with whom you need to negotiate — and your goal is to expedite fun and get along. You may be making dinner while playing a guessing game, facilitating cooperative play amongst playmates, or participating in group play yourself.

The second kind of play is called "child-centered" or "child-directed." You play alone with your child, one on one, and focus on truly connecting with your child. By centering your attention on what he wants to do and letting him take the lead, you promote your child's sense of self-worth and competence in a fashion that is unfettered by other priorities of parenting. It is an opportunity to maximize the joy quotient in relating to your child, because he gets his way, and you are relaxing into the fun, restraining yourself from teaching or solving problems for him.

While the main goal of child-directed play is to enjoy your child, you can also reap the benefits of supporting independent problem solving, enhancing creativity, and providing emotional vocabulary. When kids get enough positive attention and spend time as the center of attention, they don't need to act out to get the attention they need; giving them their way — and your full attention — is the entire point! By using the skills below to build on your child's cues, these collateral goals occur naturally as by-products of play.

Skills for child-directed play:

1. Follow your child's lead. Imitate what your child is doing, follow his instructions, and avoid imposing your own "better" or "correct" way of doing things. ("Oh, you want me to put the bed in the kitchen of the doll house? OK — your call.")

2. Avoid power struggles and competition. When you decide to engage in child-centered play, you make it clear that you are playing creatively and according to your child's rules. Don't worry about sending the wrong message about her future obligation to play by the rules of a game with others. Kids can't understand the concept of rules fully until around age five, and may still struggle with cooperatively following rules during peer play for years after that. For child-centered play, make it clear that your child can make up her own rules if she would like to (within reason). ("This is our special time when you can make up all the rules to your imaginative game. You'd like to roll the dice over and over yourself and move only your piece around the Chutes and Ladders board alone. OK. What would you like to do with my piece?")

3. Play the sports reporter. Comment on what your child is doing as if you are a reporter. Children feel admired and appreciated for their ideas, and your explicit "commentary" role helps you inhibit your own impulses to give ideas or commands. Your language may be incorporated into their play, building their language skills. ("You put the blocks in the receptacle in a particular sequence. You put the most gargantuan block in first and then smaller and smaller blocks. Well executed!") If your child asks you to be quiet, that's what you should do — but don't pull out your cell phone. They want you engaged, and even if you are placed on "mute," they'll catch you dividing your attention and you'll lose ground in building the good feeling between the two of you.

4. Be sensitive to your child's developmental abilities and cues. If a puzzle or toy is beyond your child's ability to enjoy it, you can supply other options. Younger children love rehearsal and repetition, so you may be playing the same activity over and over for a long time. I really disliked playing "London Bridge" and "falling down" on the wet grass at dusk scores of times. But somehow, my son's thrill seemed to be accentuated! Kids build confidence and mastery through repetitive play, so go with it the best you can. Accommodate their pace and tempo; they are the lead partners in this dance.

5. Think of play as a creativity lab. You encourage and praise their efforts. You do not judge, correct, or contradict your child's imaginative journeys. You may be amazed at how inventive they can get with this license and gratification. There is no "right" way of doing things, and once you suspend your sense of reality and order, you may be surprised at the trip you can enjoy, thanks to your child's navigation.

6. Encourage independent problem solving. Think of yourself as a cheerleader, instead of a fixer or a teacher. It is hard to watch a child get frustrated when the puzzle piece won't fit, but you can ask questions about options instead of giving directions or suggestions. Perhaps an easier puzzle or new toy is an option, but helping too much can result in dependency. You want them to learn creative and independent problem solving in response to frustration, not parental rescuing.

7. Laugh and have fun. They know that you are enjoying them if you are genuinely having fun and expressing it emotionally. Your child's gratification from experiencing your happiness reinforces learning and discovery during play.

Making deposits into your child's emotional bank account

In interactions with parents over time, children store positive and negative feelings in a sort of emotional bank account. Play replenishes the bank account with good feelings, praise, and affirmations. In our socialization role as parents, we impose necessary limits and routines, which amount to negative feelings and withdrawals of capital from the bank account. The bank account inevitably becomes depleted. But play can increase the balance again.

Children who are experiencing a difficult transition or veering a little off-track can benefit from extra playtime with a parent. Not only does play increase positive deposits, but, as you may know intuitively, it is also healing. When your child is vulnerable or stressed in some way, extra play as TLC helps ease her through life's inevitable rough patches.

Play as TLC (tender loving care)

The daughter of one of my friends, Molly, was struggling during the first two weeks of first grade. Although Molly normally had a pretty easygoing temperament, the teacher reported that she was oppositional in class and mean on the playground. After starting a system of negative consequences for negative reports from school, my friend checked out her ideas with me. I suggested that she nix the discipline plan and think about what might be driving the change in behavior — the transition to school, and perhaps unease about other matters she might explore. Off the cuff, I recommended that my friend state her expectations for school behavior (once) to her daughter, express her appreciation that Molly was having a hard time settling down, and plan "special time" (i.e., child-centered) play with each parent for the next couple of weeks.

My friend was a little resistant, saying that this plan would reward her daughter for bad behavior. I pointed out that since she had two adorable younger daughters at home who were getting most of her attention, this intervention was just a way of giving one-on-one time to the child who most needed it. It worked. Not only did Molly's behavior turn around in the classroom immediately, but she became even more of a delight at home.

My friend teased me for years afterward, saying that shrinks are "one-trick ponies" because we solve everything with play and special time. I love it! Guilty as charged! (P.S. It's not always this easy to turn things around, but it is a good first-line intervention for rough transitions.)

Play becomes especially beneficial when "emotion coaching" (covered in depth in Chapter 5) is involved. Emotion coaching involves noticing and naming feelings as part of a running commentary. You might notice when your child is frustrated, proud, angry, impatient, or excited. The vocabulary of feelings helps young children associate the emotional state with words, so that they can use them, instead of just acting out with negative behaviors as they mature.

Guiding multiple children in play together also benefits their developing social skills. It's important to review principles of praise (page 85), "catch 'em when they're good," and avoid comparing children to one another. It's best to be specific with praise. For example, you can say, "I like the way you waited your turn to put a track down for the trains," or "That was generous, the way you gave the bridge to your friend. You showed that you are a sharing friend." Whenever you are modeling praise or encouraging your children to give compliments to friends, you are enhancing their future friendship skills.

Good sportsmanship

Commending your child for good sportsmanship is a whole curriculum course in and of itself. You can practice "good losing" skills with kids: how to congratulate others, or reassure those who feel downhearted about bad plays. You can also help your children practice positive self-talk, so that kids learn how to bolster themselves when they feel discouraged. For instance, when a child has just blown a soccer goal, you can encourage them to say to themselves, "I can't win them all. I just need to do my best," rather than "I can't do anything right. Everybody is going to hate me."

It's easy to get mad at a kid who "blames the umpire." When kids do this, we often focus on the ugliness of blaming others, rather than on the underlying vulnerable emotions. As much as we parents dislike "victim" talk, we are better off offering empathy and encouraging positive self-talk than admonishing children, because criticism will double the shame. Comments like "You shouldn't leave the field in a huff. I was ashamed of your behavior" might be true, but it doesn't help a child to know how to overcome their bad feelings and be a good sport instead. We can encourage them to identify the feelings of failure and devise self-soothing words they can say to themselves, such as "Everybody loses sometimes. I struck out, but I can practice more." And then we encourage them to offer a "good game" salutation to winners, no matter what.

If self-blaming or blaming others has become a habit for your child, sit down with her and list some alternative ways to talk to herself. The whole enterprise needs to be embedded in empathy and compassion, because after all, their plight involves the misery of losing.

Teaching positive self-talk

When you observe your child being pessimistic, blaming, or self-critical, you can teach him how to talk to himself in positive ways when the chips are down. During a quiet time when he is receptive, develop a list of positive things he can say to himself that replace each of the typical downer statements he has fallen into the habit of repeating.

Play as the backbone of a positive relationship

Choosing to make time for playing with your child sends powerful, unspoken messages: "I care about you," "I adore being with you," and "I prioritize giving you the attention you need." By playing with children and giving them positive attention, we are providing them with preventive medicine; feeding them before they cry out that they are starving. One of the most common patterns we fall into as overstretched parents is being so glad when our kids play alone or nicely with others that we take a break and forget to give positive attention to our kids.

Children get tired of holding it together. That self-control muscle gets exhausted from tolerating the rules of social etiquette and refraining from hitting, yelling, and melting down! It's easy to find yourself derelict in giving positive attention to good behaviors and instead giving attention to negative behaviors, thereby reinforcing them. Remember, even if you think that your rebuke discourages undesirable behaviors, you are giving attention to them! To a child, negative attention is better than no attention, because it forces parents to reengage.

Your efforts pay dividends when you invest in regular positive attention for desirable social behaviors. And filling the emotional bank account with child-directed play is the ultimate booster for your relationship quality, as well as your child's general well-being. It's easy to underrate play. After all, it looks like this lightweight activity that kids do all the time. Finding time to give each of your children one-on-one attention can sometimes feel impossible. We just do our best!

The PLAY principle:

Playing is

Love in

Action from

You

Free-range play

When three- to seven-year-olds are playing together, it's tempting to think that parents need to structure play so that the children will stay happy and be nice to each other. As well intentioned as this might be, especially for younger children and hyper-lively or impulsive older ones, there are advantages to leaving some space for free-range play. Many parents undervalue the merits of "benign neglect" — allowing children to spend time alone (without gadgets), learning how to amuse themselves.

Whether kids are alone or with a peer or two, unstructured time allows kids to be creative and use their own imaginations. Without parents right there to settle disputes, kids have to figure out their own strategies for problem solving. Resilience involves bouncing back from a kerfuffle, and as long as kids know that parents will intercede to play peacemaker, they don't have to develop their own skills.

One of the biggest concerns among psychologists about the trend of helicopter parenting and ever-present screen entertainment is that children no longer have the opportunity to be bored (Crain 2004; Guldberg 2009). Boredom leads to daydreaming, which unleashes creativity. Time alone without electronics and stimulation from others gives kids the opportunity to learn to master self-entertainment and develop pastimes such as enjoying books, creating art, and making up games.

> **Bubble-wrapping kids**
> *Just as keeping a child in physical restraints would harm her motor development, keeping a child from experiencing free play, solitude without screens, and independent roaming will impede her psychological development. Think of gradually letting out the tether, so that you and your child can discover what she's capable of. Then, revel in her growing capacity for entertaining herself and handling peer play without direct supervision.*

Kids are little scientists, experimenting with cause and effect, and trial and error. There will be moments of complaining or bickering during unstructured play. I can recall episodes in which our kids used every blanket, towel, and napkin in the house to build a fort, wrecked a favorite tent in a playful "campout," and even required more than one trip to the ER for minor injuries. But these adventures were worth the trouble for what was gained from self-discovery, negotiations with peers, and independent problem solving. Controlled risk results in building competency.

SIBLING SQUABBLES

Sibling quarrels are among the most troublesome stressors for parents on a daily basis. Common causes of these squabbles may include rivalry for parents' attention, conflict in a battle of wills, and parent favoritism. Although parents of only children often fear that their kids are missing out on a necessary building block of cooperation, research reviews have not found that connection (Mancillas 2006). Still, research findings won't stop folks from attributing the cause of a kid's bratty behavior to his only-child status. Although the explanation is more likely to be plain ol' parental indulgence (which can also be extended to two and more kids in a family), myths die slow deaths.

While sibling conflicts do offer an opportunity to teach social skills, they are more often experienced as a major pain in the neck. In fact, nearly every time I give a lecture, no matter what the topic, someone in the audience will ask about sibling conflicts. They can be the bane of a parent's existence. A common parental refrain is "Could you two just play nicely together and give me a break?"

Play amongst young children who are unrelated is difficult enough; add the dynamics built into the sibling relationship, and you have quite a list of challenges for most sibs.

Scene: The living room. Five-year old Gus is playing with his little brother, "Junior," age three. They've been playing cooperatively for about ten minutes, to Mom's huge relief, until …

Junior: (screaming) Mom! Gus pushed me! Gus pushed me!

Mom: Gus, get in here now!

Gus: But, Mom, I only pushed him because he keeps taking pieces from my Lego pile. And he pushed me first.

Mom: Gus, he's three years old. I expect you to control yourself. You need to be nice. I want you two to learn to be friend, so you can support each other when you are adults. As the older brother, you need to be caring and cut him some slack.

Gus: (yelling) Mom, you always listen to him. You never listen to me!

Mom: Gus, you hurt your little brother. You always have to ruin playtime. I can't count on you to play nicely for five minutes. Why can't you understand he's just three years old? Now, go pick up the Legos.

Gus: (screaming) I hate you, Mom. You love Junior more. (Gus runs out of the room.)

Mom: I do not. You get back here right now, or it will be a lot worse for you than cleaning up the toys. You get back here or else!

This conflict can happen in any family when a parent leaves her parenting toolbox in the closet. Junior has limited abilities to control impulses — he's three — but Gus's are limited, too, when he is being shoved and his stuff is being stolen! Although this mom could be exhausted and just having a bad day (we all have our sloppy moments with sibling squabbles), there are several problems with her approach.

- *Unrealistic expectations.* Mom expects Gus to tolerate Junior's behavior and to be motivated by her value of friendship between siblings. At five, Gus does not have the cognitive capacity to appreciate future perspectives. He won't at ten, either!
- *Presumption of guilt.* Mom's first statement held Gus solely responsible for the conflict.
- *Rewarding the younger sibling.* Junior is rewarded for his actions with Gus, crying for help and getting Gus into trouble.
- *Invalidation of Gus's perspective.* Let us not forget that it is perfectly reasonable for Gus to be upset that Junior took his Legos.
- *Escalating Gus's deteriorating behavior with dismissiveness.* Mom's siding with Junior was the catalyst for Gus's added distress, his bad-mouthing Junior, and resisting the cleanup request.
- *Threats during parent-child conflict.* Making threats is not an effective way to encourage cooperation or positive behaviors.

Let's observe Mom on a good afternoon when she has her toolbox available, with tools sharpened and utilized skillfully.

Junior: (crying) Mom! Gus pushed me. He pushed me!

Mom: You two had a problem with building the tower together.

Junior: (crying and running into Mom's arms) Gus is mean!

Mom: (giving him a hug) Oh, Junior, you're upset.

Gus: I pushed him because he keeps taking pieces from my Lego pile! And he pushed me first.

Junior: I pushed, but you pushed harder. You're mean!

Mom: Gus, it's really hard to play with a three-year-old who's grabbing your stuff. Plus, he pushed you first, which makes it really hard not to push back.

Junior: (crying louder now, with tears running down his face) Mommy, Mommy, Gus is mean!

Mom: (patting Gus's arm lovingly) Hey, guys, pushing isn't the right way to handle things for either of you. What do you think you could have done instead, Gus?

Gus: Mom! I had to get him to stop.

Mom: Did you? That means you get into trouble for pushing. What else could you do?

Gus: Come and get you? But he could have wrecked everything while I was doing that.

Mom: You're right. That might have happened, and it would be really hard. (Pause) The other day when Junior lunged for your paints, you fetched the basket of fuzzy animals to distract him, and it worked!

Gus: Mom, he is such a stupid baby. He wrecks things all the time.

Mom: It's hard to be an older brother. No question about it. And Junior (hugging him close), you love to play with Gus, but neither one of you is allowed to push or hit. Let's have you both play alone for a few minutes so you can cool off and think about the "no pushing" rule.

It is difficult to begin addressing a sibling conflict with an "observation" instead of accusation (especially when there seems to be a clear conflict instigator), but it is a good way to avoid making things worse. As soon as blame is implied or assigned, the accused child will feel indicted without a fair hearing in the court of mom law. He will feel justified in pitching a fit, because he feels helpless in defending himself. In this version, Gus is frustrated with the actions of his baby brother, but he is less furious because Mom heard him out and talked with him about the predicament.

> **Addressing sibling conflict**
> *Even when you think there is a clear perpetrator, try to avoid assigning blame when you first address your quarreling siblings. Force yourself to begin with a neutral observation. Give both parties a chance to voice their feelings and perceptions, even if you will make a judgment call and give consequences as you see fit at the end of the hearing.*

In the second exchange, Mom demonstrated good judgment in ignoring Gus's bad-mouthing of Junior and sticking to the core issues of aggression and problem solving. If she had tried to take on bad-mouthing, too, she may have teetered on too much negative feedback to Gus. A five-year-old can only process so much, especially after a fight like this. And Mom is trying not to appear to favor Junior, even though she does hold a five-year-old more accountable for impulse control than a three-year-old.

In this version, Mom demonstrates her wise mind. She controls her emotions (emotion mind), and she doesn't use logic (reason mind) to lecture Gus about how bad it is to push others or good it is to have a friendship with his brother. She conveys empathy to Gus so that he can feel accepted, which keeps him calm enough to discuss alternatives to aggression. She is realistic in her goals of focusing on impulse control, validating hurt feelings, and problem solving. She knows it will be years before Gus will have the ability to think deftly when faced with such a frustrating social situation — especially with a pesky younger brother! But, just as with building other social skills, such as manners, taking turns, and empathy, it's best to accept your child's current capabilities and support movement toward realistic goals.

Sibling rivalry

By hugging Junior and acknowledging his upset, Mom struck a balance between comforting him and not overindulging his victim status — he pushed, too. Younger siblings regularly incur wrath from older sibs with their tiresome and immature behaviors. But they can be really adorable as the "baby of the family," which incites jealousy in older sibs. The younger ones may get hurt (or feign hurt), and then hurt back. Parents can easily and inadvertently reward the baby for fights, and those babies figure out very quickly how to get older sibs into trouble.

All children explore social power, and even one-year-olds may learn to show a low threshold for pain if it means they can get a big reaction. While impulses, frustrations, or a clash of wills may be the cause of sibling squabbles, sometimes it's just that kids want to get that sibling into trouble to get them back. For what, you ask?

Biological theorists emphasize competition for resources, and psychodynamic therapists emphasize the rivalry for mother or father love, but either way, siblings are in a social soup together with enormous potential for conflict. The younger one wants both to earn the older one's acceptance and to rebel against the fact that he is almost always one down by virtue of age and competence. The older sib may want a playmate and potential ally against parents in the war against authority, but fundamentally, the firstborn lost her status as number-one beloved baby the minute that new one arrived. It's a setup for rivalry!

With the young sib's burning curiosity and limited power base, he may provoke the older one because he can! For a young child, it is compelling to have the power to instigate a big shebang, like throwing a big rock in a pond. Look at that ripple effect! For younger sibs, this power may be one of their greatest weapons for punishing older sibs for the power the older one has to withhold love and attention. Likewise, the older sib might want to poke that younger sib for being an adorable baby who seems to never be held accountable for his countless offenses.

As cute as you think your little toddler's singing and babbling is, try to appreciate how irritating it is to a five- to seven-year-old who is using heaps of energy to conform to social expectations and not draw embarrassing attention to himself or give in to babyishness. You might try to reason with that older sib, but it will be ineffective and probably come off as less than empathetic and reflecting your poor understanding his world. The five- to seven-year-old has been internalizing rules for some years now, and that baby is breaking all of them! Unfortunately, your explanation that young toddlers can't follow social rules yet will escape the older sib every time. We need to pause, reflect, and recite: "We might be right, but are we effective?" Being more effective would involve practicing the art of validation.

THE FAIRY DUST OF VALIDATION

Confer with the average therapist, child development expert, or talented negotiator, and they will all tell you that validation is one of the most powerful ways of putting people at ease. As a parenting skill, it is one of the most important tools in the parental toolbox. Just like adults, when children are upset, they want to be understood. They don't want to be told how they should be more reasonable, look at things differently, or subordinate their needs to the needs of others. Maybe they can appreciate some of those principles after validation, but the first order of business during an upset is to convey that you understand their feelings.

In all of the vignettes in this book, validation is a critical step in effective problem solving. Whether difficult encounters with your children involve meltdowns over your parenting calls or difficulties in other parts of their lives, validation is an essential part of creating a bridge for connection. Handling sibling squabbles can be especially challenging for us as parents, because our buttons are pushed, and we forget to use this cornerstone skill.

Upon intervening in sibling fights, parents are often so distressed that they rush to the crux of the issue: The older child pushed the younger child, and a pleasant bout of play ended in a hot mess. Parents wish young siblings could play nicely together, but in most cases, this expectation is unrealistic for extended periods of time. (Although in some cases, extended play is possible when both siblings are endowed with mild-mannered, sociable, and flexible temperaments.)

The most important and masterful skill Gus's mom demonstrated in the second version of the sibling squabble was validation: "Gus, it's really hard to play with a three-year-old who's grabbing your stuff. Plus, he pushed you first, which makes it really hard not to push back." It quelled Gus's anger at Junior and allowed him to discuss the incident with his mom instead of flying into a rage. As effective as validation is for calming fevered emotions during conflict, it is completely unnatural when a person is angry, exhausted, or frustrated — an all-too-common state for parents of young kids!

Validation does not constitute agreement or approval; you are conveying that another person's perceptions and feelings make sense from his point of view. Of course Gus is angry that his little brother pushed him, took his Legos, and wrecked their building! Indeed, Gus engaged in other undesirable behaviors himself, but when you want to make a connection with a person, start with validation.

In any human conflict, validation mollifies angry emotions. However, if it is done in a phony, robotic, or "shrinky" manner — "I can see you are angry"— it can bomb. If it's done well, you connect with the heart of the issue for the other party. You not only convey that you "get" what made them upset or angry, but you show with some emotion that you understand and that you feel their distress deeply. As tempting as it might be to explore the cause of a problem when it is egregious (e.g., lying, cheating, stealing, hitting), starting with validation helps with calming and connecting before you move on to decide who did what, which puts people squarely in the hot seat.

Validation versus invalidation

Examples of validation:

1. Focus on listening, not responding; stay present. Your child says, "I hate my brother." You nod your head and hug her.

2. Restate what your child says, paraphrase, or attempt to reflect feelings. Your daughter says, "You love him more." You say to your daughter, "You feel like I love your brother more than you. You are mad because you think he gets off easy for being the baby."

3. Convey an understanding for what you think is really upsetting your child. "Because he is younger, you feel like we indulge him. You feel like you are always the one to get into more trouble and that I don't see it from your side — that he starts a lot of the problems between the two of you."

4. Convey that from your child's point of view, her feelings make sense. "You work so hard trying to get along with everyone and follow rules all day long. Then you see your three-year-old brother taking your toys and not getting into trouble for a lot of his behaviors. It makes you very angry that the rules are different for him than you. You are absolutely right. We have different expectations of older children and from your standpoint, it really is awful."

Examples of invalidation:

1. Reject what your child says as inaccurate. "You don't hate your brother. You love your brother."

2. Emphasize that what your child says is unacceptable. "We don't use the word 'hate' in our family. You are out of control and just acting spoiled for not getting your way."

3. Point out that your child's response is incorrect. "Your little brother is only three, and you need to cut him slack. You need to take the high road and ignore his bad behaviors. He is just trying to play with you."

4. Dismiss feelings and perspectives. "I don't love him more. I love you the same. You don't seem to understand that you are causing the problems around here with your rough and impulsive behaviors."

5. Criticize feelings. "There is no reason for you to think I love your brother more. I do so much for you and then you throw a fit and can't play nicely for five minutes so I can make dinner."

Invalidating and dismissive remarks fall out of our well-intentioned mouths regularly. It's understandable, especially when we are defensive or triggered by aversive things our young children do. However, invalidation does have a negative impact. If it is the predominant way a parent responds to negative emotions, thoughts, and behaviors, the child will feel alienated and lack trust in his parents and himself. He will feel he is not understood or accepted, which can contribute to feelings of negative self-worth and insecurity. He can't trust others to believe him to be basically good, and he can't trust others to be basically good, because his parents invalidated his (very normal) feelings.

A parent who is extremely invalidating of the feelings of a young child is putting secure attachment at risk. The child may develop problems with regulating his emotions, become sensitive to failure and rejection, and develop insecurity about his competence in the social world. Children can develop the proverbial chip on their shoulder because they feel that lack of validation chipping away at them.

Validation is connection
Validation is among the most valuable interpersonal skills one can practice in parenting (and in other relationships). It does not infer approval or agreement; it means you understand your child's feelings from her point of view. In the midst of a conflict, validation is your bridge to making a connection for problem solving.

Many parents who are learning about the importance of validating negative feelings initially feel like it is "soft" parenting, or even indulgent. Unfortunately, during a crisis, emotional triggers incite parents to go straight to the "bad thing," and the benefits of validation can take a backseat (or fly out the window). However, validation provides the connection that then allows a discussion of the issues without the child feeling criticized or rejected. Disciplinary measures may be in the mix, depending on the situation, but if you are trying to make a connection so that some important message might be received, use validation.

Supporting friendships

A child's very first friendships occur between the ages of three and seven. First, children "parallel play," which means they play side by side in a manner that is fairly independent of one another. As toddlerhood advances to early childhood, children start to enjoy playing with others, and start to develop preferences and friendships.

Friendships are usually based on similar interests. If you are surprised by the child to whom your child is drawn, it may be that the other child plays in a way that complements your child's temperament. Sometimes, opposites do attract.

Kids at either end of the temperament continuum of introversion and extroversion will have challenges with peer play. The introvert likes people, but wants time to warm up and become at ease, maybe playing on the edges of a play group instead of entering the fray. Shy kids are worried about social rejection, so they may need you to organize small steps toward socializing with playdates, birthday parties, and outings with others.

> **Respect for the reluctant!**
> *Avoid labeling your child as shy, wimpy, or a loner. Kids internalize these labels as criticisms of who they essentially are. Instead, describe what is happening for your child: It takes her longer to get comfortable with social situations.*

Kids with extroverted personalities will jump right in and interact, but this may not always suit the other playmates. Children who are highly impulsive are especially labor-intensive for parents, because they need to be supervised during those times when excitement escalates to frenzy. There is nothing like a fistfight to squelch your child's chances for another social invitation.

Playdates in your home help you evaluate your child's friendship skills. How does your child converse with her friend? How does she deal with frustration? How is she doing with sharing, resolving conflicts, or negotiating with her friend? The more challenging your child's temperament, the more challenges she will have with friendships. Furthermore, the more challenges you witness during playdates, the more you know you need to supervise and structure those playdates.

If you observe that your child has problems with assertiveness, cooperation, or frustration, you can practice social skills with puppets. You can rehearse conversation skills, and praise your child for showing interest in others, demonstrating kindness, and having good ideas for maintaining rapport. If you think your child is too much of a pleaser, you can praise her assertiveness and skillful ways of stating limits and bottom lines. The use of dolls and stuffed animals for encouraging social and emotional skills is covered in Chapter 5.

Imaginary friends

Young children engage with imaginary friends as if they think they are real, but usually understand that they are not. Just as they can pretend to be a princess or a warrior, children can pretend that they have a special friend. Imaginary friends can often serve as a window into your child's anxieties, desires, and perceptions of their world, if you listen in on their conversations. They may scold or praise their imaginary friend, just as they might do with a doll or stuffed animal while playing. Perhaps they themselves are struggling with learning appropriate behaviors and complying with rules, so they will put the friend (or doll, or puppet) in that role as a way of working on that dilemma. These imaginary friends can also provide comfort in ideal ways, because children can conjure them up in their times of need.

It is estimated that about two-thirds of three- to seven-year-olds have imaginary friends (Taylor et al. 2004). It is not a sign of loneliness or of social-adjustment problems; likewise, it is not a reflection of extraordinary intelligence. Kids with imaginary friends may be either introverted or extroverted. Either way, when children enact social play in this fashion, it's fun to watch them be creative enough to parade around and verbalize both sides of an argument, a funny conversation, or a classroom lesson.

Parents don't need to do anything about imaginary friends, other than enjoy the show! If these imaginary friends start directing you to make accommodations that are inconvenient or excessive, you might want to draw a line. Having teatime with an invisible person is one thing, but funding a whole birthday party for one is quite another. And if your child commits misdeeds and then blames the imaginary friend, you will want to reassure your child that you will support him for showing the courage to come clean. The occasion may also offer the opportunity to encourage empathy for a falsely accused friend, even an imaginary one.

NAVIGATING SOCIALLY BUMPY TERRAIN

The territory of friendship is also one of rejection, cruelty, and disappointment. Children learn important lessons from social difficulties. As long as they are not extreme or overwhelming, social bruises can build competencies, especially with you as a guide and supporter (rather than a rescuer or judge). When you observe your child's playdates with friends, you will usually note that your beloved babe isn't just receiving social bruises; he's dishing them out, too. Hopefully, you will remember this when your child comes home with only one side of the story of a social mishap.

Among parents, problematic reactions to friendship issues fall into three camps. Parents in one group criticize their child's role too much; those in the second fail to see their child's role; and the third group is altogether clueless about the need to tune into the vast hurts of the social world. These styles may originate from the parents' own histories and friendships, but the goal for parents should be to support their child's optimal social and emotional learning.

Critical parents who hear about social problems will respond to a child's complaint of hurt feelings by saying, "What did you do to deserve it?" or "Don't be such a whiner or you won't have any friends." Nothing teaches a child how to clam up about their problems in the way criticism, ridicule, and dismissiveness do.

Overprotective parents can telegraph to their children that they are frail and that peers are the source of hurt that they can't handle. Some do what I call "dumpster diving," where they interview their kids after school or playdates to see what garbage they can dig up on friends. Since almost all children will experience hurt in social relationships, there is usually plenty of dirt to offer up to these parents, who "interview for pain." Most unfortunate in this situation is that the "victim" role gets reinforced, instead of the incident serving as an opportunity to learn resilience and coping.

Social competence versus victimization
There are times when parents need to step in and intervene in social cruelty between friends, but the term "frenemy" confers an understanding that friendships are mixed bags. Watch out for "dumpster diving," "interviewing for pain," and focusing excessively on your child as a victim. If possible, look for opportunities to promote coping, savvy problem solving, and empowerment.

It's one thing to agree that children develop social intelligence by experiencing the highs and lows of relationships; it's quite another to face tough times with cruelty or rejection. We know we can't get the good without the occasional bad, but when our kids are on the receiving end of the lows, we wish with all our hearts that they could skip those social messes.

Bullying, bystanding, and vulnerability

Bullying is a repeated pattern of tormenting a child who is younger or in a vulnerable position relative to the bully. It can involve physical harm, teasing, ridicule, name-calling, and racial and sexual slurs. While cyberbullying has become recognized as a huge problem, three- to seven-year-olds should not be involved in any kind of independent use of social media. (Keep that arena solidly on your radar during the tween years.)

When kids start attending school and spending time outside the direct observation of adults, parents wonder how they will know if their child is being bullied. Ideally, your child will share this information with you. You'll want to educate your children about bullying, just as you would about other realms of safety, such as inappropriate sexual touching or solicitous strangers. You don't want to scare children unnecessarily, but you want them to understand how to handle these risks in the world. As with any problem, we want to encourage children to seek help from adults when they have a gut feeling that there is something wrong.

While approximately one-third of children in middle school report that they have been bullied, statistics are fuzzy for the three- to seven-year-old group, because they are (or should be) in the proximity of adults who prevent such behaviors. Physical and verbal aggression is developmentally normal in young children; the goal is to teach conflict-resolution skills and ways of handling intense feelings without violence. Most bullying occurs outside of the purview of adults, and it starts in elementary school. Early childhood is the time to teach children the values of kindness and empathy.

Tormenting from a bully can lead to stomachaches, headaches, school avoidance, depression, and anxiety. It can also lead to longer-term scars; unaddressed problems can get worse over time. If your child has an overt "difference" (e.g., body size, psychiatric diagnosis, visible minority status in an intolerant majority setting), she may be a target. In these circumstances, parents will want to work with the school or day care to intervene immediately. For parents of vulnerable children, a plan for preventing social discrimination focuses on creating confidence, pride, and worthiness, as well as assertiveness training.

Most children will witness bullying at some point in their childhood. Parents should educate their children about the importance of the "bystander" role and how all children have a responsibility to promote kindness. When our kids are bystanders to bullying, we want them to speak up and get help from adults. How will kids know when to address cruelty by talking back to the mean kid, and when to get help in the face of real bullying? You can help them prepare by using the technique of "play practice" (page 23). Help them practice quick comebacks to friends who cross the mean line, or standing up to cruelty on the playground. Help them know when a situation is beyond them and requires adult intervention. Think of a bunch of situations of teasing, cruelty, and bullying, and then act them out with your child, taking turns with the roles.

Social engineering

Though they might like to, parents can't really dictate their children's choices of friends after early childhood, because they are based on individual temperaments, tastes, attractions, and sensibilities. But with the three- to seven-year-old, you can still engineer social contact through playdate invitations. Parents often have their own notions about what they think is good for their kids, and they should follow their instincts.

Parents of a high-energy, envelope-pushing child often prefer to have their child spend time with friends who don't ratchet the bedlam level up a few notches. Shy, anxious children are often leery of social gatherings, since groups of children can be lively and anxiety-provoking, so parents are grateful for any friendships their children initiate themselves. Shy kids often like to play with older kids who are more mature and predictable. Alternatively, they may enjoy younger kids with whom they have a clear "alpha" role, because they can call the shots, which makes them feel secure. Since parents can observe the play of their young children, they will have an opportunity to view the blossoming of friendships and develop opinions about how their children benefit from various kinds of social contact.

The peer effect
Although excessive hovering is not recommended, neither is turning a blind eye to friendship issues. These early years are vital ones for social development, and parents need to think about the effects of negative peer influence as much as social isolation. But don't underestimate the positive influences of peers, too — belonging, recognition, and acceptance are built-in rewards for all of us.

The development of many competencies involves participation in athletics and other activities, all of which can increase access to high-functioning peers. Insisting on these healthful endeavors is as legitimate as insisting on school attendance and dental care.

On the other hand, sometimes parents overplay the importance of playdates for a child already involved in school and activities. Especially for shy or introverted children who have already clocked in a lot of social hours at school, a lot of playdates are not needed. While it is good for these kids to experience new social challenges as they mature, sensitivity to your child's temperament should guide your parental judgment calls. Shyness involves acute sensitivity to potential rebuffs from peers, so parents should caution against overtaxing their child's tolerance level.

Fears abound about negative peer influence, because parents get nervous about losing control. The hurly-burly social world outside a parent's direct influence understandably triggers anxiety, and Mama Bear and Papa Bear instincts can blind us to the positive influences of peers. Children can be mean, it's true, but more often, they teach each other about loyalty, trust, respect, kindness, empathy, respect for differences, and cooperation. Like all humans, friends are flawed creatures, but they are also a source of wonderful influences.

THE GIFT OF CULTURAL IDENTITY

When I ask parents about their cultural heritage or identity, some look blank and mystified. When they awkwardly admit that they are white and come from Maine or Iowa, it's as if they don't know that every family has a rich family lineage. The family from Iowa is proud to say that they have an Iroquoian great-grandmother. The Maine family of Irish descent knows that their ancestor couldn't get a job in the late 1800s, and they have the family heirloom— a "NINA" sign (No Irish Need Apply) — that commemorates that discrimination. And, of course, the family that is a mix of Japanese, African-American, and Pakistani heritage has its own extensive lore and history to appreciate. Since we are a nation of immigrants, we all have the potential for opening up a conversation about identity, migration, and diversity with our young children, if we are willing to explore ever farther back in our genealogies. Help your children share pride in their heritage and get ahead of the eight ball on this issue.

It's a question of values. What is important to you? Our children are inheriting a world that is increasingly diverse. We should want our children to be as intelligent about this part of life as any other, and in fact, the term "cultural intelligence" is one used in business, education, psychology, and sociology to refer to one's ability to relate and work effectively across cultures. A Caucasian Presbyterian child who is comfortable and friendly with classmates who wear headscarves, celebrate Hanukkah, or eat unfamiliar lunch food from their native country of Nigeria is going to be more successful than the child who belittles others' traditions.

What do you value of your family's rituals, and which traditions do you want to pass along? How do you want to share a sense of pride with your children related to their racial identity, cultural background, or country of origin? Children as young as two notice differences, and love to categorize according to color, gender, and dress. Just like sorting blocks by shapes and size, they enjoy making meaning of the panorama of stuff in their world.

Children also like to feel special by learning about their family's particular customs. Tell stories of your childhood, and share your rituals and traditions, even if they don't seem particularly exotic. My father gave me the cherished conch shell used for calling the farmhands in from his uncle's hops fields, even though he didn't relish the work in the fields or the fact that his widowed mother's poverty necessitated that he be raised by a paternal grandmother.

Who am I? What am I? How do others see me?
Children learn about their identities from their families and others around them. Shaped by experience, identity is not fixed. Take an active role in building a positive identity, so your child can feel a sense of belonging. Encourage your child to offer the same to those around her.

Children will make blunders that invite teaching moments. For instance, when they blurt out embarrassing comments about the unfamiliar person who has cerebral palsy or facial abnormalities, parents can discuss the fact that 10 percent of people have a physical disability, and almost 50 percent will have a psychiatric disability at some point in their lifetime (Kessler et al. 2005). When they notice people of different sizes and ethnicities, it is an opportunity to surf the Web and provide some more education on diversity. Given the possibility that any of our children could be diagnosed with a problem that requires self-acceptance, medication, and accommodation, the agenda to promote tolerance could hit closer to home than you'd expect.

Be aware that your child will learn stereotypes from the media that you may deplore. Whether its racism, sexism, or any other kind of "-ism," the world they see on TV and in other media frequently does not match up with the real world — or with your values. And given how insular our busy lives can become, it may be hard to give your kids a firsthand experience of a potlatch, a Shabbat dinner, or a tent city. But you can still teach values, and when your child demonstrates his understanding and acceptance of other cultures during his first-grade class' sharing time, you'll know that you've successfully communicated your value on cultural competence.

NURTURE VIA NATURE

For many of us, the playtime we had in backyards and neighborhood ravines are among our happiest memories. Even if we ended up with broken bones, skinned knees, or squabbles, those mishaps are woven into the fabric of cherished childhood memories. Some of the most painful rough-and-tumble bruises were social ones, but they were worth it, because escapades in nature are unique and multisensorial.

Like so many parenting strengths, monitoring safety can be both overdone and underdone. Often, a child's parents polarize on the issues of protectiveness. Does your spouse tend to support one end of the continuum, and you, the other? It's natural for one parent to try to balance out the other one, if excesses are perceived. Worrying about social dangers often increases as children age and spend more time outside adult supervision. Fear of dangers — be they physical, social, or emotional — has been magnified by depiction of the big, bad world in the modern media. You may have heard this criticism of TV news: "If it bleeds, it leads." Disaster stories sell, and the ones involving children sell more.

We are all affected by stories about child abductions and injuries. But as any sociologist, psychologist, or even news analyst can tell you, our society has never been safer. Many of us could stand to let our children's tether out a little farther, but our decision making is often controlled more by fear than the statistical likelihood of harm. It seems that we've replaced freedom in physical space with freedom in cyberspace, which we will discuss in detail in Chapter 7. Somehow, it just feels safer to let kids play inside, where you can "keep an eye on them," but this is a fallacy if your young child is online and unattended.

Physical space or cyberspace?
Sensational media stories may have swayed parents' assessments of the costs and benefits of social freedom. Are children really safer inside with gadgets? We should consider the loss of social competence that can result from less exposure to nature and less autonomy for resolving minor social squabbles.

Think about a setting in nature for social interaction and play. Imagine the building of a dam at a little stream, or the building of castles on a beach. Imagine yourself resisting the urge to intervene, except to help settle disputes. We need to be aware of what is lost by too much vigilance. As five- to seven-year-old children mature, we need to seriously question judgment calls about helicopter supervision.

Kids with parents who push them to spend time in nature are at a distinct advantage. Squeezing mud, palming stones from a creek, listening to bird calls, and gathering sticks enhance sensory development. Increasingly, there are fewer places available where children can play in the dirt under a tree or scratch chalk drawings all over the pavement, places where they can leave their mark and create fantasy worlds to their heart's content. Research has shown that time in natural settings can enhance children's attention capacities. Nancy Wells of Cornell University studied children from low-income families and found that when they moved to housing with greener surroundings, their attention spans improved (Wells 2000). Other studies by Andrea Taylor and Frances Kuo of the University of Illinois compared children who spent time walking in a park to children who walked in a parking lot, and found that the green time increased the children's ability to pay attention (Taylor and Kuo, 2009). They also found that green settings enriched fantasy play and imagination.

Imaginative play is in its heyday among children ages two–six; by seven, kids are becoming much more rational. Four- and five-year-olds love to talk out loud as they engage in play, as if they are enacting the role of commentator. With green settings serving as catalysts for kids' fantasy play, they especially enjoy making forts or creating hidden places, where they play outside the watchful eye of parents.

Kids' capacity for play is limited the minute you put a store-bought toy in front of them, because it probably has a predetermined structure. And when you take them to "pay to play" settings that are inside, expensive, and catering to child and parent comforts, you have really narrowed a child's play world. Many studies have documented that children today aren't as free to roam as the past two generations were. It's all well and good to assume our kids are safer kept inside with toys, but perhaps that assumption is based on our own sense of comfort. It's time to reexamine that assumption.

Summary

By the time your child is three, he has begun to demonstrate, in many ways, that he wants to be free from you to explore the social world. But he has also shown how much he needs you as a secure base for his next foray. Since you are his first social relationship, he draws on his trust in you to explore relationships with others. He learns pretty quickly that peers are a lot more unpredictable and surprising, and they can also be a lot of fun. And even though toddlers mainly engage in "parallel play" instead of cooperative play, every now and then they can synergize and create some magical exchanges.

Playtime with peers becomes increasingly important as children mature. Temperamental characteristics have a strong influence on comfort zones for individual children, because one child's idea of fun is another's nightmare. Friendships evolve through simpatico interests — and sometimes between children of opposite personalities, depending on the developmental needs of each child. You will not always understand it.

All children explore social power, which can involve inclusion, exclusion, cruelty, kindness, and direct or indirect aggression. Parents can help negotiate differences and expedite conflict resolution so that children learn social skills for playing nicely with each other. While only a small number of children become bullies in the real sense, parents need to promote kindness, empathy, and social responsibility, so that even as bystanders, children can take action to prevent social cruelty in all its forms.

As frustrating and stressful as sibling conflicts can be, they offer another laboratory for social-skill training. You'll want to use sibling spats to teach some mediation skills and empathy, but at times, you'll just want to give up and separate them. You're only human — you need a break, too!

Play is the "Miracle Grow" for emotional, cognitive, and social learning in early childhood. It even helps build self-control, because children need to inhibit their impulses in order to play successfully with others, abide by the rules of games, and follow agreed-upon formats for pretend games and drama. As hard as it is to find the time, playing in a child-directed manner can profoundly enhance your relationship with your child.

Don't let false perceptions of "stranger danger" keep you from allowing your child to enjoy time in nature. Kids benefit from social exploration of green spaces, although with young children, you'll want to make sure that you or another adult is present in a supervisory role. Too many parents develop a false sense of safety by keeping their kids inside, but having kids exposed to electronic trash or commercialized excess is riskier than almost any backyard. While parenting the younger child can be exhausting, many of us with grown kids would give our eyeteeth to get a few of those days back, so that we could experience the bliss of playing house or pirates or some quirky unicorn fantasy. It can be breathtaking to observe the cognitive leaps that happen during whimsical games. Peering through this window into a child's ever-expanding capacity for understanding how to cooperate with others is a wonder indeed. And when our children demonstrate increasing levels of empathy for others, we take heart that out of the happy chaos of early childhood, a socialized person is truly emerging.

CHAPTER 5

Emotional flourishing:
How should you handle your child's extreme emotions?

In our society, it's pretty much a given that parents will teach young children to bathe regularly, brush their teeth, and eat with utensils. We all agree that these skills are essential to a child's physical and social health. But we sometimes overlook a set of equally important skills for competence in the world at large: understanding and controlling emotions, and feeling empathy. We are all as much emotional beings as we are physical creatures. Teaching our children the skills of emotional health is at least as important a parenting responsibility as teaching hygiene and literacy — really!

All parents want their children to be emotionally healthy and competent, but the blueprint for this project is tough to create (much less to follow) with young children, who turn into bundles of tears, fears, and fits on a fairly regular basis. While parents often dread dealing with the disturbing emotions that generate meltdowns, the ability to name, control, and express them is an essential skill; it is the very foundation of emotional intelligence.

After all, expressing and regulating emotions is critical to being a competent adult in work settings, relationships, and life. Think about the skills you employ when you keep a cool head in hot moments at work, or negotiate a dispute with a loved one. Self-regulation is a linchpin of mental health, and one of many emotional skills that constitute emotional intelligence.

As our children grow, they become increasingly aware of feelings — their own, and those of others. They learn to name and articulate feelings, and begin to learn to effectively navigate emotionally charged moments. With young children, parents are challenged to understand what is reasonable to expect, given their child's age and stage, and also how to implement the construction of these abstract but supremely important emotional skills.

Scene: Lucia, a precocious four-year-old, gets into the car after preschool and erupts with emotions.

> **Lucia:** *(yelling in bursts) Brenda is not my best friend anymore! She wouldn't play with me at school today! She is so mean! She just wanted to play with the new kid, Sawyer. I hate Brenda. I will never play with her*

again. I will not let her come to my birthday party. I want to pull her hair out. She is the meanest girl in the world!

Mom: *(emphatically) Oh, Lucia. You are really mad that Brenda wanted to play with Sawyer.*

Lucia: *Yeah, super, super, super mad. She is so, so, so mean. I hate her. I want to kill Brenda! (Lucia lets loose with another burst of tears.)*

Mom: *You sound super upset and sad, because you've enjoyed being friends with her a lot. She was playing with Sawyer today, not with you. Tell me how it happened that you didn't play with them.*

Lucia: *(quieting now) I wanted to play with them, but Brenda said I was being pushy. I didn't want Sawyer to play with us.*

Mom: *You wanted to play with Brenda alone, not with Sawyer. What would happen if you let Sawyer play with you and Brenda?*

Lucia: *(calmer now) What if Brenda likes Sawyer more than me? I want Brenda to stay my best friend.*

Mom: *Do you have ideas about how to do that?*

Lucia: *(after some pensive moments) I'm going to take my jump rope tomorrow so we can all play with it.*

Lucia feels her emotions intensely. She is very attached to her friend Brenda. Lucia's temperamental disposition makes her prone to outbursts and meltdowns (also known as "dysregulated emotions"), and her mom has developed excellent skills for helping her cope. She knows that by focusing on feelings first, she can explore the origins of Lucia's distress and then potentially help her with problem solving.

Lucia's mom was effective because she:

- focused on feelings from the outset
- did not dismiss or invalidate Lucia when she used words like "hate" and "kill"
- did not give advice or try to solve the problem

- did not try to talk about the other children's motivations
- waited until Lucia was calm to ask for details about what happened
- encouraged Lucia to identify her feelings
- avoided premature reassurance or overprotectiveness

For decades, researchers, child development experts, and clinicians have linked emotional and social competence with academic achievement, psychological adjustment, positive relationships, and future success (Durlak, Domitrovich, Weissberg, and Gullotta 2015; Eisenberg, Cumberland, and Spinrad 1998; Morris et al. 2007; Zins, Bloodworth, Weissberg, and Walberg 2007). There are distinctions made in the fine print of the tomes written about emotional intelligence, social and emotional learning, and associated competencies, but for our purposes, suffice it to say that children benefit from these building blocks of optimal functioning.

The specific goals of people in the social and emotional learning (SEL) camp represent skills that any parent would want for their children: that they recognize and manage emotions, care about others, make good decisions, behave ethically and responsibly, develop positive relationships, and avoid negative behaviors. And there is one kind of parenting that succeeds over all others when it comes to helping kids build these skills, which all rely on emotional awareness.

Emotion-sensitive parenting styles go by several names, depending on your school of thought: "Emotion coaching," "mindful parenting," "whole-brain integration," and "wise-minded parenting." We will be covering nuggets from all of these approaches, and they all focus on a parent developing their own emotional awareness as the first step in facilitating emotional skills in their child.

EMOTION COACHING

The groundbreaking research of University of Washington psychologists John Gottman and Lynn Katz began with five-year-olds and followed them and their families for several years, examining how family interactions affected overall child adjustment (Gottman, Katz and Hooven, 1996). Their research found that children who learned to understand their feelings and master their emotions had higher academic achievement, formed stronger and more stable friendships, had fewer conduct problems, self-regulated their negative emotions more effectively, and had better physical health. In examining the parenting qualities that predicted these findings, they found a common thread, which they called "emotion coaching."

Emotions matter
Children who learn to understand their feelings and master their emotions have higher academic achievement, form stronger and more stable friendships, have fewer conduct problems, self-regulate their negative emotions more effectively, and have better physical health.

In the study, parents who emotion coached their children were found to put a priority on validating feelings and viewed negative emotions as opportunities to help their children cope. They displayed an acceptance of negative feelings that other parents might want to avoid or eliminate, such as anger, rage, resentment, and even hatred. They remained calm in the face of their children's emotional storms and showed an awareness of their own feelings, as well as their children's.

Some people might read the exchange between Lucia and her mom and think that Lucia's mom wasn't holding her daughter accountable for some pretty ugly talk. They might think that Lucia was indulged and would end up even more temperamental and bratty as a teen. They might think she should be discouraged from that kind of talk, and scolded for being a selfish friend. In this scenario, "Mama Bear" moms might want to play rescuer and arrange a three-way playdate, or worse, inform Brenda's mom that her daughter was being a bad friend by rejecting Lucia.

Any of these reactions would cause Lucia to miss out on the opportunity to learn about her feelings, identifying her fear of loss, calming down after being listened to and validated, and problem solving with her mom about steps she might take to improve the situation. Though it's easy to slip into Mama Bear or reason-mind accountability modes, the research actually backs Lucia's mom's approach.

Here's another example: Zack, age three, wants to catch the family dog's plastic toy in his mouth, pretending he's a puppy. When Dad takes the toy away, Zack screams and cries. Zack hits his father repeatedly, calling him a stinker and demanding he give the puppy's toy back.

Zack's father feels his heart rate soar to more than 100 beats a minute. He is angry that his son hit him, even though he knows three-year-olds can have meltdowns over all sorts of things. He realizes he needs to calm himself before dealing with the situation. He mentally recites the Flooding Mantra.

The Flooding Mantra
Never talk under the influence of flooding emotions.

Parents, like firefighters, police officers, and ER doctors, benefit greatly from emergency protocols. Since emotions can derail logical decision making, it is optimal for us to resort to practiced drills and guidelines, so we don't act under the influence of extreme emotions. Scolding, shaming, and yelling are common reactions to upsetting situations, when kids are rebelling or aggressive. But these reactions are not effective methods of behavioral management, and they can be harmful when used excessively. Self-calming, emotion coaching, and wise-minded problem solving are preferable and effective alternatives.

Emotion coaching, step by step:

1. Tune in to your own emotional awareness, and then to your child's.
   • Pay attention to your body and your thoughts.
   • Try to identify and name your feelings.
   • Try to identify and name your child's feelings.
   • Remember that you want to accept all feelings as valid.
   • Calm your own feelings before you address those of your child.

Zack's father realized he was first frustrated and then angry when Zack started hitting him. He remained quiet until he could regulate his own emotions before engaging Zack. He kept his mouth shut and repeated the Flooding Mantra to himself.

2. Show your child that you view negative emotions as an opportunity to connect.
   • Validate your child's negative emotions. Tell him they make sense from his perspective, and you appreciate them.
   • Identify what you think your child might be feeling and see if your child is ready to talk about his emotions.

Zack's father says emphatically, "Zack, you were enjoying playing with the toy and our puppy. I stopped the play. You are mad at Dad!" He goes on to say, "I'm holding your hands right now so that you can try to use your words. I made you mad when I took the puppy toy. Can you tell me how you feel?" After calming down a bit, Zack says, "Mad. You are a bad dad!"

3. Listen.
  • Avoid judging or criticizing your child.
  • Show your child that you understand what he is feeling.

Zack's dad says, "Tell me more about how you felt when I stopped your play with the puppy." Through his sobs, Zack says that he and the puppy were playing a game that was fun. Then Dad ruined it by taking the toy. Now, the puppy feels sad and so does Zack. Dad nods his head through Zack's explanations, while stroking his back.

4. Name the emotions.
  • Identify the feelings that your child is experiencing instead of telling him how he should feel.
  • If your child is unable to identify feelings, see if you can "read" his emotions and check out your hunch with him.
  • Repeat the feelings your child is having until you can see he is calm. Then share your feelings and use a range of vocabulary words so that over time, your child will have precise ways to express his emotions.

Dad echoes back to Zack how Zack was having fun and so was the puppy, but Dad took the toy and wrecked the fun. Now the puppy and Zack are mad and sad. Noting that Zack had become calm, his dad then says that he was worried about the germs on the dirty toy, disappointed that he had to ruin the fun, and curious about how they can find a solution to the problem.

5. Move to problem solving.
  • Redirect your child's attention to how you can work together to solve the problem.
  • Be attuned to whether your child feels like you have collaborated on an adequate solution.
  • If your child has misbehaved, explain why it was inappropriate and decide whether a disciplinary measure needs to be taken (remembering that discipline should help learning).

Zack and his dad decide to get a small toy from Zack's toy box that will be his "fetch" toy for the game when he pretends to be a puppy. Zack's dad frowns and says he was hurt when Zack hit him and called him a name. Zack's dad pretends he is a puppy and whimpers as he points to his leg (where he was hit) and his ear (where he heard he was a "stinker"). Zack mimics licking his dad's ear and leg and enjoys playing like he is nurturing "daddy puppy" for the rest of the evening. He says over and over how sorry he is for mistreating his "puppy" (father).

Zack's father feels that no other consequence is necessary for the hitting and name-calling, because Zack's demonstration of empathy for an extended time (especially for a three-year-old) reflects that he's building an awareness of others' feelings. Are you asking why Dad didn't decide on more punishment for hitting and name-calling? Good question! See page 180 for a discussion about punishment.

Feelings first
When your child becomes emotionally upset, focus on feelings first. Start by naming and validating feelings. Putting feelings into words calms emotions and allows children to engage their thinking skills for problem solving afterward.

THE BRAIN SCIENCE OF EMOTIONS

Daniel Siegel, an eminent psychiatrist and trailblazer in the field of interpersonal neurobiology, pioneered the neuroscience of secure attachment, emotional intelligence, and parent-child relationships (Siegel 2001). Similar to emotion coaching, his work endorses the importance of connecting with kids' feelings, but from the perspective of brain science. He calls his method "whole brain integration," because he uses the mapping of neural circuits to help parents understand why it is so important to encourage children to put feelings into words (Siegel and Bryson 2011).

It helps to review a little brain anatomy to understand neural processes and gain insight into what kids need from us during meltdowns and distressing experiences. The following description is extremely simplistic from a scientific perspective, but it provides a basic understanding of the brain's role in emotions. Once parents and children have this basic understanding, they can be more accepting about some of the scariest and craziest moments in our human lives. This, in turn, brings them closer to accepting emotions, harnessing them for the good, and avoiding negative spirals.

The right and left hemispheres

Our brains are divided into two hemispheres, the right and the left. The right side of the brain is where emotions are experienced and nonverbal cues are interpreted. The right side allows us to size up the big picture, as well as to interpret facial expressions, tone of voice, and gestures. The left side of the brain helps us think logically and organize thoughts into coherent sentences. Consider it our verbal side.

Imagine that your five-year-old son, George, is being rebuffed by his eight-year-old brother. When his brother closes his bedroom door to do his home-work, George cries and wails. You encourage him to express his feelings. Through his tears, he says that he is angry and sad that he can't play with his brother right now. With gusto, you match those words with understanding that he is frustrated, irate, and very disappointed that he is prevented from playing with his brother. You stick with validation, and George gradually calms down and elects to go play with his train set as a way of amusing himself.

You just helped activate George's neural circuits to move from the right hemisphere — the emotional side that registers rejection and sadness — to the left hemisphere, which allows him to put his emotional experience into words and think of alternative plans of action.

There are two absolutely crucial qualifiers for why this simple strategy worked. First, in this example, your child was not "out of control," hysterical, and beyond comprehending you. If your child was so distraught that he was screaming and could not be soothed by your initial efforts to talk to him, you would infer that another part of his brain was triggered (the amygdala; more on this in a bit) and you would have used a slightly different strategy.

A second distinction that helped this method work successfully is that you were not in a rush to move to problem solving. If the child feels the slightest coercion to "get this feeling stuff over with" or quickly move past negative emotions, he will not calm. Success at calming comes from a simple but powerful approach: Stick with validating until he calms. Be patient and accepting of negative emotions.

It can feel artificial and strange to repeat feelings over and over, saying, "You are sad that your brother won't play with you right now." However, like rubbing a soothing balm into an owie, it works. Children (and most adults) will not be capable of problem solving until they feel someone has listened to them and validated their feelings. You need to tune into and resonate with their feelings, like a human tuning fork. If you are robotic or just repeating what they say in a perfunctory manner, they'll know it! You must echo their feelings with feeling, by tapping into true empathy. To truly do this, you need to try to calm yourself.

The Getting to Calm Mantra
To help my child get to calm, I must first get to calm myself.

Shifting neural activity from the right brain hemisphere to the left
When parents lovingly encourage children to "use their words" during moderately distressing occasions, they are helping neural circuits change course from the right side of the brain to the left side of the brain. This neural shift allows them to put their emotional experience into words and think of alternative plans of action.

The 'reptilian' brain

In the lower brain area behind our eyes and extending down to the brain stem, our limbic system stores memories, regulates appetites, mediates motivation, and detects rewards and threats.

Deep in this limbic system, on each side of the brain, is an almond-size structure called the amygdala, which is considered the "reptilian" part of the brain because of its ancient evolutionary history. The amygdalae (plural of amygdala) activate with a "fight or flight" response to perceived threats. This alarm system is a vestige of a survival circuit designed for life-threatening situations in days of yore — as in millions of years ago, in caveman days, when we needed to flee from saber-toothed tigers!

Think of the limbic (emotional) system as the center city of the brain. The "fight or flight" circuit is a fast-lane superhighway. Instead of taking the slow-lane route to the thinking part of the brain, the amygdalae respond to perceived threats with lightning speed, sending messages sending and releasing hormones throughout the body to prepare for battle or to run. Why does this fast-lane system bypass the conscious-thought realm of our brain? In an emergency, we can't afford the time it takes for neural charges to travel along the slow lane. Our amygdalae are trying to save our lives!

Once triggered, the amygdalae spur us to swiftly respond to a stove-top fire, a baby jumping out of the stroller, or an impending car accident. Unfortunately, this hair-trigger circuit is indiscriminant and also sets off "false alarms." When triggered in response to the obnoxious, rude, and aversive behaviors of others, we may react with "fight" impulses — to our detriment, and to theirs. Because this a neurological fast lane, the only way to avert these hair-trigger false-alarm reactions is to calm ourselves so that neural messages can travel the slow lane to our conscious minds for deliberate decision making.

Think of all the times you and I, as adults, struggle to keep our tempers when we are furious or terrified. Now imagine how difficult it is for young children, with their fledgling brains, to calm the powder-keg "fight or flight" emotions erupting from their amygdalae!

Imagine that your four-year-old, Kayla, is having one of those awful, very bad, terrible days. She wants more screen time after she already exhausted her allowed amount. She kicks the bed repeatedly and yells, "You are a turd!" at the top of her lungs. You say that you want her to use her words to express her feelings about the rotten afternoon, but she is having none of it. When you move away, she pulls your arm. You ask her if she is ready to talk yet, but she keeps screaming. You know better than to make it worse by talking any more right now, leaving, or threatening a time-out, all of which would agitate her further or make her feel abandoned.

You stay quiet while she goes off like a Roman candle — her fiery emotions charging up, then settling a little, and then emitting more discharge, and then settling a little more. You offer a little murmur of validation or a bid for talk every now and then, to see if she can connect her feelings with words yet, but you can see it stimulates more discharge, so you stay quiet and offer nothing more than your company.

Because you have not made it worse with criticism, talking too much, or telling her to calm down, Kayla quiets herself after five minutes (which feels like 30 minutes of hell to you). When she is ready to talk (through intermittent whimpers), she talks about all sorts of upsetting things, including having her feelings hurt on the playground, in the carpool, and by her mean brother, and, most importantly, about how much she hates your rules limiting her screen time. Then you both decide it's time for a snack of apples and cheese, followed by her bath.

Kayla experienced what is called an "amygdala hijack," also known as a melt-down. Her emotions have hijacked her rational capacity. By not talking too much or trying to coerce Kayla into talking too soon, you helped her settle down, simply because you didn't make it worse! Parents often have the un-realistic expectation that they can get these upsetting and frantic outbursts to stop sooner than is possible. When parents telegraph "Oh, no, here she goes again!" their child knows it and spins even further into dysregulated emotions.

A better approach is to purr every now and then, and say, "I feel bad that you feel so bad" or "I know I'm irritating you when I talk, so I'll sit quietly until we can figure things out." Even though it feels like you can't do much to help, sometimes doing nothing is the best way to minimize the velocity of erupting emotions.

Amygdala hijacks: when thinking goes offline

When children are screaming, inconsolable, and furious that you are even talking to them empathetically, they are experiencing an amygdala hi-jack. Their "fight or flight" circuit has been triggered and has hijacked their thinking capacity. Your best recourse is to wait quietly until your child calms and can regain the ability to talk.

The fastest lane in the brain — the survival network — is stronger than other neural circuits in terms of velocity and power. As much as we dislike melt-downs, we need to appreciate that when this system is accurate about emer-gencies, it saves lives — such as when it triggers your child to slam on his tricycle brakes to avoid a car suddenly backing out of a driveway.

Your child may experience many perceived threats (i.e., false alarms) that you might want to dismiss, or that you even resent. We all struggle with being judgmental of our children or dismissive of their emotions. Perhaps it's a tan-trum over not getting what she wants (*What a brat!*). Maybe she's triggered by having to use the car seat (*Hey, it was just business as usual!*). She may have fears about coyotes (*How silly!*), dread that you'll die before morning

(*Irrational!*), or terror that everybody at school hates her (*It's just not true*). Remember, she is doing the best she can, given her emotional state. When the amygdalae are triggered, virtually anything can seem like a saber-toothed tiger — even you.

The brain's final frontier

The thinking part of the brain is called the prefrontal cortex and is located behind the forehead. It is in charge of conscious thought, planning, reasoning, decision making, and impulse control. The prefrontal cortex is not fully mature until we are in our early- to mid-twenties. We adults, with our mature prefrontal cortices, are so used to living in the world of rational and conscious thought that we frequently address our children at inappropriate cognitive levels. We can easily fail to see that our logical explanations, lectures, and reassurances are not understood by young children. That they would be is wishful thinking, but not accurate.

In evolutionary terms, the prefrontal cortex is newer than other parts of the brain, and it's the most sophisticated part of the brain in terms of its capacities. Reasoning allows us to make plans, carry them out, adjust them as needed, and devise new plans based on new information. These capacities constitute our executive functioning, which, like a CEO, helps us run the business of us. A critical part of this executive suite of thinking skills is the impulse-control system, which allows us to put the brakes on impulses and emotional reactions. Without it, we wouldn't be able to pull off plan A or plan B — or any other plan.

Because our higher-level analytic capacities make it possible to understand emotions, we can decide to override how we naturally feel about things — such as being disgusted with our child for her meltdowns — and then summon empathy and compassion. Taken as a group, these abilities, made possible by the prefrontal cortex, enable moral thoughts and actions. They allow us to understand ourselves in light of our past experiences and our higher aspirations, and then decide how we want to change our parenting styles. Other primates can't do any of this fancy stuff; they don't have our specialized prefrontal cortices.

Your child's prefrontal cortex is showing its stuff when he articulates thoughts, uses his imagination, and develops theories about the world. When the thinking brain of a six-year-old is engaged, he can feel empathy, regulate his emotions, think before acting, and decide how to behave to get a desired result.

Imagine that Tyrone, your six-year-old, wants to play with his older sister. He knows that his sister is often irritated with him. Not only does he know this from past experiences, but he also can tune into his sister's grumpy mood right now by looking at her face and listening to the tone in her voice.

Tyrone knows that his sister feels more inclined to play with him when he has attractive ideas. He decides to present a stash of his Halloween candy and invite his sister to play Monopoly, which his sister invariably enjoys because she always wins. Tyrone makes the offer of the game and candy, and voilà, he gets exactly what he wants: His sister smiles and jumps at the offer. Tyrone is rewarded for using his executive powers to make and then carry out this plan.

Wouldn't it be nice if this exceptionally useful part of the brain would mature before we reach our mid-twenties? For young children, the ability to implement a successful plan, like the one Tyrone pulled off, is erratic and extremely susceptible to being derailed by emotions, inaccurate assumptions, and distractions. Tyrone's "CEO" abilities will develop, in fits and starts and with lots of practice, over the next couple of decades. But even really smart adults can have their amygdalae triggered with false alarms, resulting in fights, rudeness, and other nasty behaviors. Almost all parents wish that their kids could control their impulses better, plan out their homework assignments more effectively, and reason through their problems more rationally. But this immaturity is what makes children ... children, and what makes them need you, in all of your prefrontal glory, to help them learn how to integrate this amazing circuitry for running successful lives.

You can't hurry logic

Attempts at rushing the development of cognitive capacities don't work. Parents need to be attuned to their children's emotional and cognitive readiness for logical input and problem-solving prompts. Optimal cognitive processing requires emotional calm.

Managing emotions, correctly reading others' emotions, and effectively putting feelings into words are core foundations of mental health, occupational success, and satisfying relationships. This isn't just the fluffy, "feel good" part of parenting. Sure, talking and stimulating analytic thinking enhance the building of intellectual capacities, but it has to be done in the context of emotional security. Social, emotional, and cognitive functions are inextricable. Our desire to enhance these cornerstones of development makes almost every day an opportunity to strengthen the wiring of the vital brain circuits that create our child's personality, character, and skills over time.

WISE-MINDED MELTDOWN MANAGEMENT

Even if we are ready to verbally process a problem, our kids may not be. As we've seen in our examples, it takes time for children's emergency systems to quiet down so they can translate their feelings into words. The abstract realm of naming and expressing feelings is challenging enough for teens and adults, let alone young children.

Children who are in the middle of an amygdala hijack will look like they are having an emotional seizure, and they generally can't be reasoned with — or have any control over their emotions — while in this state. Whether you call it an emotional seizure, a meltdown, an amygdala hijack, or something else, naming it can help you tap into empathy during these moments.

Emotional Seizure Mantra
When my child's emotions are high, I will lay low.

Until we calm this circuitry, which has released adrenaline and stress hormones for a battle or siege, we cannot get our right brain online to interpret emotions, much less our left brain for putting those emotions into words. And forget about accessing our thinking brain for problem solving! Children will learn to self-manage eventually, with maturation and with you as a model, coach, and patient supporter.

When we imagined Kayla's amygdala hijack on page 151, we described your process as you focused on calming your own physiological arousal and avoided the trap of trying to control hers. Because she was flooding, you knew to keep your mind clear of judgmental thoughts. You said validating things when it appeared that they would help. Because you were attuned to Kayla's emotional and developmental states, you knew that your goals should be patience and conveying only acceptance and empathy. You demonstrated all the skills of wise-minded parenting.

Here are the steps of wise-minded parenting during meltdowns:

Calm your emotion mind: Use a breathing exercise (see nex page) to quiet your emotions, which are sure to be triggered by your child's explosive emotions. Focus your mind on the Getting to Calm Mantra: *To help my child get to calm, I must first get to calm myself,* or the Emotion Mind Mantra: *My child is doing the best she can, given her emotional state.*

Resist your reason mind: Resist making judgments. Avoid any thoughts that focus on "shoulds," punishment of the child, or the unacceptability of the child's negative emotions. Repeat the Reason Mind Mantra: *I might be right, but am I effective?*

Enlist your wise mind: Decide what is realistic given the present situation, the emotional status of your child, your child's maturity, and his temperament. Wait until you intuitively feel confident about the right step to take. Center yourself before deciding on words or actions with these questions:

- Is he ready to express his feelings?
- Would distraction be a better first move?
- Does he just need hugs and soothing?
- Would talking about problems later work better?
- Would it be best to defer decision making about discipline, since you want to make sure it will enhance learning and not be a reflection of your anger?
- If you do speak, what validating comments can you murmur occasionally to see if you can elicit a calming response?

Since emotions are contagious, you will usually be distressed when your child is distraught or experiencing a meltdown. When a child curses, kicks, hits, or calls you names, who wouldn't be upset? You may think, He shouldn't get away with this! or He needs some discipline! These reflections of reason mind need to be resisted, since they virtually always escalate conflict.

Although most of us are compelled to try to soothe a child who is in meltdown mode, he will be like a wounded bear cub ready to claw you if you agitate him. Patience and acceptance are your best assets for handling this situation. Even though adrenaline is coursing through your veins, urging you to action, your best goal is to be present with your child and accepting of his emotional state.

The Meltdown Mantra:
Don't just do something, stand there!

This is a moment for mindful parenting, a time to focus on the present moment without passing judgment. If you are "flooding," you need to focus on taking slow, deep breaths until you can think clearly. Don't rush it. Try to not think of anything but your breathing, since thinking about the situation at hand, as disturbing as it is, will accelerate your heart rate again and render you less effective when you interact with your child.

Self-calming skills are among the most important tools in a parent's toolbox. Mindfulness practice and breathing exercises help us calm ourselves and sooth our activated arousal systems. As tempting as it might seem, don't try to get your kids to use breathing exercises during meltdowns, because it won't work. Remember: They are having emotional seizures! It's better to model breathing exercises yourself, but save the teaching for a calmer time, when your child is ready to learn. As with any skill, breathing techniques are best learned when children are not distressed.

As we described in Chapter 2, it's like the oxygen masks on a plane; you need to self-regulate before you have even a chance of helping your child. Distressed as you are by your child's screaming and oppositional behavior, there is a good chance you will not choose an optimal approach to addressing whatever problem caused this meltdown. Since, physiologically speaking, your child needs time without more stimulation to de-escalate from high arousal, almost anything directed toward him is going to make it worse. Therefore, the most important thing for you to do is to control yourself and ignore the chatter inside your head.

If your child is acting like a wild animal and having an emotional seizure, don't take the reaction personally. His name-calling, aggressiveness, outrageous threats, and hateful talk are not reflective of his character or meant to hurt you; it is his primal way of expressing his overwhelming, intense emotions. You may have some urgent matter stressing you — the need to get to work, drop kids off at the bus stop, or prepare dinner. Try to stifle that agenda, because your impatience will prolong the meltdown due to his unmet emotional needs.

Getting-to-calm breathing exercises

Paced respiration. Exhale completely and push your belly out as much as you can so you start with a full inhalation. Inhale slowly over the count of five seconds. Then breathe out over five seconds, counting "one-one-thousand, two-one-thousand ... " and up, to make sure you are pacing yourself. Repeat this breathing cycle for several minutes while trying to free your mind of all thoughts about anything other than the breathing exercise. If you prefer, instead of counting for your deep breathing, you can say to yourself very, very slowly, "Now, I am breathing in ... now I am breathing out," repeating this cycle for several minutes.

The four square. This exercise is similar to the last one, but it has four steps as you count. You first inhale over the count of four seconds. You hold your breath for four seconds. You exhale over four seconds. You rest for four seconds. Keep a visual image in your mind of your breath following a line up, over, down, and then across to your original starting point in the square.

The 4-7-8 technique. Exhale completely and push your belly out to make sure you aren't taking too short of a first breath. Breathe in slowly over the count of four seconds. Hold your breath for seven seconds (use the one-one-thousand, two-one-thousand technique for spacing, if that helps). Part your lips a little, and exhale over the count of eight seconds. If you are flooding or highly aroused, you will not have enough air in your lungs to last eight seconds. That's OK — it just shows you how much you need this exercise! Start again. When you can easily exhale slowly over the eight-second interval, you know that you have de-escalated your emotional arousal.

Ideally, all parents would become experts at meditating and practice for an hour every day. By doing so, we would develop certain parts of our brains that could decrease anxiety, depression, and irritability. We would experience more positive emotions in our everyday lives. When our kids had meltdowns, we would be able to quiet our brains more easily, avoid judgment, and ready ourselves for effective handling of their issues once they had calmed down.

Since most of us are not expert meditators (put that on your to-do list, and I will, too!), we can at least practice effective breathing techniques. The beautiful thing about choosing this strategy is that breathing deeply is incompatible with talking, yelling, and criticizing. It helps us stay out of our own way.

Performing breathing exercises takes concentration, and thus you will be less likely to hash out judgments of yourself or your child in your mind, keeping yourself upset. Once you are calm, you have a shot at choosing effective next steps for dealing with the situation. Best of all, little eyes are watching you as you model this good self-calming behavior.

We must model the emotional skills we want our children to have and help them develop emotional and social competence by giving them direct experience with qualities such as empathy and understanding from us. If ever there was a good candidate for "show, don't tell" teaching, it's empathy. In certain circumstances — such as when kids are around puppies and babies (who are not their siblings) — toddlers can be astoundingly empathic. Our species is wired for it from birth. But in the midst of distress and unmet needs, young children (and teens, and sometimes adults) will struggle to appreciate others' feelings.

The panic/calm paradox
You save time when you make time for calming during a meltdown. Even though you may think, "I don't have time for this!" when you have another demanding agenda, your child's meltdown resolves more quickly if you patiently prioritize the calming, accepting, and processing of emotions.

Causal maps

Kids' brains are little meaning-making machines. Toddlers are dominated by the brain's right hemisphere, especially through the third year. In their first few years, they are developing their language abilities, especially their ability to use words to express their feelings. Even up through their seventh year, they will be trying to figure out the world with their fledgling prefrontal cortices. One of the biggest challenges parents have is remembering that children are not little adults. Just because you explain something clearly doesn't mean your brilliant three-year-old will understand why she shouldn't put her finger in the socket, or that your seven-year-old will get why he shouldn't pop wheelies off your porch steps.

In early toddlerhood, kids are just beginning to develop their causal maps, i.e., a mental image of what causes what. If your toddler sees you push a doorbell at someone's house, he starts to understand there is a relationship between the bell ringing and a person opening the door. If the toaster bell dings, the toast is ready. But when the phone rings and nothing happens (which is the case in our house, since we rarely answer it during family time), what does that mean? Probabilities and patterns are worked out in the toddler's mind ("bells mean something"), but mysteries and inconsistencies abound.

The causal map of you

Kids develop causal maps of their world. When you come through most of the time with love, reliability, and sensitivity to their needs, you give them the emotional sense that they live in a secure and good world, despite the fact that, on a regular basis, you won't give them want they want (e.g., cookies for dinner, movies all night, and contact with you all day).

One of the most consternating mysteries for children is that you are a loving, kind, and generous parent — and then suddenly, you're not! You are your child's most secure attachment, but you constantly disappoint your dearly beloved. You don't let them mouth a dog toy, eat cookies for dinner, or explore intriguing but dangerous curiosities such as stoves, cars, and roads. You go to work or to bed without them, leaving them aching for you. Luckily, you are, for the most part, reliable, loving, and understanding. The probability they work out in their causal map of you is that you are coming through for them most of the time. And a gorgeous side benefit is that they become more competent in handling life as it is — with its omnipresent imperfections and disappointments.

A solution to opposition: choices!

Do you miss your baby, who was cuddly and content to gaze at your face all day? As the two-year-old explores and asserts her will, it's easy to become nostalgic for the good old days. It helps to remember that "the neurons that fire together, wire together." Your child's bulldozer-like drive to explore and learn is literally building gray matter. Isn't that lovely? That bulldozer drive enhances learning virtually all the time. But because your child's prefrontal cortex is immature and needs a couple of more decades for full impulse-control capacity, you have to be her guardrails in the meantime.

Sometimes it feels like your child has become relentlessly negative — or maybe you have. It comes with the turf of parenthood. Almost any nice experience you plan can go south as your child pushes for something you see as dangerous or potentially hurtful. The whole parent-child dynamic is set up for negativism and opposition, because each party has opposing motivations and expectations.

Engineering as many choices as possible for toddlers curtails power struggles. We want to empower, not overpower, our children. Creative thinking on our part can reduce many power struggles over toddlers' strong emotional need to explore their independent desires. Instead of saying, "It's time to brush your teeth," you can say, "Would you like to walk forward or backward to the bathroom?" Instead of arguing about stripes not going with plaids, you can let her wear what she likes to school. Instead of showdowns over the buckling of the car seat, you can bring it into the living room, pretend to be the baby and have your child buckle you up in funny games of role reversal. We want to continuously ask ourselves, "How can I give my child more power in this situation?"

> **Let's make a deal**
> *The toddler's drive for exploration magnifies the likelihood for show-downs and meltdowns when you need to say "no." Negotiating choices and creative deals reduces power struggles. Over time, the child learns to say "no" to herself and builds a tolerance for frustration.*

When toddlers don't understand or can't tolerate the limits set upon them, their emotional outbursts can be trying. It is regrettable that so many parents refer to this as the "terrible twos" or make jokes about the "little terrors." We need to appreciate the miraculous growth that a toddler's drive for independence produces, despite the messes that come with it.

Toddlers are like hot rods, driven to learn and experience anything and everything, and who end up crashing against parental limits. Their intense emotions are unleashed as a natural by-product. Toddlers give voice to their excruciating frustration about not getting what they want as well as confusion about what they experience as the random setting of limits by parents. Such acts as squeezing the puppy and throwing cups of water out of the tub are exciting and irresistible! So is painting the walls, their little sister, and their own bellies! The list goes on, as does their exploration and learning, as does your need to impose limits.

Why parent logic stumps children

Ramona, who is three years old, enjoys making cookies with her mom. Measuring ingredients and stirring the cookie dough are fun. As Ramona starts to dip her finger in for a yummy taste, mom whisked away the bowl of cookie dough. How could Mom be so cruel? In mom logic, she is protecting her daughter from the risk of salmonella in raw eggs. In three-year-old logic, Mom is withholding the greatest taste she has ever experienced in her life! Is Mom an enemy? No, she is a loving mommy. How does the daughter reconcile this seeming contradiction?

When Ramona asks "Why?" incessantly, she is trying to make sense of the world. The left brain wants to understand the linear cause-and-effect relationships in the world. Her right brain is feeling rage and betrayal. After Mom whips away the cookie dough, Ramona cries and wails. What can Mom do?

She can do what Zack's father did, which is first connect with feelings and then attempt to put those feelings into words. But first and foremost, Ramona's mom needs to remember that a three-year-old cannot use logic or process Mom's reasoning for dealing with her outrage.

Ramona: I want the cookie dough! Why can't I have it? Why?

Mom: You want the cookie dough so badly! You are mad because it is so good, and I want you to wait until the cookies are baked. It's so hard to wait for a tasty treat!

Ramona: I want some now. No! No! Don't take it!

Mom: It is so frustrating that we have to wait for eight minutes, and then let them cool for a few more. Waiting is so hard.

Ramona: I want it! You're mean! No! No!

Mom: What should we do for eight minutes? Shall we put more cookies on the next pan? Or should we do something else? We could wash these dishes.

Ramona: I want to put more cookies on the pan. I want to hold the timer.

When Mom gets the cookie dough out again, Ramona makes up a little song: "No, no, cookie dough. No, no, cookie dough." Mom sings along. Ramona is in the process of internalizing the rule of not eating cookie dough.

You have probably witnessed this internalization process in your own toddler when he learns not to touch a stove or walk into the street. The toddler looks at you while saying "no, no" as a half dare, half query. When you beam happily and congratulate him for his brilliant understanding about the "no-no," he replaces his temptation to violate a rule or indulge his curiosity with the thrill of your approval. Isn't socialization a beautiful thing?

Did you notice that Mom did not defend herself from Ramona's wrath with explanations about bacteria risks in raw eggs? Ramona is upset and she is three, so she won't understand that logic. Mom might introduce the concept later, despite Ramona's lack of comprehension, so that an understanding about infection and hygiene can develop over time. But right now, Mom knows to keep her response simple and focused on feelings.

Once Ramona settles a little, Mom redirects her attention to what they could do during the task of waiting. If Ramona had not calmed down enough to use her left brain, Mom would want to stay patient until she could. Surfing over to that left brain can't be rushed; otherwise, the child will toggle back over to the raging right brain to make sure her feelings are known. Since Ramona calmed down with Mom's empathy and validation, Mom was able to engage her in redirecting her attention to other ways they could distract themselves until the time came to eat cookies.

In Ramona's right brain, Mom is truly an enemy at the moment of "no." However, Ramona was not completely "dysregulated" (out of control), because she was able to verbalize her feelings pretty readily. Some kids, like Zack, may have been so upset that they would strike out at the parent, because their fast-lane reptilian brain triggered the "fight" reaction. As discussed earlier, when the deep emotional circuits are triggered and children become hysterical and start hitting, it will take more time to get their verbal and coping abilities in gear.

Toddler logic lapses
The reservoir of love and trust in the parent-child relationship runs deep — deep enough that when parent logic is not understood by the toddler, the goodness of the bond can prevail nonetheless.

Let's imagine the perspective of the children from earlier vignettes, if they could think through their experience logically (which they can't): *My parents are making no sense when they take the wonderful puppy toy and cookie dough away. They tell me they have little bad germ bugs that make them dangerous. But somehow, my own toy and the baked cookie don't have the bad germs. I don't understand how real bugs can be invisible! Oh well, I have enough good and trustworthy moments to help me tolerate these crushing moments when my parents infuriate and confuse me.*

It's sketchy as to whether preschoolers can develop a conceptual understanding of infection and germs before the age of five or six. Instead of grasping the causal mechanisms, young children learn to comply with rules about washing their hands, not sucking on sponges in the bathtub, and rinsing fruits before eating them. Likewise, they go along with baths and teeth-brushing (on good days), but, as with many routines, they humor parents by spouting off the reasons for hygiene, rather than having a real comprehension of its importance. That's fine. It works for now, because they live in a mostly trustworthy and secure environment with you. Soon, they will develop more comprehensive causal maps to help them navigate the greater independence of middle childhood.

STRESS AND ANXIETY

Scene: The kitchen, before school.

Rafiq: *No, Mom, no! I told you. I won't go to soccer!*

Mom: *But honey, we made a deal. You're in first grade. We let you drop out of T-ball. Then you refused to do anything after school in kindergarten. Now that you're in first grade, it will be good for you to hang out with classmates sometimes.*

Rafiq: *No, Mom. They'll laugh at me. I'm not any good at soccer. I'll hate it. I do already.*

Mom: *But honey, you haven't even tried it. Just try it. You promised. It's a new team. You'll have fun.*

Rafiq: *(screaming now) I won't have fun! I'll hate it! The kids will be mean to me. I'll have a stomachache. I have one right now just thinking about it. Why won't you listen to me?*

Mom: Just calm down. You're upset. That's why you have a stomachache. It's like we always say, Rafiq: You have a case of the dreads.

Rafiq: Shut up! I don't care what we call it. I won't go. I won't. You can't make me. I'll jump out of the window of the car if you make me!

Has "Just calm down!" ever worked to calm you when you're upset? I've never seen it work. Usually, it just infuriates people with its commanding and invalidating undertones. But that doesn't stop us from saying it at times when people frustrate us with what seem like irrational upsets.

Rafiq's parents have known for some time that he is shy and experiences anxiety more than other kids. He gets nervous about new things and starts to dread bad things the minute a new activity is proposed. His parents have tried to be sensitive to his temperament and have let him avoid activities that aren't really necessary for a young child, such as after-school activities and sleepovers. However, now that Rafiq is seven years old, they feel he needs to begin to face his fears.

They know that letting him avoid anxiety-provoking experiences will limit his social and emotional health, and at some point will even hamper him academically, if it evolves into an extreme form. The blowup over their soccer agreement let them know they needed a new approach. Before I describe to you how Rafiq's parents helped him tackle the problems associated with what he came to call his "sticky brain" (where fears get stuck), let's discuss the nuts and bolts of anxiety.

The biology of stress and anxiety

Stress is caused by physical or emotional provocations that require us to adjust or respond. Stressors for kids can range from mild annoyances, such as the little tags in their shirts and foods they hate, to major events, such as school changes, divorce, and parental illness. Even positive events, like a birthday party or surprise visit from a friend, can constitute stressors for some kids. Being "stressed out" happens when demands of the situation exceed one's ability to cope.

Being a little stressed can be a good thing; it gets us focused and delivers energy so we can attack a problem. If we experience this good kind of stress at just the right level right before a big event — such as a presentation, a big game, or an exam — we can achieve our optimal level of performance. The adrenaline release and narrowed focus can be adaptive and ideal for these situations.

The stress response occurs when the sympathetic nervous system is aroused, either by internal or external events. The parasympathetic system calms us back down again. But, as the bell curve graphic below shows, when our stress keeps surging and the demands on us exceed our ability to engage our parasympathetic calming system, we experience a more extreme stress response. Our performance will slide, and we will become overwhelmed with anxiety. Anxiety is a feeling of fear, worry, or unease, often caused by uncertainty.

The Stress Response

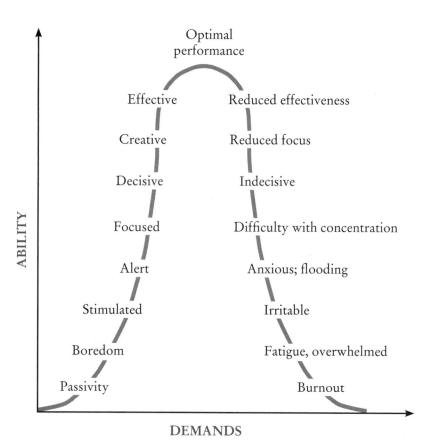

Kids get stressed by emotional triggers on a regular basis. Just putting a toddler in a car seat can lead to a meltdown. A cute baby getting attention from parents may tax the patience of the five-year-old sibling beyond her capacity to cope. A seven-year-old may be hysterical after a dream about gremlins. Unfortunately, parents commonly try to point out that these stressors should be "no big deal!" But this response is dismissive. Kids can't help being triggered; their triggers are their triggers!

Although the triggers for anxiety may be different for adults and children, the physiology is the same. Heart rates soar, breathing gets faster, muscles tense, and sweating may occur. Adrenaline is released, readying the body for a fight or for flight. Depending on the situation and the temperament of your children, they may be more inclined to attack or to run away. With a lot of stress and anxiety, they may have stomachaches, headaches, diarrhea, or excessive tiredness. Psychological tolls may include panic, difficulty concentrating, irrational outbursts of anger, feelings of doom, obsessive worry, clinging, tantrums, and refusal to participate in activities.

Parents will want to consult a mental health practitioner if a child is experiencing these symptoms with frequency, persistence, or intensity, or if they interfere with his ability to participate in the activities of daily living. There is a continuum of depressive and anxious symptoms; in the normal range lies a lot of everyday emotional upheaval that parents will want to address by enhancing their child's coping strategies.

Anxiety basics

- **Anxiety is normal.** Everyone experiences anxiety, because uncertainty and scary threats are part of living.
- **Anxiety can be either adaptive or maladaptive.** Detection centers in the brain perceive both real dangers (a screaming kid who was pushed off the slide) and false alarms (a yelp of glee on the slide). Anxiety is adaptive when it motivates kids to prepare for tests, make up with friends after a squabble, and practice for a performance. It's maladaptive when those false alarms create so much fear that kids refuse to go on field trips or participate in any activities.
- **Anxiety is temporary.** Like gravity, anxiety goes up, and it always comes down. It can be extremely uncomfortable — and can even feel life-threatening — but it will resolve when the heart rate can come down to normal levels again.

- **High anxiety leads to avoidance.** Due to the emotional discomfort associated with anxiety, children (like adults) have a natural motivation to avoid anxiety-provoking situations. Avoidance can become a bad habit, because it means kids miss opportunities to face their fears. And because avoidance leads to a drop in panic-induced accelerated heart rate, kids learn to associate avoidance with safety.
- **High anxiety drives kids to beg for rescue.** Whether dread is associated with separation from parents, vaccinations, or new social activities, kids will go to any length to get the parent to allow their escape or avoidance of the dreaded experience. (This parental behavior is called "symptom accommodation.")
- **High anxiety is contagious.** Because emotions (especially between loved ones) are contagious, parents can be so affected by their children's anxiety — experiencing their own accelerated heart rates, panicky thoughts, and amygdala hijacks — that they give in to their child's desire for escape.
- **High anxiety leads to excessive seeking of reassurance.** Although it may seem counterintuitive, constant reassurance does not work to allay anxiety; exasperated parents can end up impatient and rejecting, which then exacerbates the child's anxiety!
- **High anxiety does not abate with talk alone.** Since extreme anxiety is experienced in the emotional brain regions, a parent's logical opinion about safety usually does not suffice. In fact, talking about how fun or benign school or dance class will be can lead to more anxiety (and arguments), not less.
- **Anxiety is best addressed with coping strategies.** Children need to be exposed to circumstances that make them irrationally afraid in stepwise fashion, with calm and accepting parental support. With a variety of coping techniques, they need to learn through facing their fears that they are safe. Anxiety will attenuate only when they experience the ebb of their anxiety in the presence of that threat (e.g., day care, dance, field trips, sleeping on their own, preschool, birthday parties).

When your child is experiencing stress or anxiety, modeling healthy coping techniques — such as breathing exercises and self-calming methods — is essential, but so is investigating the potential causes that may exist in your child's social or family world. Short-term stressors can be normal experiences, such as school transitions or fighting with a friend. But long-term stressors are another kettle of fish.

Research has shown that chronic stress in early life can have lifelong effects on health and emotional adjustment (Anda et al. 2006). The anxiety felt by children who experience stressors ("adverse childhood events") such as major marital discord, abuse, and alcoholism in childhood can transform their neuroendocrine systems such that they may have compromised self-regulatory (self-calming) capacities. In other words, the nervous system has discharged so many stress hormones throughout the body for so long that it has overwhelmed the body's ability to calm, regulate, and compensate for the load. The stress has literally worn down the health of the whole body.

The prefrontal cortex is altered by chronic stress, leaving children less able to concentrate and learn in school, and more likely to develop depression and anxiety. Young children are very sensitive to the effects of stress and trauma, which is why parents want to protect their children from overload. They also want to help children learn to cope with typical challenges, and make stress management a top priority for the whole family.

BUILDING RESILIENCE

When you know your child is fearful of some new experience, the best thing to do is make a plan for facing the fear. You can't eradicate all of the anxiety; the goal is to manage it. As the parent, you can't promise that they won't feel rocky when you drop them at preschool, but you can convey that you are confident that they will make it through and be safe until you return.

Expressing positive but realistic expectations is more difficult if you have absorbed some of their panic and share their dread. Don't forget the Getting to Calm Mantra: *To help my child get to calm, I must first get to calm myself.*

Resilience is the ability to deal with and recover from stress. Children become strong by developing coping strategies for stressors that naturally occur in life. They gain self-esteem by mastering anxiety and enhancing their competencies with every new thing they don't avoid.

Temperament plays a part in determining a child's resilience. Some children are more susceptible to being negatively affected by normal stressors, but sensitive parenting can mitigate long-term impact (Belsky, Bakermans-Kranenburg, and van IJzendoorn 2007). A common metaphor in the literature on resilience uses dandelions and orchids to describe child sensitivity to stress (Kennedy 2013). Orchids need a lot of care, and dandelions are hardy by nature. Orchids are tender children who have low thresholds for being triggered by stressors. With their fear systems activated by new experiences or typical stressors, sensitive children will need their parents to demonstrate lots of patience and skills for getting to calm. However, with the right TLC and attention during childhood, orchids can grow up to be as successful, persistent, and productive as dandelions — maybe more so!

> **Tending tender orchids**
> *Like orchids, some children are highly sensitive to stress and benefit from extra care. They will also benefit from gentle nudges to develop emotional skills for resilience. We strive to parent the child we have, and if we have an orchid, we become good orchid nurturers, even though it requires more work.*

Facing fears

What's involved in helping children face their fears? In the earlier vignette, Rafiq's extreme reaction to soccer — literally saying that he'd rather die than go to soccer — let his parents know they needed to change tactics. They developed an agreement with Rafiq, which included the following techniques of exposure and guided imagery, and also breathing exercises and rewards.

Exposure is a key ingredient to anxiety management. Using this technique means that Rafiq will be exposed to his scary thoughts or feared experiences and then use coping techniques, instead of avoidance, to deal with his fears.

Rafiq listed his "dreads" for his parents, and they worked out ways that he could cope with each one. For the fear of being laughed at, his parents did play practice with him so he could practice witty comeback lines. His favorites were "If you think I'm goofy at this, you should see my dad!" and "You have a great laugh."

Rafiq made a list of "what ifs," and he and his parents wrote out solutions or "evidence for and against" the possibility that these dreaded events would occur. For example, Rafiq was afraid his mother might be late picking him up. They played detective and called the coach to ask whether he had a policy of leaving kids alone at the field (not a chance, of course). The process of developing these coping tools helped Rafiq experience little victories; he vanquished the spikes of anxiety he experienced with these stressors.

Guided imagery involves bringing to mind a positive story that allows the child to envision a positive outcome. When sports psychologists use this technique, they have athletes visualize themselves performing the perfect golf swing, tennis serve, or butterfly stroke. It's a way to direct your imagination, tap into the power of positive thinking, and instigate a positive self-fulfilling prophecy.

For his guided imagery, Rafiq and his dad wrote a story about a boy named Rafiq who dreaded soccer practice. Good and bad things happen to him in the practice, such as falling on his face and kicking the ball haywire, and also being cheered for good passing. The hero boy copes successfully with his hardships and goes home feeling great, because he was no better or worse than most of his teammates, he conquered his fears, and he had some fun. Dad read this story to him every night until they started making up other Rafiq the Superhero stories, which focused on humor, fantasy, and ... you guessed it, conquering other fears.

Positive reinforcement included copious praise from Rafiq's parents for his taking on this challenge, extra time with his parents as they practiced breathing techniques together, and, last but not least, a reward. Rafiq's mom agreed to buy new cleats for him after he completed ten days of practice. This was a big deal, since he hated using his brother's hand-me-downs and his parents thought buying new gear was unnecessary. But his parents acknowledged that for Rafiq, conquering his fear of new endeavors took courage and bravery, and was deserving of a prize.

> **The breakfast of champions: guided imagery**
> *When Olympic athletes prepare for big events, they use guided imagery, not just because it helps them to prepare mentally for excellent athletic technique, but as a method for managing anxiety. Guided imagery depicts positive mastery, which helps to crowd out dread and negative self-talk. With your child as author, write a story illustrating his mastery of a challenge or fear and read it at story time.*

Family stress

Research has established the link between parent problems (e.g., divorce, marital discord, economic strike, cumulative life stressors) and child functioning, even though the pathways by which the harm occurs is still in question (Crnic, Gaze, and Hoffman 2005). Some parents cope better than others, and some kids are harder to parent than others. But the take-home message is that whatever reduces stress on families will help children. And since stress is so common for modern-day families, parents need to prioritize healthy self-care.

People commonly ask whether child anxiety is more prevalent these days.

Many people think so. Adults typically recount how in their youth, they walked long distances to school, took buses alone, and rode their bikes all over town. Memories deceive, but your average survey of peer groups of parents will reveal that kids did seem to have more independence and less anxiety in the last generation or two, compared to current (safer than ever) times.

We have a lot on our plates: jobs, carpools, child activities, domestic responsibilities, healthy meals … and the list goes on. And although we only have to be good-enough parents, our ambitious goals and ramped-up lives can derail our wishes to become less frazzled, frenzied, and frightfully busy. How stressed are you?

Parent stress checkup

Yes No

- ☐ ☐ Do you feel like you are yelling a lot?
- ☐ ☐ Do you feel resentful of your kids or partner?
- ☐ ☐ Do you feel a lot of pressure about getting basic things done?
- ☐ ☐ Do you feel excessively depleted in your ability to cope?
- ☐ ☐ Do you get very stressed about situations with your family?
- ☐ ☐ Do you feel like your family life is chaotic?
- ☐ ☐ Are you worried about finances, health, or your children?
- ☐ ☐ Do you lack emotional support for dealing with your challenges?
- ☐ ☐ Do you feel dissatisfied with your life?
- ☐ ☐ Are you highly irritable with your children or partner?
- ☐ ☐ Are there major stressors that you are afraid you can't cope with?
- ☐ ☐ Are you in a bad mood a lot of the time?
- ☐ ☐ Do you wish you could run away from your responsibilities?
- ☐ ☐ Do you feel guilty about your family life?
- ☐ ☐ Do you often experience physical symptoms of anxiety (accelerated heart rate, fatigue, stomachaches, or headaches)?
- ☐ ☐ Are you overwhelmed with all the things you have to do?
- ☐ ☐ Are you hypersensitive about things that didn't bother you before?
- ☐ ☐ Do you have a lot of "shoulds" on your mind that make you feel bad?
- ☐ ☐ Do you feel as though being busy keeps you from being present with your children?
- ☐ ☐ Do you feel like you hardly ever get to relax and be calm?

If you said yes to more than a few of these items, you are probably suffering from stress. If you are stressed, your children are absorbing stressful feelings from you, and the feedback loop (in which you then absorb their anxiety) can make you feel even more stressed! In this vicious circle of anxiety, each person's stress exacerbates that of every other person. Perhaps you need some radical self-care for starters, and then worry about your kids. Remember the old oxygen-mask metaphor.

> **Tonic for modern living**
> *What can you eliminate from your calendar of activities? Remember that your children need you in a calm state more than they need playdates, lessons, or shopping excursions. They need less of "Just a minute" and more of "Hey, let's relax." One of the greatest gifts you can give your children is a calm home environment.*

Current thinking among researchers is that stress gets into your immune system and can change it for life (the field is called "psychoneuroimmunology") (Hertzman and Boyce, 2010). Research indicates that stress can literally turn on the genetic potential for physical and mental illness. Stress restricts learning potential and therefore, academic potential. Extreme stress obliterates one's capacity to experience joy and other positive emotions.

This is not a call to eliminate stress from our lives, because we can't, and as stated earlier, a certain amount of stress focuses our attention and galvanizes us for top performance. The goal for parents and children alike is to follow the middle path, pursuing experiences that enrich us, embracing challenges that help us grow, and placing a high value on calm time and restorative activities that help us stay healthy and resilient.

Shuttling kids to activities, spending time in cars, and running on a deficit of good old-fashioned playtime are some of the culprits that contribute to anxiety in child rearing. Another problem is that with fewer kids being born to most families, and later ages for childbearing, parents have a lot resting on high-performance parenthood. Parenting can become a competitive sport, with the trappings of excessive enrichment activities, pressure for perfection, and the pursuit of excellence in everything.

Anxiety caused by an overpacked schedule for children is only one part of the problem. Many parents are challenged to get dinner on the table and spend time with their kids, given their work schedules and other demands in their lives. Certainly, universal preschool and quality child care options would buffer the stress for everybody in our society, but identifying all the sources and solutions for societal stress on families is outside this book's purview.

The role of positive emotions

Every family can benefit from a clear-eyed assessment of their individual and family-wide emotional states. What are sources of stress? Is there time for laughter, loving, and fun? Has home become a boot camp? Do the kids (or you) have emotional outbursts that signal that you need to back up, assess the overall situation, and make a plan for problem solving or stress reduction? Do you regularly experience positive emotions such as joy, reverence, awe, gratitude, and love?

Have you heard the line "There is no health without mental health"(Prince et al. 2007)? It's true. There is getting by, and then there is thriving. If you or your kids are not thriving, consider the inventory of what's going on and make some new plans. Children who are emotionally flourishing live in the optimal range of mental functioning, in which they are most likely to enjoy the fruits of learning, resilience, creativity, and well-being. Kids who are stressed out and depressed are at the opposite end of this continuum; they are barely getting by, struggling, or failing to cope.

Families that are failing to thrive often include parents who deny problems, employ "magical thinking" that significant problems will go away on their own, and delude themselves that parental stress does not hurt child health.

> **Parent stress is kid stress**
> *Parents are the source of their children's security. Research has shown that kids suffer when their parents are extremely distressed, whether the source is marital discord, depression, or anxiety. Parents need to de-stress for their kids' sake!*

Healthy families are not without problems; everyone has problems. Welcome to the human club! The difference is that healthy families deal with their problems. One of my hopes in sharing the vignettes in this book is that they can inspire readers with new ideas for overcoming their own challenges.

Emotions can be messy, confusing, and often disturbing. If we pay attention to our own bodies and inner thoughts, we will have clues about when we have problems we need to solve. If we stay attuned to our children, we'll know when we need to help them with their difficulties. Overcoming challenges builds resilience and competences.

A counterbalance to day-to-day stress is doing things that elicit positive emotions. Sometimes we need to remind ourselves to pursue experiences that can unleash them! You can make a list of positive emotions and set goals to do things that will trigger them. We feel positive emotions when we are absorbed, courageous, ecstatic, purposeful, altruistic, adaptable, generous, content, passionate, powerful, empathic, serene, and kind — to name but a few. What activities elicit these emotions in you and your family members? Make a point of doing more of those endeavors!

Stress relievers for kids and parents

See if you and your family can do three things from this list every week.

Reading	Dancing
Music	Yoga
Drawing, painting	Guided imagery
Puzzles	Mindfulness or meditation
Watching animal videos on YouTube	Writing in a journal
	Riding bikes
Sports	Play activities
Board games	Listing three good things
Cooking	from today
Playing with pets	Writing a gratitude letter to
Knitting	someone
Playing an instrument	Volunteering
Gardening	Calling a friend
Puzzles	Doing a favor for someone
Singing	Going to a movie
Crafting	Writing
Walking	Hiking

Play is the opposite of worry. We need to make play a priority, because our brains (and our kids' brains) default to the worry side.

Negative and fearful emotions are hardwired by evolution to be stronger than the positive emotion circuits in the brain, because nothing is more important from an evolutionary perspective than surviving dangers. Food, comfort, and reproduction can happen tomorrow, but you must run right now if a saber-toothed tiger is after you. With all the triggers in modern society, our minds can be tricked into thinking life is filled with terrible threats (such as our kid not being put into the higher math class, or being cut from a team, or not having enough playdates).

Most people like the idea of stress relief, but feel like they don't have enough time to pursue this important goal. Technology, media entertainment, the invasion of work into home life, and other stressors rob families of opportunities to have experiences that stimulate positive emotions. When in doubt, have a date with your wise mind.

The wise-minded solution for stress excess

If your stress level is sky high and you've been crabby, negative, and distracted with your kids all week, you know in your heart that you don't want to postpone doing something about it. You notice your emotion mind reacting to high stress and your reason mind minimizing or rationalizing the toll, and you need to summon your wise mind.

Your emotion mind is telling you things are out of control and you can't possibly slow down and enjoy some positive activities with your children. Your reason mind is telling you that you need to get things done, that stressful lives are normal, and you'll have some positive time with the kids over the weekend.

Your wise mind evaluates your stress level and your values, feels empathy for both you and your children, and figures out a plan. You and your children need calm, loving moments tonight. Will it be a dancing to favorite music, visiting a friend in pajamas with some popcorn, or a board game while wearing silly costumes? Maybe you'll read funny poems, have a messy bubble bath, or make a video for Grandma. You have a choice.

Summary

Every chapter in this book addresses the topic of emotion. That's no surprise; virtually every aspect of our existence involves emotions. Mackenzie couldn't get to sleep because of her anxiety about sleeping on her own. Liam's frustration about not touching the magazine resulted in a tantrum in the grocery store. Gus was enormously vexed and jealous of his younger brother. And Ramona and Rafiq had emotional outbursts for their own perfectly valid reasons, even though a dismissive parent might just say, "Oh, c'mon. This is no big deal. Get over it."

Emotionally attuned and skilled parents see negative emotions as opportunities for helping their children understand their feelings, and learn to cope and solve problems. Children will experience frustration, fear, hate, resentment, disappointment, and anxiety throughout childhood and adulthood. Young children are in a sensitive period of learning to recognize and deal with their feelings, but also of absorbing the effects of stress.

A couple of centuries ago, parents were successful if their child survived and learned the family vocation. Now a parent's job involves teaching social and emotional intelligence, so that young people can develop self-awareness, read others' emotions, collaborate, do well in school, and become capable of having long-term, intimate relationships. Building emotional skills requires a huge commitment of time, patience, personal skill, and modeling. Not for the faint of heart, this agenda is far more sophisticated than the one most parents thought they were signing up for when they decided to have cute little babies. Emotional outbursts and meltdowns are more plentiful — and more disturbing — than most parents imagined.

Knowing the neuroscience of emotions can be helpful, because it enables us to have realistic expectations for our young ones' nascent abilities to rein in emotional outbursts. It also helps us understand why we need to calm the emotion circuits in the limbic system before we can begin to put feelings into words.

Emotions are contagious, with our brains often firing neurons in our limbic systems in tandem with our children's upsets, and vice versa. This fact helps us know that we can only help our children during outbursts if we have first quieted our own physiological arousal. During amygdala hijacks (theirs and ours), we need to practice our getting to calm skills.

In this ramped-up culture of ours, we all need healthy coping strategies and stress reduction capabilities. Any family that manages to take time for play, fun, and positive emotions on a regular basis is way ahead. Parents and children affect each other with their positive and negative emotions, which have an undeniable influence on health and relationships. Parents who understand the importance of emotional health and make it a family-wide priority are wise, indeed.

CHAPTER 6

Character:
Is your discipline building a caring, moral child?

No one wants to raise a spoiled brat — or any child whose behavior departs significantly from standards we deem right, good, or appropriate to expect. No kids are truly "bad"; they just lack skills, or have developed bad habits — maybe because their parents unwittingly fell into some of their own. And your expectations about acceptable behavior can be way off the mark if you don't know child development norms for the three- to seven- year-old. Furthermore, let's not forget that some children are really hard to raise, because of the challenges built into their temperament (page 60). But in general, kids don't develop good habits without some fairly skilled efforts on their parents' part.

Good character is the result of good habits that are internalized and maintained, driven by a set of values. During early childhood, those good habits are primarily developed by parents teaching responsible behaviors and modeling character virtues themselves. Since teaching sometimes includes imposing discipline, we are going to delve into the controversial realm of punishment and all the ways it can go haywire, even in the most loving and devoted families.

Scene: It's time to do chores, and seven-year-old Eliza is having none of it. Eliza's mom is fed up with her daughter, whom she describes as oppositional, defiant, and spoiled rotten.

Mom: *I asked you three times to clean your room, and you blew me off. I've had it! You can forget going to that birthday party on Saturday.*

Eliza: *You are the meanest mom who ever lived! You are a witch! I hate your stupid rules. I like my room the way it is.*

Mom: *You call me mean? Look at all the stuff in this room. Who is responsible for your cushy life? You are so spoiled. I can't even get you to clean your room.*

Eliza: *And I can't get you to shut up! All you do is yell at me!*

Mom: You are so disrespectful! If I ever spoke to my parents the way you speak to me, I would have gotten a spanking! Start cleaning your room right now or else!

Eliza: Just get out of my room! You suck!

Mom: You asked for it. You are now grounded all weekend!

When I met Eliza's mom, she was furious, and so was Eliza. Like many children who have become defiant and unruly, Eliza had learned to retaliate against what she has experienced as rejection, criticism, and constant punishment for her negative behaviors. A parent may feel entitled to punish and lecture about bad behavior when life with kids turns into a state of constant rebellion, but children have their own ways of fighting back. They disobey, "act out" their anger with misbehaviors, and develop potty mouths. The negative feedback loop begets more of the same, keeping the power struggle going, until it escalates to open warfare. Both parties have valid reasons for feeling anger, but in a parent-child relationship, the responsibility to be the bigger person falls squarely on the adult.

As Eliza's mom described to me how out of control her daughter's behavior had gotten, she used phrases like "lacking a moral compass" and "lacking character." When I asked her to expound on what she meant, she explained that she was worried about her parenting because it was her job to teach Eliza to "do the right thing" and be self-disciplined. Even though her approaches weren't working, her fierce aversion to the idea of raising a spoiled kid had her using spanking and other punitive measures. Her tactics exemplified the authoritarian parenting style (page 67).

THE DOWNSIDES OF PUNISHMENT

While there is a place in the parenting toolbox for punishment, it is often the most misused and misunderstood strategy for behavior management. There are far more effective and positive strategies at your disposal. The pie chart on page 9 is a good illustration of how much parents should tip the balance towards positive approaches to influence their children's behavior – and how sparingly they should use punishment and consequences. When a child misbehaves, it's far more effective for parents to find a way to support the development of desirable behaviors, rather than resort to punishments for undesirable ones.

While most American parents do spank their children ages three and older, it's pretty clear such punishment is at best ineffective, and at worst, harmful. Corporal punishment (spanking) is linked to negative outcomes, including conduct problems, psychological difficulties, and substance use during adolescence (Afifi et al. 2012; Gershoff 2013; Kazdin and Benjet 2003). The American Academy of Pediatrics has taken a firm position against the use of spanking, because there are so many alternatives for influencing behavior that don't run the risk of physically harming children or modeling physical aggression. Parents who don't spank but punish by yelling or threatening instead can leave just as many harmful psychological marks (Straus and Field 2003).

Pitfalls of punishment

Punishment teaches what not to do, rather than what to do.

Punishment can put an end to a behavior in the near term, but in the long term, the behavior can bubble up again, either because the child is motivated to retaliate or lacks an opportunity to learn the desired behavior.

Punishment as a major strategy to influence behavior deteriorates relationships. No one wants to cooperate with someone who seems like a tyrant.

Modeling negative approaches to problem solving, especially ones that include criticism, aggression, and vengeance, can result in the child using these same behaviors with peers.

Punishment is often motivated by anger, righteous indignation, or revenge, because the parent is intensely frustrated with a child's misbehavior. Since emotions are contagious, this can lead to a negative spiraling of behaviors.

Punishment as a primary disciplinary tool is discouraged by virtually all child development experts, for several reasons. First of all, positive reinforcement is simply more effective. Since any parental attention can reinforce behavior, even punishments can unintentionally reinforce the very behaviors you want to see reduced. For instance, if you punish your child for pestering a sibling, get ready to see more pestering.

Second, punishment is often associated with negative parent-child interactions and power struggles, and together, these dynamics can make the behaviors worse. They interfere with the child's security and trust in parents. Once a child's trust has deteriorated, it can be hard to win it back. In short, using negative consequences still has a role in shaping behavior, but its overuse (or underuse) can cause real problems.

MOVING ON FROM POWER STRUGGLES

How does a parent wind up with a punishment-heavy disciplinary style? The approach used by Eliza's mom exemplified a very typical pattern. During my evaluation, she described the narrative she had been reciting in her mind (for years) that children should respect their parents, comply with rules, and appreciate that insistence on obedience is for their own good. The more Eliza dragged her heels on chores and rebelled, the more Mom piled on the punishments that didn't work.

Eliza's dad described himself as the quiet type; he had completely deferred to Mom as the major caregiver. But the constant conflict in their home had him concerned, and he was more than ready to support a change in disciplinary approach.

How did these parents build the behaviors they wanted to see in Eliza? And probably more importantly, how did they recover from the negative feelings that resulted from the previous excessive use of punishment? First, Mom infused Eliza's schedule with more child-directed play and positive time with her (page 115). Next, she set up a behavior program using the ten guidelines on page 17, rewarding her for chores completed at a certain time on certain days. Eliza named the agreement "The Deal." If chores were done on time, she gained points toward buying little figurines she collected and adored. If Eliza missed the deadlines for chore completion, she earned no points.

Eliza's mom agreed to cut down drastically on her nagging and negativity (her goal was to eliminate it by 80 percent!). Eliza's mom worked hard at avoiding nagging, instead using the "The Deal" to motivate Eliza to comply with expectations. She reminded Eliza just once of "The Deal," and either Eliza got chores done on time and earned her points or she didn't. Eliza's mom also applied the "First work, then play" rule (page 57) and let Eliza play with her figurines only after she completed her homework.

The drastic negativity overhaul
When home has become a war zone, consider eliminating 80 percent of your negative verbal output. Cut out criticism, nagging, and reacting to undesirable behaviors. Instead, employ techniques from the positive parenting toolbox to encourage the desired behaviors.

By eliminating most of her negative verbalizing and punishment, and instigating positive methods to influence desirable behaviors, Eliza's mom was on her way to overhauling her negative interaction patterns. Eliza's parents learned that the benefit of using these behavioral methods was a more positive home environment.

Our biggest goal was to help Eliza feel good about her relationship with her mom again and help her feel that "Mom is on my team." Kids can tolerate occasional bummers like time-outs, earlier bedtimes, and extra chores for their misdeeds, as long as those measures are a very small part of an overall positive parenting plan, taken in the context of a loving, supportive relationship.

Is your disciplinary style backfiring?

When emotions are unleashed, children need to learn how to calm down and avoid destructive behaviors. So do parents. Lapses on both sides make discipline one of the toughest challenges in parenting. As described in the last chapter, parents should prioritize emotional calming and coaching if the child has a meltdown.

Sometimes, the best way to handle a tantrum is to treat it as an emotional issue, and employ a "getting to calm" intervention (page 42). Other times, it's best to tackle the overall behavioral issue; in those cases, a measured dose of negative consequences can enhance learning. And often, the child will benefit from both responses from the parent. Ideally, the course you choose will be determined by your careful discernment of how the child can best learn, given the particular circumstances. But because our emotions can be swiftly triggered by kids' tirades, our discernment can evaporate with our soaring heart rate.

Remember, the Latin root of the word discipline is discere, which means "to teach." Many kinds of harsh punishment, such as anger-motivated spanking, only teach children about anger — their own and their parents'. When parents take this route, it results in children who are more focused on parental cruelty than their own wrongdoing. Thus, the punishment backfires, teaching the child fear instead of self-control and rule compliance. By contrast, the goal of positive discipline is to teach children how to behave, manage feelings, and learn from mistakes.

The first rule of punishment

Anger about child misconduct can result in an impulsive decision to dole out a harsh punishment, which is not an effective means of shaping behavior. Never decide on punishments when under the influence of negative emotions.

Ideally, you will think deeply about your punishment strategy for your children. You won't react by imposing harsh consequences when you are angry. When you are angered by your child's behavior, calm yourself so you can figure out whether a negative consequence will actually help learning. Make sure that punishments are only a small part of a mostly positive parenting approach. And if you realize later that the punishment has been excessive, you can always apologize and re-think your decision, showing your child you are able to take responsibility for mistakes.

Remember Zack, the three-year-old who threw a tantrum and hit his father when forbidden to chew on the puppy toy (page 145)? The father calmed himself and took time to decide what to do. He redirected Zack to choosing a different toy for puppy play and reenacted the puppy-play situation. Zack demonstrated genuine empathy for his dad, showing sincere regret for calling him names and hitting him. Punishment was not necessary for teaching.

If Zack was routinely aggressive despite receiving lots of attention from his parents for positive behaviors, they might want to institute a time-out program (see page 192). But deciding on a program of negative consequences for misbehaviors should be a deliberate process, carried out when heads are cool.

Sloppy discipline = sloppy parenting

When parents use punishment as the centerpiece of their efforts to influence behavior, they are missing out on one of the most important strategies for promoting and maintaining desirable behavior: positive reinforcement. However, using too few negative consequences to deal with aggression and rule violations is also a problem.

Parents who have difficulty with discipline fall into two major camps: those who need to set more limits ("permissive" parents), and those who use threats and punishments excessively ("authoritarian" parent: see page 67). Of course, there are other problematic subtypes, such as the parent who bounces from permissive to authoritarian in an inconsistent manner, or the one who neglects to parent at all.

Your self-awareness is critically important. Are you too quick to react with anger and punishment? Are you anxious about setting limits for fear that your child will hate your guts? Do you punish in the heat of battle, but then feel guilty and opt out of doing anything about the misbehavior?

If you don't feel good about your disciplinary approach, your first step is to examine how you encourage desirable behaviors. It may help you to review the section on positive parenting (page 8) and think about out how it can apply to your own parenting.

Discipline course correction
Your love and approval are the most powerful motivators for eliciting the behaviors you want from your child, and discouraging the behaviors you don't. But if you feel as though you've got plenty of high-quality time with your child and he still regularly disobeys, blows you off, or shows aggression, negative consequences are needed to discourage the behaviors.

Some parents may think they are discouraging negative behaviors by talking about how harmful or wrong they are, but this talk may be incomprehensible at best and rewarding at worst. These parents may lack the "authority" piece in the authoritative parenting style proven to be so effective in rearing children. They may talk about the importance of character and behaving well, but small children benefit more from behavioral shaping than diatribes and logic. Imposing negative consequences for breaking rules is a necessary tool in the parenting toolbox. While authoritarian parents value obedience over feelings, permissive parents are so weak-kneed or worried about displeasing their children that they have an aversion to setting limits and the negative emotions that come with that turf.

Often the parents most passionate about "building character" are the ones most attached to punishment as a means of attaining it. Even though they end up consulting me because punishment hasn't worked, they are still convinced that authoritarian parenting is the best way to build virtues. That couldn't be further from the truth, but the passionate amongst us aren't always persuaded by research.

NATURAL AND LOGICAL CONSEQUENCES

The beauty of using logical negative consequences for teaching desired behaviors is that they teach children to take responsibility for their behaviors. They are used most effectively with children about five years and older, because at that age, kids can understand the cause-and-effect relationship between their behaviors and consequences. But even a toddler can start to figure out a causal map when he loses a toy because he uses it to bop his infant sibling.

Natural consequences are those that occur as a direct result of your child's behaviors, without your playing the punisher role. The parent simply does not intervene and lets natural forces do the disciplinary work. For instance, if your son doesn't get up with his alarm or your "wake up" notice for his morning routine, he is late to school. In preschool and kindergarten, the teacher might offer a disappointed greeting: "Please try to be on time tomorrow." Most children do not like disappointing their teacher or being out of step with their peers.

The natural consequence for a child not eating his lunch is that he is hungry in the afternoon. Children can tolerate a little hunger. The natural consequence for not wearing his coat as you requested is that he is cold. (You know that colds aren't caused by being cold, right?)

> **A disciplinary easy street**
> *Natural consequences teach children valuable lessons. Other than tolerating some mild distress in your child — which is the teaching part for him — you don't have to do anything!*

Natural consequences are as underused for behavioral shaping as punishment and talky warnings are overused. Why? Parents would rather lecture and rescue than let natural consequences do the heavy lifting for shaping behavior. A bit of discomfort goes a long way toward teaching kids lessons, but many parents are too uncomfortable with that pinch. But ironically, a parent's belittling lecture about irresponsibility and thoughtlessness can pinch a lot harder than natural consequences. Another downside to the lecture: Parents become the bad news, instead of the hunger, chill, or teacher's scowl.

When parents use logical consequences for teaching a lesson, they use a consequence related to the misbehavior to help the child learn from mistakes. For instance, if your daughter plays roughly with the cat, the penalty is that she loses the opportunity to play with the cat for a while (rather than, say, having to go to bed early). A logical consequence for your son losing his sweatshirt would be for him to earn the money for a new one or get one from a thrift store (rather than losing story time). If your daughter bikes outside her allowed area, then she loses access to her bike for a day (rather than losing screen time). You link the consequence directly to the behavior.

Negative consequences 101

• *If power struggles are common in your family, consider an overhaul by using mostly positive approaches to influence behavior.*
• *Punishments should be mild and only be combined with positive reinforcements that teach desirable behavior.*
• *Punishments, time-outs, and negative consequences should be immediate, mild, and brief. What's mild? If your child has extreme and prolonged emotional reactions to a punishment or expresses that she feels parental rejection, you are not in the "sweet spot" for learning. Review techniques for emotion coaching (page 144) and wise-minded parenting to brush up on skills for coping with meltdowns and building emotional competence.*
• *The younger the child, the shorter the duration of the consequence should be. A minute per year of age is a common rule of thumb for time-outs (see page 192 for more). For children younger than five, one day is plenty for losing access to a privilege like a bike, screen or toy.*
• *Do not decide on discipline when you are angry; you are likely to overdo it.*
• *Do not be afraid to repair or retract a punishment that is excessive. Consistency is important, but carrying out a punishment that is too harsh is nutty. Plus, you'll get to model another desirable parental behavior: admitting to mistakes. "I was wrong to decide about discipline when I was upset." Be proud if you deliver that line.*

When children are given logical consequences as a punishment, it's important to consider the right dose. You're heard that maxim "The punishment should fit the crime." The general principle is that if you underdose or overdose your child on negative consequences, he will miss the sweet spot for learning.

Ignoring: Harder than it seems

Let's face it: It can be hard to ignore low-level, annoying, and negative behaviors, such as whining, baby talk, thumb sucking, stalling, pouting, and complaining. We always need to consider there is a meaning behind such behaviors — most likely that they are just revealing normal feelings! But the great bulk of these irritating behaviors will go away naturally if you don't shine your spotlight on them. Sometimes this valuable tool is called "planned ignoring," to emphasize that you don't ignore to punish or as a reaction to behaviors you don't like. You ignore in a planned way, because you've realized your attention to annoying behaviors is actually rewarding to your child.

It is important to remember that ignoring should not be used with anger, since that may reinforce the behavior, too! Since most negative behaviors are perfectly normal, we truly want to accept them as temporary. The pouting may reflect disappointment that they don't get cookies before dinner. The whining may reflect that they are frustrated, tired, or angry about not getting their way. The stalling may be because they're tired of some taxing daily routine. The screaming may reflect that they are overwhelmed at this minute with everything, both within and outside of them.

While you may want to emotion coach if you have a hunch that there is a problem underlying the display of emotion, many annoying behaviors merely need to be tolerated. It's time for your "getting to calm" curriculum! Otherwise, you might reinforce the behavior with your attention, or worse, you may admonish your child for normal and valid feelings. It is natural for you to pay attention to whining, rudeness, potty talk, arguing, talking back, tantrums, and teasing. Natural — but not recommended! As reviewed in detail in Chapter 1, any attention amounts to reinforcement of those behaviors. Paying attention is like a spotlight; by focusing your attention on the child, you unwittingly increased the likelihood that the behavior you dislike will occur a lot more often.

Talky mommy

Six-year-old Jack and his mom came to my office because of too much fighting, noncompliance, and a perceived lack of discipline. Jack's mom described how he called her names, screamed at her when he didn't get his way, and would not cooperate with chores, homework, or screen limits. She didn't believe in time-outs or sticker charts, which she called bribe systems.

It became clear that this mom's main method of discipline was talking. She tried to plead and beg Jack into compliance. The result was endless arguments, power struggles, and, of particular importance a lack of effective discipline. After my initial conversation with Mom about her concerns, we shared a playtime together. What I observed was a constant chatter of negativity erupting from Mom as Jack played games and fooled around in my office.

Jack's mom shared that she understood the irony of her situation. She had hoped to avoid punishments and time-outs as a way of averting a "rupture in the relationship," only to end up in constant battles, which were certainly leading to wear and tear on those involved. Mom was great at giving Jack choices and showing warmth and love, but without the important quality of limits and boundaries, both she and her son felt out of control.

I introduced the concepts of positive attention, ignoring, and targeting some negative behaviors to eliminate. Although Mom claimed that she "picked her battles" and ignored benign negative behaviors, in actuality, she was highly reactive to Jack's low-level infractions. When he started looking at my play materials, she scolded him. When he stayed on task with an exercise I gave him, she didn't acknowledge him. When he started rolling on the floor (which I found acceptable for a bored six-year-old), she pleaded with him to stop. When he responded by snorting like a pig, they began arguing about his behavior.

Jack's mother committed herself to learning how to ignore low-level annoying behaviors and praising Jack for on-task behaviors. She reminded herself to "catch him while he's good," giving attention to Jack when he was helpful and compliant with routines and rules. She put effort into not responding to Jack when he tried to engage her with whining and complaining.

Initially, Jack's mom had to be prepared for the ignored behaviors to get worse. To understand why this happens, you need to understand the concept of "intermittent reinforcement." Imagine an experiment in which a pigeon sporadically receives pellets for pecking at a bar (i.e., intermittent reinforcement). The pigeon pecks like crazy to get as many pellets as possible.

Suddenly, the pellets stop coming. What happens then? The pigeon (or any other animal) will peck at that bar with even more intensity. The pigeon's motivational systems intensify effort, since pellets have always been delivered with enough pecks. This process of intensified effort once the delivery of goodies has been extinguished is called "extinction surge."

Whether it's an elevator button, a doorbell, or a pedal on a water fountain, if something doesn't deliver the expected response, we usually intensify the behavior in an effort to push the system into giving us what we want and what we are used to getting.

Does this remind you of a child who gets attention for whining or throwing a tantrum when she doesn't get what she wants? If your kid is used to getting your attention by begging or whining, she will accelerate that behavior to increase the probability of getting that reinforcement. In the initial stages of withdrawn reinforcement (such as a parent's attention), the child will go all out to hook the parent back in.

The power of ignoring

Your attention is powerful reinforcement. When you stop paying attention to annoying behaviors, such as whining, arguing, or begging, it triggers more effort on the child's part to get that attention. Initially, your child will burst forth with a tsunami of those behaviors that previously hooked your attention. After the surge abates, wait a bit, try to engage him in another activity and give lots of attention to the behaviors you want to see more of. If you are consistent, and the annoying behaviors lack other sources of reinforcement, these behaviors diminish will over time.

Effective ignoring occurs only when you give your attention to the positive opposite of undesirable behaviors. You withdraw attention from undesirable behaviors and instead pay attention and praise your child when she is exhibiting the desired behavior. For instance, instead of commenting on negative behaviors like picky or sloppy eating, you wait until she doesn't display those behaviors and then tell her how much you enjoyed eating with her. Instead of reacting to her whining, you engage with her fully when she isn't whining. Instead of scolding your son for dawdling, you increase your praise when he stays on task. Internalizing self-discipline is the hardest job children undertake; they deserve a lot of credit.

Parents need to distinguish between the constructive use of ignoring and the threats of neglect and/or abandonment. Let's say a dad gives his child, who is climbing on a jungle gym, a couple of reminders that they need to leave the playground at a certain time, but the child refuses to climb down. The dad says, "If you don't get off right now, I'm leaving without you." The child persists in climbing on the jungle gym. The dad thinks he is ignoring dawdling behavior by walking off, but the child feels terrified. As with harsh punishment, the child may appear chastened by this method, but it may leave a scar of distrust. Withdrawals of love, threats of abandonment, and spanking have short-term impacts but create other problems affecting secure attachment.

There are plenty of behaviors that aren't good candidates for ignoring, including harm to others or property, stealing, noncompliance, or signs of emotional difficulties, such as depression and anxiety. And many times when children are upset, we want to help them through it with emotion coaching. But a lot of behaviors are appropriate for ignoring, especially irritating scowls, low-level sassiness, and ordinary upsets stemming from frustration. You'll want to get your spouse, grandparents, or other adults on board with your game plan to avoid saying things like "Wipe that look off your face!" Consider writing down the behaviors you wish to ignore so that everybody knows what and how to ignore them. And if, upon reflection, you later consider that those behaviors relate to hurt feelings, be sure to circle back for some empathy when the time seems right.

The myth of the spoiled kid

Parents who complain about their spoiled kids sometimes miss the irony that they are referring more to their own regrettable behaviors than their child's. A child cannot become "spoiled" without an indulgent adult supplying an excess of goodies. Parents who buy their children goodies every time they go to the store, on the way home from school, or when they attend other activities are creating expectations. Children will beg you to "gimme" (keep the goodies coming). Just like suffering the "extinction surge" of a child's emotions when you withdraw the reinforcement of your attention, you will experience the same when you stop delivery of material goodies.

> **Dealing with the gimmes**
> *Get ready for some wails if you are going to discontinue giving in to the gimmes. Let your child know ahead of time if you are going to stop buying goodies upon your child's pleas or demands, and then prepare to be tested. Practice your own "getting to calm" skills, gird yourself for the torrent of emotions that accompany an extinction surge, and rest assured that if you are consistent, your child will learn that gimmes don't work anymore.*

If your kid is used to getting a goody or your attention by begging, they will intensify that behavior to increase the probability of getting the goody. If all of a sudden, your daughter doesn't get the candy at the store when previously this was a given, chances are she'll let loose with some mighty big wails (extinction surge) to see if you'll cave.

If you can't think of good validations, breathe deeply until you can. You can even apologize for getting into the bad habit of giving goodies (or not setting a regular bedtime routine, or whatever indulgence you're weaning her from). She may not understand the apology, but your sweet tone will convey that you don't enjoy inflicting the pain that comes with this switcheroo.

Time-outs: The good, the bad, and the ugly

The most important thing to know about time-outs is that they only work if children have enough "time in" with their parents, that is, plenty of positive and nurturing family time (Morawska and Sanders 2011). A systematic review of 41 studies found that time-outs can be very effective in increasing compliance when executed infrequently, without anger, and with certain kids in certain circumstances (Owen, Slep, and Heyman 2012). Did you note all of those qualifications? Because time-outs can be so fouled up, they have gotten some bad press lately, which is well-deserved. However, used correctly, this method can stop the undesirable behavior from skyrocketing.

The good: Time-outs create a pause when things are getting out of control. Time-out means "time out from positive reinforcement." It is another version of ignoring, because it means you are ending the reinforcement of your attention, or your child's aggressive or destructive behaviors (e.g., hitting, throwing things, damaging property).

While some parents may prefer an alternative negative consequence, such as the withdrawal of privileges, the advantages of a time-out are that it is immediate, serves as a time to "calm down" when the child needs it, helps the child practice effortful control (i.e., toggling from revved up to cooperating with the time-out), and avoids a delay in punishment, which may be confusing to the young child. Yanking screen time or dessert may seem like a preferable consequence to you, but a toddler may not understand the cause-and-effect link to slugging a sister earlier in the day.

Implementation of time-out

1. Identify target behavior. Time-outs should only be used for certain behaviors that have been thoughtfully targeted for this intervention, such as noncompliance with a parental directive in the counting method (page 70) or as a consequence of aggression. If you are using it for aggressive behavior, don't give "reminders," because it would be giving a second chance to one of your nonnegotiable rules about "no hitting."

In deciding the length of time for the time-out, some parents use the rule of thumb of one minute per age of the child. Some parents just use one minute across all ages.

2. Designate a time-out location. Decide with your child on a place that can serve as a cooling-off (or calming-down) location. Consult your child in your initial meeting, but make sure that there are absolutely no negotiations during the actual implementation. It is ideal if the location is a bottom stair (it is immovable!) in a room that you will stay in so that she doesn't feel banished, and where you can direct your attention to something else during the time-out.

3. Describe the time-out process. Tell your child that it will last for one minute from the time he stops yelling or screaming. You will use a timer.

The options are threefold: If he goes to the location in a cooperative manner, he stays there for one minute. If he doesn't, you will then take him to his room (or another) with the door open for one minute, as long as he is quiet. If he is yelling, the door will be closed by you and opened the instant he quiets and from that moment he only stays there for one minute.

If your child spirals into an amygdala hijack or emotional seizure and is too out of control to comply with the time-out, sit with him quietly, following the guidelines on page 156. Once he has quieted, try to gently escort him to his one-minute time-out. If the ordeal has been so emotionally draining that neither one of you can manage it, chock this failed effort up to the fact that kids can't comply with anything when they are flooding emotionally.

When this method works the way it is supposed to, once children learn how short and easy the first version of time-out is, they will generally cooperate fairly quickly. In the third version, if the child is so upset that he is yelling from behind the closed door, open the door every 30 seconds and whisper a reminder, "I get to open the door for a one-minute time-out as soon as you quiet down." This procedure reminds your child that you are obeying a rule of time-out, and that you are on his side. You are giving him an incentive to quiet down (i.e., the door will open and the timer will start). The whispering shows your child that you are not angry, and he may quiet down just so he can hear what you are saying.

4. Use "play practice" to simulate how time-out works. You can swap roles, practice each version of time-out, and talk about why you are employing it for rule infraction. Avoid using words like "bad" and "good," and be specific about why you've decided on the counting method for noncompliance or using a time-out for aggression. Although a three-year-old won't understand the logic, she will "feel" your good intentions and learn how benign the process is by simulating it with you. Your loving tone while you practice will set her up to understand this in not about rejecting her; it is a consequence for revved-up behaviors that require a time-out from attention and business as usual.

5. Evaluation. If you are giving more than two or three time-outs every day, consider that you may have a bug in the program. There are several possible explanations:
 • You may not be spending enough time giving your child positive attention and engaging in child-directed play, which leaves the "bank account" of good feelings at a deficit, unable to afford a withdrawal.
 • You may be showing anger during time-outs. Your child may be insecure or anxious in her attachment to you and thus may feel rejected by the way the method is implemented.

• Your child may have a highly sensitive temperament, and, in spite of your neutral and supportive handling of the time-out, he may not be able to self-regulate and calm down with this method. His flooding in response to the time-out may mean that you need to handle the targeted behavior like an "emotional seizure" (page 155). In this case, you may want to withdraw a privilege as a consequence instead of using time-outs.

• The frequency of your child's noncompliance or aggressiveness may suggest that she would benefit more from a behavioral program with rewards than one with time-outs. In this situation, you would give rewards for intervals of time in which the targeted behavior did not occur. For instance, she gets "points" and/or stickers for every half-hour that she is cooperative and does not display aggressive behavior. Review the section earlier in the book (page 16) about why behaviors you may think should come naturally to children still deserve rewards. If your child has a revved-up personality, remember the Acceptance Mantra, and that she is doing the best she can given her emotional state, even though she needs to do better. Believe it.

While some say that time-outs help children reflect on a misdeed, I don't think that's the case. How much reflecting does a high-energy four-year-old do? However, when used well, time-outs serve as an opportunity for the child to stop the misbehavior and experience a consequence for the targeted transgression before rejoining the play. You can talk all you want about "We don't tolerate hitting in our family," but that will not stop the impulses of a four-year-old who gets aggressive during physical play. Neither will a time-out, but at least it can serve as a temporary pause in the accelerated fight, and teach the child that there are consequences to rule violations.

One of the boys I worked with likened his time-outs to a penalty box, "like in hockey … do the crime and pay the time." He told me he liked it better than getting yelled at all the time. And he understood that he "gets hyper a lot" when he plays, loses control, and needs a place to cool off.

Used correctly, time-outs can be an effective tool for the whole family. They can be used logically to interrupt negative behavioral patterns among adults as well as children. Who among us doesn't get riled up and stressed out occasionally?

Model time-outs and emotional intelligence by saying: "I am grumpy from my day at work. I worry that I'm going to take it out on you guys. I didn't like way I just snapped at you. I'm sorry. I am going to take a five-minute time-out and come back with the intention of putting my best foot forward. Here I go." And make sure you don't disappear to do e-mail or look at your cell phone. Instead, do a guided imagery with your eyes closed, imagining reuniting with your family with your best self.

The bad: It's important to emphasize that you should not use the time-out method with a punitive attitude or a harsh, banishing tone. This will backfire. When parents are angry and send their child to their room or another place, it can scare the child. The child will not learn any lesson other than to be afraid of banishment or to internalize shame.

Another downside is when time-outs are used without also using the emotion coaching methods described in the last chapter. Although you might want to use time-outs for cooling down behavioral outbursts like hitting, you also want to help children put feelings into words and one day, you hope, express their feelings verbally instead of physically.

The ugly: Time-outs can be used excessively. They can also start to be part of the parent chatter of threats and criticism. How often have you heard a parent say, "Do you want a time-out?" and "If you don't stop this minute, I'll give you a time-out!"

It's also ugly when a parent lectures the child after she finishes her time-out. Double jeopardy! In many cases, the child will benefit from putting feelings into words after a calming time-out. Ideally, the parent would engage in some emotion coaching (page 144) and right/left brain integration (page 149). But lecturing her about how wrong her actions were after the time-out is dirty pool.

And it's ugly when parents get frustrated that the time-outs don't put an end to targeted behaviors. Kids get riled up (the high-energy ones will get really riled up), and impulsive behaviors will occur and recur. Children may get some good self-control practice, but they don't suddenly develop mature brains just because you implement a nifty time-out program.

Time-out for loving kindness
When the parent greets the child after a time-out with kindness and conveys an accepting spirit, the child will learn that time-outs really are a chance to reset, reboot, and start over with a clean record.

Sometimes, parents watch their kids bounce out of time-outs happy as can be and wonder if the consequence had any impact. They wonder whether hitting should result in a bigger wallop of a consequence if their children are so carefree after the time-out. However, this resilient response is just what you want to see, because it shows that they self-calmed successfully. Chances are it did make an impact, and the child has already shifted gears. It's time to get back into the fray of things. Yippee!

In determining whether you want to use this method, you must exercise your wise mind, because the qualifications for using it are essential: It should be infrequent, conducted without anger, and in the context of mostly positive parenting. As you summon your wise mind (and avoid the reactivity of the emotion mind and the harsh judgment of the reason mind), you will choose this method if it feels right to you.

There should be no physical coercion or dragging of kids to time-out. If the method isn't feeling like a successful method for discouraging, stopping, or interrupting certain behaviors, go back to the toolbox and consider other tools. But in your evaluation of time-out, be sure to have realistic expectations. As discussed in Chapter 2, it takes about two and a half decades for the self-control "muscle" to fully develop in the prefrontal cortex. Your best outcome for the use of time-outs should be that your child learns to pause, comply, calm, and reset. However, that doesn't mean that amped-up noncompliance will be eliminated, especially if your child has a temperament wired for high energy and/or emotional intensity.

As children mature, parents will increasingly discourage undesirable behaviors with the use of other logical consequences. They will also increasingly encourage reflection and mutual problem solving through empathic talking, listening, soothing, and respectful conversation. However, with toddlers and young children, who have limited capacity for abstract reasoning, they learn to curb impulses through direct measures you take to discourage them. In their best versions, time-outs help kids and adults get to calm.

HOW DO YOU BUILD CHARACTER?

Character is defined as the group of traits that result in good behavior. Researchers who study character examine virtues that put people on the path to a good life; one that is happy, meaningful, and fulfilling. While a discussion of character in the three- to seven-year-old may seem premature, I maintain that it is the very best time to establish good habits, self-discipline, and a lifestyle that promotes the development of virtues. We covered many topics related to self-control in Chapter 2; now, let's examine the other traits that contribute to the development of character.

While temperament is influenced by biological tendencies related to patterns of feeling, thinking, and behaving, character is molded by your experiences. Your child's character is developed in many ways: with your family routines, how you have fun and relax, how family members show their love, what you do on the weekends, how you and your friends celebrate achievements, how you respond to issues of racism, sexism, and other "-isms," and how you respond to mistakes of character.

For several decades, psychologist Martin Seligman at the University of Pennsylvania has studied happiness, character, and the virtues that contribute to a life well lived. Along with Chris Peterson, Nansook Park, and other leaders in the field, Seligman has identified seven character strengths that are associated with leading engaged, happy, responsible, and successful lives (Peterson and Seligman 2004). These character strengths are: zest, grit, optimism, self-control, gratitude, social intelligence, and curiosity.

While their research has not focused on parenting per se, it consistently highlights the importance of parents modeling the virtues that they want to see in their children. It also emphasizes the significant role that enriched educational and social opportunities play in the development of a strong character.

Once you leave the annals of academic research conducted on virtues, an obvious question surfaces from the trenches of real-life parenting: It is one thing to talk about values such as honesty, kindness, and curiosity, but what do you do when you struggle with the lack of those behaviors in real life? We all acknowledge that child rearing is messy, and that children experience self-control challenges for at least two decades. We know that we want to blow on the embers of kindness and empathy so that we can get the virtue fires burning. However, if we talk too much about virtues or our children's shortcomings, we run the risk of getting fewer of exactly the behaviors we are trying to promote. Some deficits require swift and immediate action; others need a light application of guilt while steering clear of shame (lying, cheating, stealing and hitting come to mind). How best to handle these common virtue deficiencies?

The infuriating habit of lying

One of the most frequent questions I hear when I give public talks is "Why do young kids lie?" That's an easy one: Because they can! I like getting this question, because the best way to handle a lying habit can be counterintuitive, so it's helpful to get some pointers. First, let's start with what's normal for this age.

At some point at about two or three years of age, children begin to tell lies to cover up transgressions. Kids lie for the same reasons adults lie: They want to get out of trouble, spare people's hurt feelings, impress others, or gain something. It takes some mental agility to lie under the duress of parental scrutiny, because kids have to remember what they've said and attempt to make the story plausible.

A study of two- and three-year-olds illustrates how common it is for them to lie (Talwar and Lee 2002). After telling a group of children not to peek at a toy placed on a table behind them, an experimenter left the room. A videotape of the action revealed telling results: Ninety percent of the children peeked! About two-thirds of them concealed their peeking by either lying or refusing to answer when questioned. By the ages of four–six, children were less likely to peek and less likely to lie, because by this age, they have more self-control and they know that it is wrong to lie.

The honest truth about lying
A toddler's lying is an experiment. As they realize that they are individual people with individual minds, they experiment with telling a lie. Perhaps they have the power to get their sibling into trouble ("She broke the cup"), get themselves out of trouble ("I didn't break the cup"), or make up a whopper ("The cup broke itself!"). Luckily, parents' displeasure and the toddlers' learning that the whoppers don't get them off the hook curb this habit naturally.

When their toddlers discover the little thrill of lying, parents need to make it clear from the start that lying is wrong. They need to explain in simple terms the importance of telling the truth and then praise them when they cough up the truth instead fudging or telling a fib, because it's hard for them to do.

As common as lying is, most school-age kids learn the value of honesty, feel bad about lying when they do it, and feel relieved when they come clean to supportive parents. Ideally, parents model honesty and are consistent in telling the truth themselves. They seek to understand the motives behind lies when they occur (e.g., sibling rivalry, fear of punishment, anxiety about homework) while conveying the ultimate importance of honesty.

Effective management of a lying problem

Six-year-old Rayburn had a bad habit of lying, which brought his family into my practice for an evaluation. His parents had made it clear to Rayburn that they valued honesty and that consequences for any misbehavior would be doubled if he lied about it. Rayburn's lying did not abate.

Rayburn's temperament was sociable and impulsive; he had lots of energy for athletics, friendship, and school activities. Rayburn had difficulties in executive functioning, which made it hard for him to focus on goals and stay on task. His impulsivity made the lying problem worse; not only did he get into more trouble than the average boy of his age, but he would also spout tall tales to try to cover his tracks. Try as they might, his parents were ineffective with their punishments, lectures, and reasonable explanations about the importance of honesty. So what finally turned Rayburn around?

First, we talked about the "catch 'em when they're good" maxim. Rayburn's parents balked a bit on praising him for telling the truth, because they thought honesty should be automatic. It isn't. If telling the truth about homework means that you have to do homework instead of getting screen time, it can be awfully tempting to lie.

Second, these parents needed to temporarily suspend their focus on lying as a moral breach and instead address it as a behavioral one. Psychologists define guilt as feeling bad about bad behavior, and shame as feeling like you are a bad person. This is key. Rayburn, who had been lying for at least two years, was solidly in the second camp. He told me, "I'm a bad liar, and my parents hate me for it."

Why is Rayburn's comment important? Rayburn felt so ashamed about his lying that he covered up his ears and would scream when the subject came up. If he can't even talk about his bad habit, how can we help him stay conscious of it, recognize his triggers, exercise a different decision at certain moments, and turn this habit around? As paradoxical as it may sound, we needed to help him feel less bad about his bad habit, so that he could tolerate addressing it. He needed to spend more of his willpower on overcoming his impulse to lie, rather than wasting it on trying to deal with his shame.

Rayburn is not a bad boy, but he did have a bad habit. Getting access to goodies or getting out of trouble are both extremely enticing. We needed to make the truth irresistible. Like any habit that is very reinforcing — playing instead of getting ready for bed, stealing from Dad's coin dish, or pestering a sibling — the reward for doing the positive opposite needs to be more powerful than the behavioral habit. In Rayburn's case, built-up bad feelings from his long history of wrangling about the truth had left him with a very strong compulsion to avoid the whole messy subject. Overcoming his avoidance of this topic would be as challenging as getting an aerophobic American to get excited about flying to London for a vacation. The concept of honesty sounds good, but first, the fear of being in trouble has to be addressed.

Rayburn's dad acknowledged that his son's dishonesty pushed his buttons. His own father had had multiple extramarital affairs, and he watched his mother's suffering and was aware of the subsequent tremendous financial burden left on her after her husband abandoned the family and she worked to support four children. Rayburn's mom believed that her husband's reaction to their son's impulsivity and lying was extreme, but she wanted to support him. When she defended their son's behaviors by saying, "But he's only six!" her protestations rankled her husband. He was convinced that Rayburn's character flaws needed to be nipped in the bud before he became deceitful like his grandfather.

Like many parents, this dad reacted forcefully, based on his own history. In deploring his father's dishonesty, he flipped 180 degrees to such an extreme position on honesty that he couldn't appreciate the normalcy of Rayburn's initial lying at four years of age. Neither did he understand Rayburn's impulsivity to lie as a way of covering up his many behavioral infractions, or his denial as a reflection of his deep shame about lying. With built-up anxiety about his lying, Rayburn was unable to reach the sweet spot for learning about the importance of telling the truth.

Family-of-origin issues
If you detested some characteristic in your own parents' behavior — dishonesty, permissiveness, cheating, or harsh punishment — beware of the pendulum swinging too far to the other extreme in your own parenting.

A central goal for Rayburn's parents was to first reverse Rayburn's shame about being a bad person and then to develop the skill of truth telling. His dad had done a lot of reflecting about the father he wanted to be after never having experienced a loving father in his own childhood. By understanding a bit more about child development, his own reactivity, and his son's temperament and shame, this dad discovered empathy, which kick-started a fairly rapid improvement in Rayburn's habit.

Deflating shame

To help this family, I explained two techniques I use for establishing a "reset, reboot" in kids' minds about habits they are ashamed of. These habits could include lying, stealing, soiling their pants, masturbation, or thumb-sucking as six- or seven-year-olds.

First, the parents apologize to the child. If you're surprised by this first step, imagine the child's reaction! That's the point. Whether the problem is lying, soiling, or stealing, the apology is for not solving the problem with the child — yet.

If the problem has been handled ineffectively, and unpleasant feelings have become entrenched, an apology can open up a thought in the child's mind that perhaps "I'm not that bad." The apology is surprising, unexpected, and a breath of fresh air. It also allows a clean slate for new problem solving.

Rayburn's father said, "Rayburn, I'm sorry that we have not helped you more with the lying habit. I feel really bad about it. As your dad, I want you to be successful. I've been able to help you with math, basketball, and folding laundry. But I've failed miserably in helping you with your habit of fudging the truth. I apologize. I hope you'll give me another chance." Rayburn did not cover his ears and yell.

The reset, reboot apology

When parents are entrenched in trying to change a child's bad habit, especially one riddled with shame, you can switch the focus from their bad habit to your failed attempts at helping them. If your problem-solving efforts have failed, apologize for that. When parents go in with a sincere and heartfelt apology and convey empathy to their child, it can open up channels for new problem solving.

The second step was for Rayburn's parents to assume a "coaching" approach to building Rayburn's capability to tell the truth. The pre-coaching phase consisted of explaining to Rayburn that they knew lying was automatic for him, so they needed to get his attention in a very compelling way every time he was going to practice telling the truth. They knew how much he wanted to avoid feeling bad when he made a mistake, so they were going to become "cheerleaders for the truth" when he was in this situation.

Dad described his first victory with Rayburn. Rayburn had used his laptop without asking, which his father knew by looking at the computer's history. This was a flagrant violation of their family rules. Rayburn's father practiced his coaching approach with what he described as a basketball coach's exhilarated tone:

Rayburn! OK, buddy, now listen up. I know you can do this. Here's what I'm looking for. I'm about to tell you something that I've learned. Something you did. Something I know you did, from evidence. Now here's what I'm hoping I can hear from you: "Yeah, Dad, I did that." Now, this might be harder than dunking three baskets in a row, but you can try. I know it's hard. Are you ready, Buddy, are you ready?

As you can see, Dad is stalling for time, building Rayburn up, getting him psyched for what's to come. By chatting him up in a positive way, Dad is creating a lure. Rayburn can absorb his dad's approval and excitement, and the positive emotion of this coaching helps to offset Rayburn's fear of being a bad boy. Dad's coaching was undoing shame. And it worked.

Rayburn still got docked some screen time for using Dad's computer, but the parents celebrated his breaking the link between transgressions, shame, and automatic lying. Overcoming maladaptive habits is hard, hard work. Don't you have some experience with this? We all struggle with efforts to clobber bad habits and initiate good ones. To show solidarity with Rayburn, his parents took the TV out of their bedroom so they could get more sleep. They explained to Rayburn that they were working on their temptation to stay up too late at night. Rayburn said, "Hey, we are bad-habit busters. We're a team!"

> **Coaching for good**
> *As natural as it is to react to character flaws in children, it can entrench children in shame and impede headway toward establishing positive opposites (desirable virtues). Try to set up low-stakes situations for your child to demonstrate character strengths such as grit, kindness, or generosity, and take on a coach/cheerleader role. Get excited about your child's capacity to achieve small goals. This conveys optimism, creates a self-fulfilling prophecy of success, and builds a "You can do it!" faith that compels them toward achievement.*

Is being happy more important than being caring?

A recent survey conducted through the Making Caring Common project at the Harvard Graduate School of Education investigated children's perceptions of their parents' values. Most parents think they are conveying the message that caring for others is important, but apparently the message just isn't getting through. Many kids believe that personal happiness and achievement are more important than caring for others.

In a sample of more than 10,000 middle school and high school students from across the country, only 20 percent said that caring for others was an essential value for their parents. This survey result was surprising, because in a previous study of parents, 96 percent said that moral character in children was "very important, if not essential," and that they wanted their children to be "honest, loving, and reliable." Valuing both achievement and caring doesn't have to be an either/or proposition, but students were three times more likely to agree than disagree with the statement: "My parents are prouder if I get good grades in my classes than if I'm a caring community member in class and school." The older the child, the less the student thought his or her parent valued caring over personal happiness and achievement.

With increased global competitiveness, parents are anxious about academic performance, which can translate to grade consciousness (if not obsession) among children. Think about how often we all hear parents say, "I just want my child to be happy." Compare that to how often we hear, "I really want my child to be honest and kind."

How do your comments to your children reflect a value of honesty over academic performance, or kindness over personal happiness? If your child had neglected to read an assigned book, would you let your child watch a video of a book's story the night before the test instead? Or would you let a bad grade be a "natural consequence," so that your child could learn the importance of honesty? Would you stick to your rule that your child should walk the newspaper up the driveway to the elderly neighbor's door, or would you let her get out of it when you couldn't stand her whining about it anymore? It's easy to talk about values, but the real lessons happen when the going gets tough.

BASICS OF RAISING CARING, MORAL CHILDREN

Is your parenting optimal for raising kids that reflect your values? Here are six things to consider.

1. Model caring behaviors toward family and others. We need to demonstrate our values about caring for others by the way we spend our time. Maybe we'll persuade our child to sit with an outcast at lunch. Maybe we'll take food to the homeless shelter. Maybe we'll be late for work because we've taken a lost dog home. Have you ever told your child, "The most important thing to me is that you are kind?" What do you talk about at the dinner table? What are you interested in, and what do your children hear you say that reflects your values? Do they hear you talk about your friends' new acquisitions and achievements, or about the sacrifices they make to take care of their parents or children?

2. Create rituals for gratitude. Remember that old-fashioned ritual of saying "grace" before a meal? You don't have to be religious to establish a routine for gratitude. Not only is it a good practice to commune at mealtime and recount gratitude for the day, it's beneficial to your health. With all the worries that can crop up at the end of the day, it is good to focus our attention on the "glass half full" things we are grateful for and the people we appreciate. Help your children get into the habit of writing little (or big) thank-yous in letters, texts, or e-mails. Establish a bedtime routine of recounting the good things that happened during the day.

3. Practice caring actions. Create opportunities for young children to practice caring for others. Whether it is pet care, helping with younger siblings, or tagging along with you for your own volunteering, actions of caring always count more than verbalized values. Take a new neighbor some cookies. Show your child how you are donating money online to victims of the latest disaster. When the time comes, inconvenience your child with the expectation that he babysit for a needy parent in a crisis when he'd rather not. When you act on your values in particularly inconvenient times, you show your genuine dedication to the ethic of caring.

4. Be a media critic. Children continually absorb messages from the media about the importance of wealth, appearance, being cool, and being accepted. Critique these media messages with your children. Tell them your values, ask them what they think of what they are seeing and hearing, and help them learn values by thinking through ethical dilemmas. What happens when the girl hero sticks up for the outcast and then loses her best friends? How do people feel about obese characters? What messages are being received about dumb blondes and macho men? Watching videos is a time to teach kids about the values you want to see — and not see — in your children. How are they going to know which is which without you riding in the saddle beside them, navigating the Wild, Wild West of media?

5. Praise moral behavior, but don't give rewards. When children are given a reward for moral behavior, you may be encouraging them to act for external reasons rather than from internal motivation. Instead, offer praise, which communicates that qualities such as generosity and kindness are worthwhile for their own sake.

6. Avoid shaming kids for normal and messy negative emotions. Instead, encourage appropriate expression, self-control, and positive opposites. As explained in Chapter 5, negative emotions are valid. But we want to encourage a child's growing verbal, self-regulation, and problem-solving skills. The "gimme" and "me first" aspects of childhood are normal, but parental repugnance and unhelpful lectures can result in more, not less, of these behaviors. Parents may be sincerely committed to character development, but also be clueless about how normal self-interest is. Moreover, parental attention to a child's selfish inclinations doesn't inspire more caring behavior. Better to ignore or issue a very short rebuke than to be dismissive of or scolding for natural emotions. Shaming can lead to complicated feelings of self-loathing and resentment toward parents. It can also delay progress in building cherished virtues.

I describe good character this way: knowing the good, loving the good, and doing the good. In other words, there is moral knowing, moral feeling, and moral action. One of the most enduring themes in the realm of character education is that parents teach moral values more through their actions than their words. In fact, preaching can be less effective than modeling generous, giving behavior while saying nothing at all.

Promoting empathy

At its core, empathy is the ability to share the emotions of others and to imagine what another person feels. Emotional awareness and empathy are the drivers for many of our moral actions, and this has its roots in human development. As we evolved as a social species, we were dependent on each other for survival. It became adaptive for us to detect one another's feelings, and in fact, literally feel each other's pain; it motivated us to take care of one another, so that the group had a greater chance of survival.

The brain regions that process our own experiences of pain are also activated when we observe other people in pain. A study of seven- to twelve-year-olds conducted by Jean Decety, a neurobiologist at the University of Chicago, showed that when the children were presented with images of people getting hurt, their brains registered the experience in their brains as if the pain was being experienced firsthand (Decety 2010). Watching one person deliberately inflict pain on another caused even wider activation of brain regions, reflecting emotional upset and moral reasoning.

But we don't need research to tell us our little ones feel empathy. You've seen your child reach out to soothe a baby, help you with a task, and share her toys. You've also wished for more of the same.

A child's ability to feel and convey empathy is influenced by her attachment history (see Chapter 1). If a parent has tuned into his son's emotional states in the first few years of life, nurtured him in a responsive way, and provided for his needs in a "good enough" way, he will most likely be secure and have the capacity for empathy. Secure children develop a "theory of the mind" and intuit what others are feeling, thereby setting up a precondition for caring behaviors. Here's your son's empathy and logic working well on a good day: "That kid just fell down and cried. When that happens to me, I'm hurt and upset. I bet that kid is, too! I would be glad if someone offered me their nice toy. I think I'll offer him my toy to play with."

Making others feel better when they are hurt makes children feel better, but that doesn't mean they can do it on a regular basis. This can be confusing for parents, who may fear that their child has a deficit when in fact, they may be having just a lapse. But this happens to adults as well. When very moral people like you or me are in a hurry, distracted, or emotionally overwhelmed, we do not tune into the feelings of others as effectively either, and unfortunately, we can miss a chance to be helpful, too.

Got guilt?

Some parents' own childhood histories can complicate matters. Those who were shamed as children may be afraid to express their disappointment in their children's behavior, even though it is an appropriate response to undesirable behaviors.

Guilt is a natural and adaptive response to having done the wrong thing, which helps children self-correct (Kochanska et al. 2009). Parents raise caring children by expressing disappointment and explaining why the behavior is wrong and how it affects others. They can also give their children a chance to repair and rectify the situation — an important part of the lesson. Children need to know how they can achieve a moral identity — in other words, how they can become caring, helpful, and generous people. Allowing kids to feel a little guilt is a good thing, but be careful not to overdo it, or they might miss the sweet spot for learning.

> **A little guilt helps**
> *What's the right amount of guilt for learning standards of behavior? With too much emotion and guilt, children can't process or learn from your feedback. With too little, they won't learn, either. Guilt is a healthy response to missing the mark on standards of good character. When you see your child genuinely reflective and regretful about a behavioral shortfall, you will intuitively know it. Guilt is a natural form of self-discipline.*

The beauty of conveying the right amount of disappointment is that it includes information about disapproval as well as high expectations for improving their behavior: "Since you are a kind child, I know you didn't mean to hurt Grandma's feelings. You can express your thanks for the present later."

Moral misses such as stealing, hitting, lying, cheating, and selfishness raise the ire of parents, as they should. Finding the right balance for learning can be tricky. Because parents can be horrified at those moral misses, they can overreact, and then have to work to undo the shame. Other parents may handle their embarrassment by turning a blind eye and doing nothing. Once entrenched, patterns can worsen, and reversing the tide can be even more difficult.

If your child has a bad habit and you're unsure of how to address it, don't hesitate to seek a consultation. You go to the medical doctor when you have a broken leg, right? Why not visit a child-development specialist when your child has some fracture in character development?

Summary

Good character is cultivated by good parenting, supportive school experiences, positive peers, a nurturing environment, and the practice of virtuous behaviors. Aristotle opined that we are what we repeatedly do, which is one way of emphasizing that actions mean more than words.

Feelings drive behavior. Sometimes children will be generous, empathic, and kind, and we will praise them for being helpful and kind people. Sometimes they will miss the mark and hurt others, emotionally and perhaps physically. We will ask them how they think the injured person feels, and they will ideally identify the emotion accurately. We will both help them rectify the situation and express our faith that they can learn from the experience.

Character strengths are learned by parents' modeling and by giving children the opportunity to practice virtues such as grit, gratitude, and generosity. Big lapses are plentiful, and parents need to help their children learn from mistakes, feel a little bad about it, and then figure out ways to improve. We want neither to treat misbehaviors lightly or overfocus on them; a little guilt is part of self-discipline, but shame can harm irrevocably.

Knowing the norms of child development is important. Before we ever think that a child's behavior is reprehensible, we should check our developmental handbooks, because most the time they are acting their age.

Kids cannot abide hypocrisy. When parents do not practice what they preach, even young children know it and become deaf to lectures and exhortations. On the other hand, when admired parents stumble on their own good intentions and apologize, they are exercising a character strength — humility — which is valuable to children, who stumble on a constant basis. Children trust parents who admit they aren't perfect and share their own mistakes. Modeling self-acceptance and an earnest effort to improve is another great parental habit — but only if it is truly earnest.

Young children naturally put their parents on a pedestal. This placement falters considerably by the tween years, so we should use our powerful influence to our advantage during these impressionable years. Children are ever watchful of their parents' behaviors and are compelled to imitate them. Use this influence wisely!

CHAPTER 7

Physical health:
When you worry about screen excess (and other unhealthy habits)

When pediatricians, psychologists, and child development specialists assess the health of children, they use a wide-angle lens, taking into account everything from screen exposure to gun safety, vaccinations, and sleep hygiene. They also consider the emotional well-being of the whole family, because a child's health is largely influenced by his home environment.

Generally speaking, the factors that influence your child's physical health fall into the following broad categories:

- Exercise
- Nutrition
- Time spent in nature
- Sleep
- Technology management
- Sex education
- Safety precautions
- Stress management
- Religious or spiritual involvement
- Recreational and leisure activities

Technology management, one of the most controversial arenas in modern parenting, affects child development in powerful ways — even from birth. Because of the influence of technology on a parent's life, it inevitably affects the infant's life and mushrooms over time as the child grows to become a consumer himself. In addition, technology affects every other domain on the list above. And because screen use is extremely rewarding for kids, it can be exceptionally difficult to control, making it one of the biggest potential sources of family conflict.

Scene: It's Saturday afternoon and Mrs. Lee walks in on her husband and son watching a baseball game on TV. Mr. Lee has his phone and tablet on the table next to the chips and pop. He has his laptop open, as does Steven, who is seven years old and playing a video game.

Mrs. Lee: Is this what you call quality time? We arranged this afternoon so you could spend special time with your son. And you are both plugged into screens! Why aren't you playing baseball instead of watching it? We're turning into a family of couch potatoes!

Mr. Lee: *Give us a break. This is a playoff game! This is how guys bond.*

Steven: *Yeah, Mom. We're having fun. Leave us alone.*

Mrs. Lee: *(addressing Mr. Lee) Great, now I'm the bad guy! You're undermining our agreement on screen time. We agreed that we are worried Steven could become a screen addict if we're not careful. Plus, we agreed to move more, eat less, and unplug. We need to be aligned!*

Mr. Lee: *This is a special occasion. Look, will you please just let me enjoy my Saturday with my son? Cut me some slack, will you? We were figuring out batting averages and doing some math.*

Steven: *Yeah, Mom. We were having fun until you got here.*

Whose side are you on as you read this story? Perhaps both, to some degree. Or perhaps you identify with Mrs. Lee, because you worry more about screen time than your spouse does. Or maybe you identify with Mr. Lee because you think your spouse overestimates the evils of screens (or you just plain hate nagging).

What is a family battle over screen time doing in a chapter about physical health? Like many parents, the Lees have an overweight son. They appreciate that he is becoming a computer whiz, but they worry about his increasingly sedentary life. He also has tantrums when they set limits on screens. Although the Lees are polarized about how serious Steven's problems are, they do agree that Steven's emotional and physical well-being are negatively impacted by screen time — and by their fighting and eating patterns. Real work lies ahead in agreeing on policies and implementing change.

This type of family dynamic is called "parent polarization," or "parent splitting." It can happen in relation to every topic and child issue in this book, and it can contribute to marital conflict, child misbehavior, emotional problems, and even divorce. Frequently, a parent's biggest frustration isn't with their child's behavior; it's caused by a failure to reach consensus with their spouse.

Unity is essential. It enables parents to work together toward a consistent and effective management approach to issues. We'll get to some effective approaches to resolving parent polarization in a bit; first, let's delve into the hot topic of screens.

THE POWER OF TECHNOLOGY

Screens are everywhere, virtually all of the time. Surveys show that children between the ages of eight and eighteen spend an average of seven and a half hours per day on entertainment media, including TVs, smartphones, and other devices (Kaiser Family Foundation, 2010). And for some kids, many of those hours are spent using multiple screens at the same time. They are plugged into gadgets, dividing their attention to avoid missing out on compelling social or entertainment media. While most kids younger than eight years of age haven't entered the social media world (yet), they are primed for a media-centered life, because they play with screen things from the moment they can hold mommy's cell.

There are benefits of technology, it's true; it connects children to learning tools and keeps them in touch with parents and supportive friends. It's also true that playing electronic games is fun and often harmless. And just as parents in previous eras gratefully plopped a child in front of the TV for a few minutes of peace, today's parents use gadgets to help keep kids happy in the car or the waiting room or anywhere else parents need to get their kids out of their hair.

The problem is that electronic interactive gadgets are the most powerful reward machines of all the playthings in the history of humankind. They stimulate the release of dopamine, the neurochemical associated with pleasure, which is discharged in the brain in anticipation of rewards. Through millennia of evolution, the release of dopamine ensured that we would be motivated to seek out food, warmth, sex, and safety for our survival. These days, it also ensures that we seek out other rewards, such as new goodies, drugs, and yes, media. Dopamine creates a surge of ecstasy and a desire for more — right now!

Electronics and dopamine squirts
There is a reason that you (and your children) struggle to power down cell phones and other media gadgets: They stimulate the release of dopamine, the neurochemical associated with pleasure and rewards.

The enormous appeal of computer games

Games are devised to be perfectly calibrated to a user's desire for rewards, tolerance for failure, and motivation to stay engaged to get more rewards. Based on the user's behavior, the game adjusts rewards, finding the user's "sweet spot" for motivation and delivering rewards at the ideal level of intermittent reinforcement. Users will win enough to stay highly reinforced, fail enough to keep motivation maintained at intense levels, and derive enough status and satisfaction from the game's prize systems to receive exceedingly big amounts of gratification.

The intermittent schedule of reward delivery keeps users yearning and craving for more. As we all know, many adults and children have trouble managing their drive to get doses of this drug (oh, excuse me, neurochemical) through electronic machines. Some adults are every bit as hooked to their e-mail, Twitter and other social media, and cell phones as kids are to their games and gadgets.

Big pot calling the little kettle black
Differences exist among us as to what we find rewarding — TED talks, ESPN news, celebrity gossip, texts, shopping websites, or work — but electronic machines deliver jolts of dopamine when gadgets make our personal favorites available. Why do parents complain so much about their kids' yen for screens when they are not much better?

It is ironic that parents are appalled when their children become manically attached to their electronic rewards. Adults possess greater impulse control and cognitive maturity for decision making, but we get hooked on our personal favorites as much as kids do.

A big problem is that adults fail to understand the power of tech reward systems. If we faced this fact, we'd set up systems to automatically turn the tech off, since our emotional drive for these rewards results in an inability to "just say no," despite our stated family goals and values.

Are you in control?

A 2013 survey funded by the Department of Education sounded a major alarm about the power of screens (Michael Cohen Group 2013). It polled 350 parents about the play habits of their children ages twelve and younger. Sixty percent of the parents reported that their kids' use of screens was their children's primary play activity. Lesser playthings were dolls, puzzles, board games, play vehicles, action figures, arts and crafts, and blocks. Gadgets have nearly made the toy chest of yesterday obsolete.

A family TECH health policy:

Take time to learn it.

Exercise control over it (so it doesn't control you).

Consider filters, tracking, and automatic turn-off settings

Harness the best, limit the rest.

It took thirty years for television sets to become accessible to everyone; in just a fraction of that time, cell phones and tablets are in the majority of households. Where are we headed with this screen trend? The screen invasion into our play culture is expected to continue and intensify. Here are a few important facts to remember:

• Technology enthusiasts emphasize the benefits for children's problem-solving skills, hand-eye coordination, spatial skills, strategic thinking, and executive functioning. Child advocates warn of technology's negative impact on play, face time, family life, and social and emotional competence. Both camps have research that supports their positions.
• When used appropriately and discriminately, technology and interactive media are effective supports for learning in the classroom and home.
• Virtually all experts in the fields of psychology, child development, education, and pediatrics advise parents to scrutinize the content of children's media and impose time limits. Digital tools should not replace play and responsive interactions with teachers, parents, and peers.
• Parents need to understand the technologies and social media their children are exposed to before their children become consumers, so they can monitor, protect, and limit effectively.
• Video games can have both positive and negative effects on children. As with any game that develops skills, the impact depends on the game content, fellow players, and the child's level of preoccupation. One of the biggest downsides to gaming is the time it takes away from other important developmental activities.
• Heavy consumption of TV and media by children is correlated with negative consequences for academic skills, attention, and behavior. But parents

are the mediators for access and exposure, which challenges the notion that the media is inherently the problem.

• Parents should consider the "marketization" of children with every purchase of media products (TVs, online games, videos, "educational" toys, etc.). Ads are targeted at children such that kids will want products that purport to enhance their social standing and increase their status and sense of belonging. Selling to children and encouraging materialism is built into the commercialization process.

• Just as physical fitness, nutrition, and sex education are part of health maintenance, so is media education. At developmentally appropriate levels, children need to be educated about what they consume, how to discern quality, and the dangers and benefits of this powerful dimension of our modern lives.

Most child development experts agree that children between the ages of three and seven should have no more than two hours of screen exposure per day, and less is better. It's not that two and a quarter hours will turn their brains to mush; it's that screen exposure can easily become a slippery slope. One cartoon becomes a Disney movie, and one computer game becomes five more, and ... well, you know. Kids crave this rewarding source of entertainment. They badger their parents for more and more, and throw fits after being unplugged. Parents cave because they want peace.

THE SOLUTION TO TECH TOXICITY

Like any powerful tool, technology can be used to positive or negative effect. The goal for parents is not to dread, demonize, or deny the benefits or dangers of technology; the goal is to be a wise-minded manager of this mighty medium, protecting children's interests while helping them become shrewd consumers. Despite all of the advantages of electronics, don't ever forget that some company made bank the minute you coughed up your credit card.

Beware of tech creep
Technology has advanced the quality of our lives in myriad ways, but it can also behave like a bandit. It can invade your home, steal time that should be spent with loved ones, and replace the pleasure once derived from family interaction with pleasure derived from a machine.

Technology and media literacy for a parent involves knowing how to use it, prohibiting excess use, and preventing it from interfering with life and family values. Authoritative parents who maintain firm boundaries and who care deeply about protecting their relationships with their children are well positioned to negotiate the challenges of tech creep — that insidious process by which technology bleeds into every aspect of our lives.

Guidelines for technology use and media consumption:

• *Limit your child to no more than two hours a day spent in front of all electronic gizmos, including TVs, DVDs, videos, video games (handheld, console, or computer) and computers (outside of homework).*
• *Make deliberate choices regarding TV programs and games. Settings with automatic turnoffs are handy.*
• *Don't use the TV for background noise when you are not watching a program. It can interfere with learning among young children. Consider the beauty of silence and music as alternatives, because they can become lost pleasures in the multiscreen world in which we live.*
• *Watch what your children watch and know their games before you buy them. Don't allow exposure to media without supervision. Younger children often need help understanding what they've seen on TV.*
• *Follow the recommendations on video games' ratings. If children appear aggressive following video gaming or start to avoid other types of play, restrict access.*
• *Don't watch violent shows or TV news when young children are present. They can't distinguish between fact and fiction, and they can become anxious despite your attempts to explain and reassure.*
• *Eat meals at a table without the TV or cell phones turned on. Your children need your eye contact, your interest, and opportunities to learn the art of conversation.*
• *Model moderation regarding technology and media exposure.*
• *Review your policies with child-care helpers, relatives, and the parents of your children's friends.*

Authoritative parents who know technology well enough to be good screeners and limiters are at a huge advantage. The term "digital divide" used to mean the separation between those who have a computer, and those who do not. Now that virtually everyone uses some form of screen, I believe the new digital divide is between kids whose parents limit access and kids whose parents don't.

Moderation is the name of the game. As in the rest of life, our habits define our character. Your child's exposure to media of any kind, especially in bulk, will have an effect on her brain, learning, and values.

Our consumption habits — of food, goods, and media — reflect our values and also our health. If we are truly invested in the good care of ourselves and our children, there simply should not be excessive use of screens.

The last six chapters recommended time allotted for sleep, play, chores, math, reading, nature, exercise, and other activities that promote character, positive emotions, and healthy routines. I've also emphasized making time for down time, so that kids can learn how to entertain themselves without screens, handle boredom, and become creative. I've also described the importance of allotting more time for morning and evening routines, because providing guardrails and positive supervision takes loads of patience with young children, most of whom are distracted and at least somewhat resistant.

Parents also need time for discussions, volunteering, self-care, and socializing. How can we do all this important stuff if everyone in the family is glued to screens? If we walk the walk, not just talk the talk, the math is clear: The hours of media consumption and gadget use must be limited.

The road less traveled

Many people would say that limiting a child's screen exposure is a question of values. It's important to start with that value, but as with exercise, family dinners and regular sleep, it is also a question of your own executive functioning and self-control.

When you make goals and policies, do you follow through? Are you consistent? Do you manage your own screen exposure and execute screen limits with your children? For family tech use to be successfully limited, that prefrontal cortex of yours has to be in good working order to enable you to plan, make goals, remove obstacles, tweak your managerial system, negotiate skillfully with your spouse, and control your emotions.

Lest you think I'm turning into a taskmaster, a preachy shrink, or a Luddite, let me assure you that I'm a typical adult in 21st-century modern America.

I love my screens. I struggle with efforts to balance my life. (Ask my kids! And my husband is even worse!) But we work at it.

Most adults have busy lives and come home tired, stressed, and a bit overwhelmed by the domestic duties of getting their kids fed, homework supervised, and bedtime accomplished. Add to that work e-mail, personal stressors, chores, and other life responsibilities, and it's no wonder almost everyone turns to screens! It's an easy way to veg out. It can curtail quarreling among siblings. Some of us have a weakness for entertainment, others for social media, and still others for after-hours work.

Here's a dirty little secret: Playing with electronic stuff is often more fun than interacting with kids. Playing "Duck Duck Goose" or cooking with messy, impulsive kids can test your patience, but toddlers love messes and wild play with parents. And reading the same book over and over to a toddler isn't that fun either. Pulling the plugs to play with kids truly does become the road less traveled. It takes brute willpower. In fact, it can take as much fortitude as changing up nutrition and exercise habits, depending on your (and your child's) particular reward and vulnerability pattern.

> **The dirty little secret of good parenting**
> *Sometimes it takes extraordinary willpower to do the right thing and shut down screens. We love our kids, but often, playing with them isn't as gratifying as our screens. Shut 'em down anyway.*

CO-PARENTING AS A UNIT

Parenting is a partnership. Like two CEOs running any business, if you and your spouse aren't in agreement on policies and implementation, the business will falter. Not only will the child lack clarity on rules and expectations, but polarized parenting teaches the child which parent is the softie and which one is the hardliner. Inevitably, the child will seek an alliance with the softie against the hardliner.

Let's revisit the Lee family at dinner as they struggle with their other bone of contention: nutrition and food choices. The left column is the conversation, and the right column identifies the problems in the family dynamic.

Content (what is said)	**Process** (the underlying dynamic)
Mr. Lee: Do you really want that cookie when it is so close to supper?	Dad's question would be better presented as a directive to not eat the cookie.
Steven: Yeah, I want more.	Dad did ask about hunger.
Mr. Lee: How can you be hungry when we had so many snacks during the game?	Dad shames his son about a decision he himself made to allow access to snacks.
Mrs. Lee: See what happens when you don't follow the rule on snacks? Why don't you two walk the dog and get some exercise?	Mom takes advantage to impose a penalty: her "I told you so." Her reaction to Dad's passivity is to be the taskmaster.
Steven: Stop bugging me, Mom. I have to finish this game! Sheesh!	Like most kids involved in a game, he is incapable of just turning it off.
Mr. Lee: I'll walk the dog.	Dad wants to avoid a blowup.
Mrs. Lee: (yelling) Why are you always indulging him? He needs to get off his behind!	By rescuing his son and defending him against Mom, Dad has infuriated Mom.
Steven: Mom, you are a grouch.	Kids often protect their protector.

Did you note the number of problems in this conversation? Did you identify with making any of them? Virtually all of us have committed at least a couple of these errors:

- Asking a question that should have been a directive. Instead of "Do you really want that cookie?" Mr. Lee should have said, "Do not eat that cookie. It's too close to dinner time."
- Blaming a child for a behavior that the parent instigated (e.g., supplying junk food, which primes them for wanting more)
- Asking kids to do things that are unlikely to result in compliance. For example, at age seven, it is unrealistic expect a child in the midst of a family

squabble to stop an engaging tech game and start a chore.
• Undermining a co-parent in front of a child about a policy on which the parents have agreed
• Rescuing a child from a chore that he is supposed to do
• Triangulating, or joining with a child in an alliance against a co-parent. In this instance, Mr. Lee comes off as the "good cop" and wants to complete his son's chore to rescue him from the "bad cop," Mom.

Families are emotional systems. We have complex and ambivalent feelings about icky dynamics we share with other family members. We engage in all sorts of dysfunctional behaviors, knowing on some level that they are sloppy and wrong, but trudge along day after day, not knowing quite how to fix them. Spending time in problem-solving meetings with our spouse is the right thing to do, but we avoid them when we dread confronting negative feelings and difficult issues. As with many healthy habits, doing the right thing is really hard. It's easy and natural to avoid things that are difficult and anxiety-provoking.

Addressing parent polarization

The Lees disagree about how to handle food, media, and exercise expectations; your family may engage in disputes about homework, bedtime routines, and sibling aggression. Any issue that generates anxiety and strong emotion can polarize parents. Even when parents start out with similar values, they can be driven apart by conflicts over time. The softie gets softer about the policy because the hardliner appears so rigid; the hardliner gets harder because the softie appears so permissive. The "good cop/bad cop" dynamic of the Lee family is one of the most common patterns among parents.

The period of child rearing when kids are three to seven years old brings parental differences to the surface. With all the challenges and upheaval of this developmental period, almost every couple experiences marital conflict over one policy or another. Distress amplifies whatever tendencies parents have — whether it's avoiding conflict, micromanaging, or expressing extreme emotions — making it more likely that the other parent will react to that exaggerated trait.

Resolving polarization requires that parents recognize their plight, enter into negotiations, and give up a little ground to reach a middle position. When intense feelings about child welfare are at stake, parents may get bogged down and want to persuade one another of a "better" or "right" position. However, unless a mutually agreeable policy can be reached, everyone loses. When parents argue incessantly, the child suffers from the negative emotional climate.

While some parenting policies can clearly cause harm to children, my experience is that many children suffer more from parent polarization than whatever policy is causing it. When parents can't resolve their differences by themselves, it's a good time to consult a parent counselor. In fact, given how important marital health is for the satisfactory functioning of the child and family, couples should consider marital enrichment programs or couples therapy when dynamics start to slide. Empirically supported couples counseling is effective, but not if parents delay and let the problems grow beyond their treatable states (Jakubowski et al. 2004; Johnson and Lebow 2007).

The polarization conundrum

When you and your co-parent disagree on a policy, the disagreement itself is often worse for the child than whatever position the two of you are currently arguing about. Often, your child would be better served if you split your differences and implemented a policy in lockstep unity than she would if you stuck to "your principles," resulting in an impasse rife with resentment on both sides. But strong emotions about parenting do not always allow such an easy solution.

Problem solving 101

Entering into negotiations often isn't easy, especially when you are sure you are right, and you are worrying about the health of your child. All participants in this intimate and long-term job of parenting must expect to sacrifice and be adaptable. Optimally, we reach for enough humility to allow ourselves to incorporate another's ideas as a counterbalance to our own excesses. If you are as frustrated as Steven's parents, you may need to purge some hostility before attempting to negotiate a policy. Before you start discussions, it's advisable to summon your wise-mindedness and ponder the Reason Mind Mantra: *I might be right, but am I effective?* and this one, as well:

The Compromise Mantra
It's more important to get along well than to get what I want.

Problem-solving steps

• *Schedule a relaxed time for a meeting and bring paper or a white board.*
• *Prepare to use your best communication skills, such as listening, validating, and the "sandwich" technique (see page 106). Reread the section on emotional self-control (see Chapter 5).*
• *Pick only one problem to solve and agree on a specific goal.*
• *Generate options. Brainstorm many ideas with a wide range of creative and even silly alternatives to break up the polarization and negative feelings of past arguments.*
• *Evaluate the options without passing judgment. What are the costs and benefits of each option? Try to swap positions and write down the benefits of your spouse's ideas and vice versa.*
• *Make a plan. Start with a small and specific goal, and make sure both you and your spouse feel confident that you can follow through on implementation.*
• *Write down the details of the agreement.*
• *Identify potential obstacles to success and make a plan to overcome them.*
• *Plan another meeting to evaluate the implementation.*
• *Expect to adjust the plan.*
• *Praise yourselves for collaborating, giving up ground, and being open and flexible for the good of your child.*

Sometimes it is beneficial to do a little homework on recommended policies or health habits for kids before the meeting. You can seek information from books, reputable online sources, and valued consultants. Agree on this process with your spouse, because if you cite your friends or play the expert, this step can backfire. Imagine the most admirable and respected people you know watching a video of your interaction; this can help you stay mindful of using your most skillful and polite skills while negotiating your parenting policies. Treat your spouse as if he or she was your most important client.

The YouTube trick

A good way of staying mindful and respectful with your communication is to imagine that you are being videotaped for a YouTube segment or reality show that will be aired to a million viewers, including every person you admire.

EATING AND PHYSICAL ACTIVITY

Picky eating, sneaky eating, and eating junk food are contentious issues for many families; when your pediatrician tells you your child is overweight or obese, your concern mushrooms. You wonder whether your child will suffer a miserable childhood as an outcast with low self-esteem, or even a terrible adulthood and an early death — all your fault, of course. Scare tactics that call for overhauling daily habits of eating and exercising can drive the sanest of parents to pull their hair out. Better to start with a humble goal of taking small steps in the right direction.

Childhood obesity has more than doubled in the last thirty years. In 2012, more than one-third of children and adolescents in the U.S. were overweight or obese, and the weight problems were likely to have started before kindergarten (Cunningham et al. 2014). The list of long-term consequences is formidable, including conditions ranging from cardiovascular problems to diabetes to cancer. The formula for the solution is simple (less caloric intake and more physical activity), but the implementation is complex (organizing one's family routines to prioritize the planning of healthy meals, regulating access to junk food, and ensuring lots of exercise).

Get them moving

By the age of five, children should be engaged in one hour of physical activity a day, according to the American Academy of Pediatrics. Following through on this recommendation can be good news for parents who need — and want — more activity themselves. If logic ruled the day, family members would just cut down on screens and get on their bikes, walk the dog, run in the park, or go to the gym. But because emotions, demands of our complicated lives, and fatigue generally rule, most of us are not getting anywhere near that recommended sixty minutes of aerobic activity per day.

Everyone knows that exercise is good for children and adults. The relationship between improved learning and exercise has been well documented, even for children who are overweight. Recently, researchers have also been able to show that vigorous physical play activities for children ages eight–nine made a remarkable difference in their executive functioning, which encompasses the ability to make and complete plans (Castelli et al. 2011).

This nine-month study compared a group of students with an average age of nine that participated in a routine of playing physical games for at least sixty minutes a day to a group of same-age students similar in fitness who did not. The children wore pedometers and were tested with elaborate instruments that measured their ability to pay attention, avoid distractions, and toggle back and forth between cognitive tasks. As expected, the children in the exercise group were more physically fit than the comparison group. But the big finding was that the children who had the best attendance at these play sessions had the best cognitive scores. The study proved that what's good for kids is essentially what children have done for generations: They play outside every day, like whirling dervishes, until Mom calls them to dinner.

School districts are cutting back on physical education, either for budgetary reasons, or to make room for other curricula. It's up to parents to figure out ways to get their kids moving, whether it's on the home front or lobbying for physical education classes at school (ideally both). During the preschool years, parents should make sure that recreation involves physical activity, not just games on the couch. Setting up routines for physical activity will help.

Becoming overwhelmed by big goals can paralyze people and stop them from doing anything. It's important to start with an achievable goal, get people to join you (e.g., your friend or spouse and another kid), and make it enjoyable. If screens are your child's favorite thing in the world, make access contingent on the bike ride first (or whatever she is willing to do). It's worth scouting for an activity that your child likes. Sometimes parents become exhausted in this pursuit, but with persistence they discover something that captures the family's fancy. Maybe it will be tandem bikes, geocaching, Frisbee, or kickball.

Healthy eating as a priority

Parents of obese children need to consult their physician so that they make changes that are not detrimental to their children's health. Because I've treated so many adolescents with eating disorders, I'm very aware that intense emotions swirl around the child who eats too much, too little, or the "wrong" kind of food.

It's easy for parents to get caught up in their reason mind, and talk, talk and talk about healthy eating, which may very well result in overweight children actually eating more, because they are so ashamed of their hankering for certain high-calorie or processed foods. Parents often get hooked by their emotion minds and react with distress, hostility, or judgment when they see their children pile on seconds, pick at their food, criticize food, or refuse to eat. These reactions are ineffective at best; at worst, they can be harmful. Children's eating habits can easily push parental buttons, so it is good to reach for some wise-minded approaches.

Ellyn Satter, a highly regarded researcher and nutritionist, has written both scientific articles and books for parents about nutrition. She created a model she calls the "division of responsibility," which describes the roles that parent and child should assume in eating (Satter 2007). According to Satter, it is the parent's job to decide what, when, and where to serve the child. It is the child's job to decide how much and even whether to consume that food. Voilà! Food war over. There are very few malnourished middle-class children in the United States, and those few will see their doctors for true eating disorders or physical maladies.

Satter recommends these following guidelines, which are also endorsed by the American Academy of Pediatrics.

It is the parent's job to:

• choose and prepare food;
• provide regular meals and snacks;
• make meals pleasant;
• model how to eat and behave at the table;
• be patient with children's process of eating without catering or preparing à la carte meals;
• accept that children will develop the body type that is right for them, if you fulfill your responsibilities.

It is the child's job to:

• decide how much — if any — of the food presented to them they will eat.

As Satter's research and decades of clinical expertise demonstrate, these guidelines will, over time, result in children eating the amount they need and behaving well at mealtime. I heartily suggest you consult her website and books if you have difficulty with feeding your child (see Resources).

Stop talking about food
When it comes to healthy eating, as in so many arenas of child rearing, parents can easily get into the habit of talking too much. They can also get into arguments, power struggles, and endless negotiating. Bottom line: Stop talking, put healthy food on the table, and leave it at that. Enjoy the meal!

SAFETY AND RISK

I'm a big advocate of the safety recommendations promoted by the American Academy of Pediatrics. Its evidence-based information gives you guidance, so that you don't have to suffer the anguish of wondering what's healthy for kids. Let this venerable institution do the literature review for you! (See Resources).

Since the health of a child largely depends on the behavioral choices that her parents make, pediatricians and behavioral consultants like me have a long history of working together. We know that it's not just parental choices that make the difference in child health, it's also the health of the family system — the quality of the fish tank in which the little fish swims.

Research has shown that childhood events and the quality of relationships (or lack thereof) literally get under your skin (Anda et al. 2006). Toxic interactions during childhood harm a child's immunological system and can influence health outcomes for the rest of her life. For instance, the stress of marital conflict or fractious divorces leaves its mark psychologically and physically. Conversely, a loving, stable home environment provides essential nutrients within that family fish tank that contribute positively to security and long-term health.

Whether you're wondering about guns, dangerous toys, or bicycle safety, it's good to discuss policies with your co-parent before problems surface in your home, or at the home of your child's playmate. You can find excellent guidelines on the American Academy of Pediatrics' website (see Resources). To put those policies into action requires skill, so let's focus now on the process of implementation. We'll begin with the common example of driving with screaming or misbehaving kids.

Handling car travel

The confined space of a car can be the scene of considerable havoc. Parents can issue directives to kids to stop hitting, yelling, or throwing, but even toddlers know that you have less power in the car. See if you identify with the following:

Mom: Peter, stop screaming! Stop trying to undo your seatbelt!

Peter: (screaming) Lorraine won't stop punching me!

Lorraine: (screaming) I'm patting him. I'm not punching!

Mom: If you two don't stop this minute, I'm going to put you both to bed an hour early tonight!

Peter: (in an ear-piercing scream) But it's Lorraine's fault!

Mom: I can't drive safely when you're screaming. You must stop this minute! We could have a serious accident. Is that what you want? I've had it with you two! You're losing your screen time!

Presumably, by now you know that threats about later punishments don't work, because young children live in the "now." Plus, threats can be like red capes in front of a bull — they accentuate anger, because kids feel misunderstood and abandoned by their loving parents. Even validating statements can amplify anger, because you aren't fixing the problem they are screaming about. The counting method and distraction aren't as effective as usual because, well, you're driving a car, and lack the freedom and flexibility needed to manage a time-out, or redirect your child's energies into other activities. To make matters worse, kids often enjoy driving parents a little crazy by causing a rumpus in a car, not realizing that it could result in the car going off the road.

Kids like power. Toddlers and young children often lack it. They're controlled by powerful others all day (especially you). When a child screams or punches a sibling, they watch the reactions they get. Attention springs eternal from obnoxious behaviors. Parents tell their children that screaming in the car is dangerous, but kids don't have the cognitive wherewithal to understand that logic, especially in the midst of battle. Thus, talking about it may just fuel their appetites for power. Remember: All attention can be reinforcing.

Why kids go crazy in the car
Kids seek power. In its innocent form, kids are experimenting with cause and effect, and learning about their capacities. But in its messy other version, they delight in pushing buttons, especially when they have more power than usual. Car seats may restrain their torsos, but not their mouths and hands.

There is an (almost) foolproof method for ending a car rumpus. It only takes one or two times to teach children not to scream in the car. It's a little awkward and dramatic, but it works. It's logical and doesn't punish. It's responsible. And it takes very few words. Like many effective interventions with young children, it's more about action than words. And since kids are surprised by the action you're taking, you get their full attention, so they can learn to stop the rumpus.

The car fire drill

If you have a fiery emotional climate in the car, it's not safe to drive. You need a fire drill. Since the only person you can control is yourself, and since trying to control fiery emotions usually sparks a powder keg of more negative emotions, you should be the one to take a time-out. It's best to tell your children about the "fire drill policy" in advance — perhaps in a meeting at home — so that when you first employ it, they won't be unduly upset by your actions. The key to success is to accept that children have upsets in cars and to avoid becoming either "power coercive" with threats and punishments or verbose with explanations about safety that kids can't comprehend — especially when they are distraught.

Here is what you can say as you implement a car fire drill:

1. "When you scream or fight, I can't drive safely."
2. "I will ask you to stop, and if you can't within the count of three, I will inform you that we need a car fire drill."
3. "I will pull over at the soonest safe opportunity."
4. "I will get out of the car and close my door."
5. "I will sing, pray, or enjoy a mindfulness exercise for one minute while leaning against the door."
6. "If you are screaming while I'm leaning on the door, I will restart my self-soothing minute, beginning from the time you stop screaming."
7. "After my time-out is finished, I will resume driving."

8. "We will not talk about the screaming" (so that we don't stir up another fire).
9. "I will be as calm and kind as I can manage during this fire drill."
10. "I accept you completely for having these emotionally fiery moments in the car. It is my responsibility to conduct a fire drill to ensure driving safety."

Why is this method effective? Because you get their attention better with action than with words. They don't want their parent to pull over; it's weird to have your parent leaning against the car door for even a minute. But because the parent is not mean and rejecting — and in fact, he's even accepting of how normal it is for kids to have negative emotions and assertions of power — the children are not harmed by this intervention. Since the parent doesn't yell, threaten, or punish, one could argue that using the car fire drill results in less anger directed at the child.

Even three-year-olds can learn not to scream. Explanations or sharp rebukes don't work if kids are really upset. (Would they work on you?) This method works because it's surprising and it directs children's attention to the car safety precaution the parent is maneuvering: pulling over (even if it means exiting a highway).

I taught the car fire drill method to a mom who had two scrappy (now very successful adult) siblings who drove her nuts when she was driving. She called her problem "war on wheels." After mastering her car fire drills, she gave me a gift: a toy magic wand with reflecting streamers and a button that starts up pleasant little whistles, a spinning top, and light sparkles. This mom is a nurse who works at a pediatric hospital. You can imagine how distressed babies are when they wake up after surgery in the hospital setting. They are usually screaming, and can't be easily soothed by loving touches and cooing. But sometimes a magic wand can help. When the nurse pushes the button on the wand, the babies are so surprised by the wonderment of the multisensory display of fun sounds and colored sparkles that they are stunned into quieting so they can take it all in. The emotional centers of their brains "attend" and subsequently, they can respond to the soothing of the human touch and voice. Surprise can be an asset when it doesn't hurt, but rather alerts children to attend to something unique.

Why did I say that the car fire drill method was almost always effective? Because it won't be, if parents become embroiled in conflict with their children and argue about the truth (reason mind), or fly off the handle (emotion mind). Wanting to lecture about the truth of safety and yell when extremely upset is normal, but it is not effective.

Some parents have a really hard time not being mad at their kids — even young ones who can't control their emotions on demand. Having kids screaming and fighting in a car is extremely stressful. When we flood (physiological arousal and a heart rate of more than 100 beats a minute), we become confused. In this state, our black-and-white thinking makes us feel victimized by our shouting, uncooperative kids. Thus, we can end up treating our children like the enemy (e.g., "You are going to make me have a wreck!" "You need to get yourself under control!").

It is not fair to expect kids to understand or act differently than their little messy selves in these moments. Therefore, if parents express their anger or go negative with their kids while using this method, it won't work. They will freak out that Mom or Dad is punishing them with the car fire drill.

Parents should never drive under the influence of fiery emotions — theirs or their child's. Stopping and calming just makes good sense!

Summary

One of the new frontiers of understanding in health science relates to something Leonardo da Vinci said centuries ago: "Realize that everything connects to everything else." Every chapter in this book is intertwined. There is no health without mental and emotional health. And children's physical health is influenced not only by the bodies they were born with, but by the interaction and confluence of all the predictors of health represented in our last six chapters: secure attachment, efforts to build self-control, doing well at school, emotional and social competence, and character-building routines. Recent studies confirm that children absorb the stress of their environments, just as their bodies can absorb toxic chemicals. A certain amount of stress can activate and energize, just as exposure to certain pathogens can strengthen antibody and immune responses. But like an overload of toxins, excessive stress overwhelms and diminishes learning, performance, and every other aspect of physical and mental health.

Children flourish with parents who demonstrate particular parenting strengths, but they are also naturally quite resilient. One advantage of the decades I've spent treating so many families is that I get to observe how a lot of kids — in a lot of different family situations — turn out. Even with a messy divorce, some excess of punitive style, or a touch of indulgence, the majority of kids become well-adjusted adults. Secure attachment and steadfast love and support are the central determining factors in raising healthy kids. Banish perfectionistic expectations of yourself and embrace the fact that you only have to be good enough.

As much as the "good enough" rule should reassure us as we go about our messy lives, most of us have hunches that our lives and our kids' lives can be a bit better with some adjustments in our parenting. Don't we all need some improvement? With the various quirks of our temperaments, undesirable habits inherited from our families of origin, and co-parent combustion, most of us have plenty of material to inspire some "growth opportunities."

We protect children from influences that we know can be harmful, but we also want to expose them to challenges, so that they can become hearty and capable. A certain amount of free-range parenting allows kids to learn from mistakes, develop competencies, and cultivate their creative potential.

Parents can become so mired in conflicting opinions that they coast even while suffering through child-rearing problems. The key is to access your wise mind by first getting to calm and quieting your emotion mind. Then, quiet the judgmental chatter of your reason mind. Only then can you reflect on realistic goals and problem solving with your wise mind.

Understand that doing nothing can be a fine option; if the time doesn't feel right to change your parenting approach right now, take a break to reflect and relax. Trust your intuition. The true power for enacting change lies in accepting yourself and your child — exactly as the two of you are. This glorious, messy, frightening, and intensely rewarding job of parenting isn't for the faint of heart, it's true, but it helps to remember the wise words of Dr. Benjamin Spock: "Trust yourself. You know more than you think you do."

Notes

Chapter 1

Cassidy, J., and P. Shaver, eds. *Handbook of Attachment: Theory, Research, and Clinical Applications.* Guilford Press, 1999.

Compton, S. N., J. S. March et al. "Cognitive-Behavioral Psychotherapy for Anxiety and Depressive Disorders in Children and Adolescents: An Evidence-Based Medicine Review." *Journal of the American Academy of Child and Adolescent Psychiatry* 43 (2004): 930–959.

Hawkins, J. D. et al. "Effects of Social Development Interventions in Childhood 15 Years Later." *Archives of Pediatrics & Adolescent Medicine* 162 (2008): 1133–1141.

Hebb, D. *The Organization of Behavior: A Neuropsychological Theory.* Wiley & Sons, 1949.

In-Albon, T., and S. Schneider. "Psychotherapy of Childhood Anxiety Disorders: A Meta-Analysis." *Psychotherapy and Psychosomatics* 76 (2007): 15–24.

Kabat-Zinn, M., and J. Kabat-Zinn. *Everyday Blessings: The Inner Work of Mindful Parenting.* Hyperion, 1998.

Kaminski, J. W., L. A. Valle, J. H. Filene, and C. L. Boyle. "A Meta-Analytic Review of Components Associated with Parent Training Program Effectiveness." *Journal of Abnormal Child Psychology.* (2008): 567–589.

Kazdin, A. *Parent Management Training: Treatment for Oppositional, Aggressive, and Antisocial Behavior in Children and Adolescents.* Oxford University Press, 2005.

Kazdin, A., and C. Benjet. "Spanking Children: Evidence and Issues." *Current Directions in Psychological Science* 12 (2003): 99–103.

Kiesner, J., T. J. Dishion, and F. Poulin. "A Reinforcement Model of Conduct Problems in Children and Adolescents: Advances in Theory and Intervention." *Conduct Disorders in Childhood and Adolescence*, edited by Jonathan Hill and Barbara Maughan. Cambridge Press, 2004.

Kumpfer, K. L., and R. Alvarado. "Family-Strengthening Approaches for the Prevention of Youth Problem Behaviors." *American Psychologist* 58 (2003): 457–465.

Linehan, M. M. *Dialectical Behavior Therapy, Skills Training Manual.* Guilford Publications, 2015.

McMahon, R. J., and R. L. Forehand. *Helping the Noncompliant Child: Family-Based Treatment for Oppositional Behavior.* Guilford Press, 2003.

Moon, R. *Sleep: What Every Parent Needs to Know.* American Academy of Pediatrics, 2015.

Price, A. M. H., M. Wake et al. "Five-Year Follow-Up of Harms and Benefits of Behavioral Infant Sleep Intervention: Randomized Trial." *Pediatrics* 13 (2012): 643–651.

Sanders, M. R., K. M. T. Turner, and C. Markie-Dadds. "The Development and Dissemination of the Triple P—Positive Parenting Program: A Multilevel, Evidence-Based System of Parenting and Family Support." *Prevention Science* 3 (2002): 173–189.

Schore, A. N. "The Effects of a Secure Attachment on Right Brain Development, Affect Regulation, and Infant Mental Health." *Infant Mental Health Journal* 22 (2001): 7–66.

Velting, O., N. Setzer, and A. M. Albano. "Update on and Advances in Assessment and Cognitive-Behavioral Treatment of Anxiety Disorders in Children and Adolescents." *Professional Psychology: Research and Practice* 35 (2004): 42–54.

Webster-Stratton, C., M. J. Reid, and M. Stoolmiller. "Preventing Conduct Problems and Improving School Readiness: An Evaluation of the Incredible Years Teacher and Child Training Program in High Risk Schools." *Journal of Child Psychology and Psychiatry* 49 (2008): 471–488.

Winnicott, D. W. "The Theory of the Parent-Infant Relationship." *The International Journal of Psychoanalysis* 41 (1960): 585–595.

Chapter 2

Baumeister, R. and J. Tierney. *Willpower: Rediscovering the Greatest Human Strength*. Penguin, 2012.

Brackett, M. A., S. E. Rivers, and P. Salovey. "Emotional Intelligence: Implications for Personal, Social, Academic, and Workplace Success." *Social and Personality Psychology Compass* 5 (2011): 88–103.

Bradley, S., D. Jadaa et al. "Brief Psychoeducational Parenting Program: An Evaluation and One-Year Follow-Up." *Journal of the American Academy of Child and Adolescent Psychiatry* 42(2003): 1171–1178.

Duckworth, A. L., C. Peterson et al. "Grit: Perseverance and Passion for Long-Term Goals." *Journal of Personality and Social Psychology* 92 (2007): 1087–1101.

Larzelere, R. E., A. S. Morris, and A. W. Harris, eds. *Authoritative Parenting: Synthesizing Nurturance and Discipline for Optimal Child Development*. American Psychological Association Books, 2013.

Mischel, W., and O. Ayduck. "Willpower in a Cognitive-Affective Processing System: The Dynamics of Delay of Gratification." *Handbook of Self-Regulation: Research, Theory and Applications*, edited by R. F. Baumeister and K. D. Vohs. Guildford, 2004.

Mischel, W., Y. Shoda, and M. L. Rodriguez. "Delay of Gratification in Children." *Science*. 244 (1989): 933–938.

Moffitt, T. E., L. Arseneault et al. "A Gradient of Childhood Self-Control Predicts Health, Wealth, and Public Safety." *Proceedings of the National Academy of Sciences* 108 (2011): 2693–2698.

Rothbart, M. K., S. A. Ahadi, and D. E. Evans. "Temperament and Personality: Origins and Outcomes." *Journal of Personality and Social Psychology* 78 (2000): 122–135.

Shoda, Y., W. Mischel, and P. K. Peake. "Predicting Adolescent Cognitive and Self-Regulatory Competencies from Preschool Delay of Gratification: Identifying Diagnostic Conditions." *Developmental Psychology* 26 (1990): 978–986.

Chapter 3

Brummelmann, E., S. Thomaes et al. "On Feeding Those Hungry for Praise: Person Praise Backfires in Children with Low Self-Esteem." *Journal of Experimental Psychology: General* 143 (2014): 9–14.

Diamond, A. "The Evidence Base for Improving School Outcomes by Addressing the Whole Child and by Addressing Skills and Attitudes, Not Just Content." *Early Education and Development* 21(2010): 780–793.

Duncan, G., C. Dowsett et al. "School Readiness and Later Achievement." *Developmental Psychology* 43 (2007): 1428–1446.

Dweck, C. *Mindset: The New Psychology of Success*. Ballantine Books, 2007.

Halpern, D. R., L. Eliot et al. "The Pseudoscience of Single-Sex Schooling." *Science* 23 (2011): 1706–1707.

Hart, B., and T. R. Risley. *Meaningful Differences in the Everyday Experience of Young American Children.* Paul H. Brookes Publishers, 1995.

Kastner, L. S., and J. Wyatt. *The Launching Years: Parenting Strategies from Senior Year to College Life.* Three Rivers Press, 2002.

Kelley, S., C. Brownell, and S. Campbell. "Mastery Motivation and Self-Evaluative Affect in Toddlers: Longitudinal Relations with Maternal Behavior." *Child Development* 71 (2000): 1061–1071.

Lepper, M., and J. Henderlong. "Turning 'Play' into 'Work' and 'Work' into 'Play': 25 years of Research on Intrinsic Versus Extrinsic Motivation." *Intrinsic and Extrinsic Motivation: The Search for Optimal Motivation and Performance*, edited by C. Sansone and J. M. Harackiewicz. Academic Press, 2000.

Luthar, S. S. "The Culture of Affluence." *Child Development* 74 (2003): 1581–1593.

Pashler, H., M. McDaniel, D. Rohrer, and R. Bjork. "Learning Styles: Concepts and Evidence." *Psychological Science in the Public Interest* 9 (2008): 105–119.

Ramirez-Esparza, N., A. Garcia-Sierra, and P. Kuhl. "Look Who's Talking: Speech Style and Social Context in Language Input to Infants Are Linked to Concurrent and Future Speech Development." *Developmental Science* 17 (2014): 880–891.

Roseberry, S., K. Hirsh-Pasek, and R. M. Golinkoff. "Skype Me! Socially Contingent Interactions Help Toddlers Learn Language." *Child Development* 85 (2014): 956–970.

Scholastic. scholastic.com/readingreport/key-findings.htm

Tominey, S., and McClelland, M. "Red Light, Purple Light: Findings from a Randomized Trial Using Circle Time Games to Improve Behavioral Self-Regulation in Preschool." *Early Education and Development* 22 (2011): 489–519.

Zins, J. E., M. B. Bloodworth, R. P. Weissberg, and H. J. Walberg. "The Scientific Base Linking Social and Emotional Learning to School Success." *Journal of Educational and Psychological Consultation* 17 (2007): 191–210.

Chapter 4

Crain, W. *Reclaiming Childhood: Letting Children Be Children in Our Achievement-Oriented Society.* Holt Paperbacks, 2004.

Guldberg, H. *Reclaiming Childhood: Freedom and Play in an Age of Fear.* Routledge, 2009.

Kessler, R. C. et al. "Lifetime Prevalence and Age-of-Onset Distributions of DSM-IV Disorders in the National Comorbidity Survey Replication." *Archives of General Psychiatry* 62, no. 6 (2005): 593–602.

Mancillas, A. "Challenging the Stereotypes About Only Children: A Review of the Literature and Implications for Practice." *Journal of Counseling and Development* 84, no. 3 (2006): 268–275.

Sanson, A., S. A. Hemphill, and D. Smart. "Connections between Temperament and Social Development: A Review." *Social Development* 13, no. 1 (2004): 142–170.

Taylor, M. S. et al. "The Characteristics and Correlates of Fantasy in School-Age Children: Imaginary Companions, Impersonation, and Social Understanding." *Developmental Psychology* 40, no. 6 (2004): 1173–1187.

Taylor, A. F., and F. E. Kuo. "Children with Attention Deficits Concentrate Better After Walk in the Park." *Journal of Attention Disorders* 12, no. 5 (2009): 402–409.

Wells, N. M. "At Home with Nature: Effects of 'Greenness' on Children's Cognitive Functioning." *Environment and Behavior* 32 (2000): 775–795.

Chapter 5

R. F. Anda et al. "The Enduring Effects of Abuse and Related Adverse Experiences in Childhood: A Convergence of Evidence from Neurobiology and Epidemiology." *European Archives of Psychiatry and Clinical Neuroscience* 256, no. 3 (2006): 174–186.

Belsky, J., M. J. Bakermans-Kranenburg, and M. H. van IJzendoorn. "For Better and for Worse: Differential Susceptibility to Environmental Influences." *Current Directions in Psychological Science* 16, no. 6 (2007): 300–304.

Crnic, K. A., C. Gaze, and C. Hoffman. "Cumulative Parenting Stress Across the Preschool Period: Relations to Maternal Parenting and Child Behavior at Age 5." *Infant and Child Development* 14, no. 2, (2005): 117–132.

Durlak, J. A., C. E. Domitrovich, R. P. Weissberg, and Thomas P. Gullotta, eds. *Handbook of Social and Emotional Learning: Research and Practice*. Guilford Publications, 2015.

Eisenberg, N., A. Cumberland, and T. L. Spinrad. "Parental Socialization of Emotion." *Psychological Inquiry: An International Journal for the Advancement of Psychological Theory* 9, no. 4 (1998): 241–273.

Gottman, J. M., L. F. Katz, and C. Hooven. "Parental Meta-Emotion Philosophy and the Emotional Life of Families: Theoretical Models and Preliminary Data." *Journal of Family Psychology* 10, no. 3 (1996): 243–268.

Hertzman, C., and T. Boyce. "How Experience Gets Under the Skin to Create Gradients in Developmental Health." *Annual Review of Public Health* 31 (2010): 329–347.

Kennedy, E. "Orchids and Dandelions: How Some Children Are More Susceptible to Environmental Influences for Better or Worse and the Implications for Child Development" *Clinical Child Psychology and Psychiatry* 18, no. 3 (2013): 319–321.

Morris, A. S. et al. "The Role of Family Context in the Development of Emotion Regulation." *Social Development* 16, no. 2 (2007): 361–388.

Prince, M. et al. "No Health without Mental Health." *The Lancet* 370, no. 9590 (2007): 859–877.

Siegel, D. J. "Toward an Interpersonal Neurobiology of the Developing Mind: Attachment Relationships, 'Mindsight,' and Neural Integration." *Infant Mental Health Journal* 22, nos. 1-2 (2001): 67–94.

Siegel, D. J. and T. P. Bryson. *The Whole-Brain Child: 12 Revolutionary Strategies to Nurture Your Child's Developing Mind*. Delacorte Books, 2011.

Zins, J. E., M. R. Bloodworth, R. P. Weissberg, and H. J. Walberg. "The Scientific Base Linking Social and Emotional Learning to School Success." *Journal of Educational and Psychological Consultation* 17, nos. 1-2 (2007): 191–210.

Chapter 6

Afifi, T. O. et al. "Physical Punishment and Mental Disorders: Results from a National Representative U.S. Sample" *Pediatrics* 130, no.2 (2012): 1–9.

American Academy of Pediatrics. www.healthychildren.org/English/family-life/family-dynamics/communication-discipline/Pages/Where-We-Stand-Spanking.aspx

Decety, J. "The Neurodevelopment of Empathy in Humans." *Developmental Neuroscience* 32, no. 4 (2010): 257–267

Gershoff, E. T. "Spanking and Child Development: We Know Enough Now to Stop Hitting Our Children." *Child Development Perspectives* 7, no. 3 (2013): 133-137.

Kazdin, A. and C. Benjet. "Spanking Children: Evidence and Issues." *Current Directions in Psychological Science* 12, no. 3 (2003): 99–103.

Kochanska, G. et al. "Guilt and Effort Control: Two Mechanisms that Prevent Disruptive Developmental Trajectories." *Journal of Personality and Social Psychology* 97, no. 2 (2009): 322–333.

Making Caring Common Project. http://sites.gse.harvard.edu/making-caring-common/resources-publications/research-report

Morawska, A., and M. Sanders. "Parental Use of Time Out Revisited: A Useful or Harmful Parenting Strategy." *Journal of Family Studies* 20, no. 1 (2011): 1–8.

Owen, D. J., A. M. S. Slep, and R. E. Heyman. "The Effect of Praise, Positive Nonverbal Response, Reprimand, and Negative Nonverbal Response on Child Compliance: A Systematic Review." *Clinical Child and Family Psychology Review* 15, no. 4 (2012): 364–385.

Peterson, C., and M. E. P. Seligman. *Character Strengths and Virtues: A Handbook and Classification.* Oxford University Press, 2004.

Straus, M. A., and C. J. Field. "Psychological Aggression by American Parents: National Data on Prevalence, Chronicity, and Severity." *Journal of Marriage and Family* 65, no. 4 (2003): 795–808.

Talwar, V., and K. Lee. "Development of Lying to Conceal a Transgression: Children's Control of Expressive Behavior During Verbal Deception." *International Journal of Behavioral Development* 26, no. 5 (2002): 436–444.

Chapter 7

Anda, R. F. et al. "The Enduring Effects of Abuse and Related Adverse Experiences In Childhood." *European Archives of Psychiatry and Clinical Neuroscience* 256 (2006): 174–186.

Castelli, D. M. et al. "FIT Kids: Time in Target Heart Zone and Cognitive Performance." *Preventive Medicine* 52, supplement, (2011): S55–S59.

Cunningham, S. A. et al. "Incidence of Childhood Obesity in the United States." *The New England Journal of Medicine* 370, no. 5 (2014): 403-411.

Jakubowski, S. F. et al. "A Review of Empirically Supported Marital Enrichment Programs." *Family Relations* 53, no. 5 (2004): 528–536.

Johnson, S., and J. Lebow. "The 'Coming of Age' of Couple Therapy: A Decade Review." *Journal of Marital and Family Therapy* 26, no. 1 (2007): 23–28.

Kaiser Family Foundation. http://kff.org/other/event/generation-m2-media-in-the-lives-of

Michael Cohen Group LLC. "Survey on Ownership and Usage of Touch Screen Devices among Parents of Young Children." Prepared for the U.S. Department of Education Ready to Learn Program, June 2013.

Satter, E. "Eating Competence: Definition and Evidence for the Satter Eating Competence Model." *Journal of Nutrition Education and Behavior* 39, no. 5, supplement (2007): S142–S153.

Resources

Emotional connecting, emotional intelligence, and mindful parenting

Gottman, J. M., L. F. Katz, and C. Hooven. *Meta-Emotion: How Families Communicate Emotionally.* Lawrence Erlbaum Associates, 1997.

Gottman, J. M. and J. Declaire. *Raising an Emotionally Intelligent Child: The Heart of Parenting.* Simon and Schuster, 1998.

Kabat-Zinn, M. and J. Kabat-Zinn. *Everyday Blessings: The Inner Work of Mindful Parenting.* Hyperion, 2014.

Salzman, A. *A Still Quiet Place: A Mindfulness Program for Teaching Children and Adolescents to Ease Stress and Difficult Emotions.* New Harbinger Publications, 2014.

Siegel, D. and M. Hartzell. *Parenting from the Inside Out: How a Deeper Self-Understanding Can Help You Raise Children Who Thrive.* Tarcher, 2013.

Siegel, D. and T. Payne Bryson. *The Whole-Brain Child: 12 Revolutionary Strategies to Nurture Your Child's Developing Mind.* Bantam, 2012.

Siegel, D. and T. Payne Bryson. *No-Drama Discipline: The Whole-Brain Way to Calm the Chaos and Nurture Your Child's Developing Mind.* Bantam, 2014.

Anxiety and anger management

Cohen, L. J. *The Opposite of Worry: The Playful Parenting Approach to Childhood Anxieties and Fears.* Ballantine Books, 2013.

Greene, R. W. *The Explosive Child: A New Approach for Understanding and Parenting Easily Frustrated, Chronically Inflexible Children.* Harper Paperbacks, 2014.

Harvey, P. and J. A. Penzo. *Parenting a Child Who Has Intense Emotions. Dialectical Behavior Therapy Skills to Help Your Child Regulate Emotional Outbursts and Aggressive Behaviors.* Harbinger Press, 2009.

McCurry, C. *Parenting Your Anxious Child with Mindfulness and Acceptance: A Powerful New Approach to Overcoming Fear, Panic and Worry Using Acceptance and Commitment Therapy.* New Harbinger Publications, 2009.

Rapee, R., et al. *Helping Your Anxious Child: A Step-by-Step Guide for Parents.* New Harbinger Publications, 2008.

Behavioral management

Kazdin, A. *The Everyday Parenting Toolkit: The Kazdin Method for Easy, Step-by- Step, Lasting Change for You and Your Child.* Mariner Books, 2014.

Phelan, Thomas. *1-2-3 Magic: Effective Discipline for Children 2-12.* Parent Magic, 2014.

Webster-Stratton, C. *The Incredible Years: A Trouble-Shooting Guide for Parents of Children Aged 3-8.* Umbrella Press, 1992.

Child development

Carlsson-Paige, N. *Taking Back Childhood: A Proven Road Map for Raising Confident, Creative, Compassionate Kids.* Plume, 2008.

Lieberman, A. *The Emotional Life of the Toddler.* Simon and Schuster, 1993.

Steinberg, L. *The Ten Basic Principles of Good Parenting*. Simon and Schuster, 2005.

Couples relationships

Gottman, J. M. and N. Silver. *The Seven Principles for Making Marriages Work*. Harmony, 1999.

Hendrix, H. *Getting the Love You Want: A Guide for Couples*. Holt Paperbacks, 2001.

Child health

American Academy of Child and Adolescent Psychiatry: aacap.org

American Academy of Pediatrics: healthychildren.org

American Psychological Association: apa.org/pi/families/children-mental-health.aspx

Children and Nature Network: childrenandnature.org

Koocher, G. P. and A. M. La Greca, eds. *The Parents' Guide to Psychological First Aid: Helping Children and Adolescents Cope with Predictable Life Crises*. Oxford University Press, 2010.

Moon, R., ed. *Sleep: What Every Parent Needs to Know*. American Academy of Pediatrics, 2015.

Satter, Ellyn. *Your Child's Weight: Helping Without Harming*. Kelcy Press, 2005.

Play

Brown, S. and C. Vaughan. *Play: How It Shapes the Brain, Opens the Imagination, and Invigorates the Soul*. Avery, 2010.

Crain, W. *Reclaiming Childhood: Letting Children Be Children in Our Achievement-Oriented Society*. Holt Paperbacks, 2004.

Playworks: playworks.org

Preparing for the tween and teen years

Ginsburg, K. R. *Building Resilience in Children and Teens: Giving Kids Roots and Wings*. American Academy of Pediatrics, 2011.

Kastner, L. S. and Wyatt, J. F. *Getting to Calm: Cool-headed Strategies for Parenting Tweens + Teens*. ParentMap, 2007.

Kastner, L. S. and K. Russell. *Wise-Minded Parenting: Seven Essentials for Raising Tweens and Teens*. Parent-Map, 2013.

Technology

Common Sense Media: commonsensemedia.org

Pew Internet and American Life Project: pewinternet.org

Rosen, L. D. *Rewired: Understanding the iGeneration and the Way They Learn*. Palgrave Macmillan Trade, 2010.

Steiner-Adair, C. and T. H. Barker. *The Big Disconnect: Protecting Childhood and Family Relationships in the Digital Age*. Harper, 2013.

Achievement

Dweck, C. S. *Mindset: The New Psychology of Success*. Random House, 2006.

Tough, P. *How Children Succeed: Grit, Curiosity, and the Hidden Power of Character*. Houghton Mifflin Harcourt, 2012.

Index

About ParentMap

ParentMap is a media company that inspires, supports, and connects a growing community of wise-minded parents by publishing intelligent, trusted and thought-leading content to equip them for their essential role as their child's first and most important teacher. ParentMap's unique social-venture business model drives its vision and day-to-day operations, ensuring that publication readers and website visitors are given the most current information related to early learning, child health and development, and parenting. In all of its work and through all of its resources and publishing channels, ParentMap is dedicated to providing outstanding editorial content, advocating for children and families, and contributing to community.

Visit us at *parentmap.com*.

Other ParentMap titles:

Spare Me 'The Talk'!: A Guy's Guide to Sex, Relationships, and Growing Up By Jo Langford, M.A.

Wise-Minded Parenting: 7 Essentials for Raising Successful Tweens + Teens By Laura S. Kastner, Ph.D. with Kristen A. Russell

Getting to Calm: Cool Headed Strategies for Parenting Tweens and Teens By Laura S. Kastner, Ph.D., and Jennifer Wyatt

Beyond Smart: Boosting Your Child's Social, Emotional and Academic Potential By Linda Morgan

Northwest Kid Trips By Lora Shinn

ParentMap books are available at special discounts when purchased in bulk for premiums and sales promotions, as well as for fundraisers or educational use. Contact *books@parentmap.com* for more information.